# SOFTWARE

## *for Your*

# HEAD

# SOFTWARE

## *for Your*

# HEAD

*Core Protocols for*
*Creating and Maintaining*
*Shared Vision*

JIM McCARTHY

MICHELE McCARTHY

✦Addison-Wesley

Boston San Francisco New York Toronto Montreal
London Munich Paris Madrid
Capetown Sydney Tokyo Singapore Mexico City

The publisher offers discounts on this book when ordered in quantity for special sales. For more information, please contact
Pearson Education Corporate Sales Division
201 W. 103rd Street
Indianapolis, IN 46290
(800) 428-5331
corpsales@pearsoned.com

Visit Addison-Wesley on the Web: www.aw.com/cseng/

*Library of Congress Cataloging-in-Publication Data*
McCarthy, Jim.
    Software for your head : core protocols for creating and maintaining shared vision / Jim McCarthy, Michele McCarthy.
        p. cm.
    Includes bibliographical references and index.
    ISBN 0-201-60456-6
    1. Computer software development management.   2. Teams in the workplace.   3. Group problem solving.   I. McCarthy, Michele.   II. Title.

QA76.76.D47 M3875 2001
005.1—dc21

2001045093

ISBN 0-201-60456-6
Text printed on recycled paper
1 2 3 4 5 6 7 8 9 10—MA—0504030201
First printing, December 2001

*This book is dedicated to those who by their
daily acts of courage sustain the advance of freedom and bring
closer the day of its absolute triumph.*

# CONTENTS

# ACKNOWLEDGMENTS

We would like to thank the people who have contributed to The Core: the BootCamp students; the staff of McCarthy Technologies, Inc.; the members of McCarthy TeamworX staff over the years, its various partners, and associated consultants; and the many corporations who invested with us in the development of their employees and in the vision of this work.

We would also like to thank particular people who have contributed to the book itself: Mike Hendrickson believed and was patient; the many reviewers who added insight; Linda Rising, who made the words work more efficiently; Dan McCarthy, who made visual what was only verbal; and Tyrrell Albaugh, who shipped the damn thing.

# The Core V. 1.0 Background

We didn't create The Core. Instead, we watched it grow. We did, however, along with John Rae-Grant, create the set of initial conditions under which The Core protocols, or something very much like them, would almost certainly emerge. Over the years, we have maintained healthy conditions for Core evolution. Along the way, we also pruned the tree from growing into a few false directions. And we added resources: our own money, time, focus, and stamina. We protected it. Took notes. Tried it out. Passed it out.

A proper credit also has to include the hundreds of product developers and other students from around the world who contributed to The Core's development over the years. Crediting one person or segment of contributors exclusively would be inaccurate, however. The real story is both simpler and more complex.

The emergence of The Core was in some measure a result of our experiences in 1994–95. We were working for a commercial software company, leading a development team of approximately 150 people. We used a homegrown aphorism to help us try new ideas:

*Team = Software*

That's the idea. Because of its many virtues, despite its deficits, and regardless of others who have had the same thought, this maxim became a bit of a mantra for us. During stressful times, when we were tempted to retreat from the overwhelming complexity of the software development tasks; when the confusion and disorientation were really getting to us; when schedules were slipping and goals receding and prospects were looking pretty grim indeed. Then, just when we needed it most, someone in our group would invariably come up with a new idea, would provide a fresh point of view based on "Team = Software." "I get it," he might say, and then rattle off some new application of "Team = Software" that could apply to our situation. Occasionally, these ideas were profound; more often they weren't. They were almost always useful, however.

The essence of the "Team = Software" philosophy is that the behavior of a team maps directly to the qualities of its product, and vice versa. If you want a product with certain characteristics, you must ensure that the team has those characteristics before the product's development.

We also realized that everyone has a product or provides a service. Everyone produces a concrete expression of his value system that carries that person's virtues and vices out into the world.

What was our leadership team making? We moved through the hierarchical levels in our organization and answered two pertinent questions at each interesting point: Who is the team here? And what is its product?

Let's call the team of frontline developers the Level I team. Level I makes the actual product. The managers of this team constitute the Level II team. Its product is the Level I team. When applying the "Team = Software" philosophy, the team on one level is the product of the team at the next higher level. If the Level II team sees an undesirable trait in the Level I team, it must be an expression of or reflection of Level II teamwork and the Level II team members. This pattern applies to teams at all levels, right up through the corporate ranks.

This idea may seem clever, obvious, fanciful, or just plain wrong-headed, but to us it was certainly helpful. Using this model, no one can hide from accountability. In our situation, even though we were bosses, we could not fault a team for lacking a virtue, unless and until we had personally demonstrated it. Nor could we expect any remedy that we weren't personally modeling. On the one hand, this realization was depressing, because there really was no escape: Responsibility inevitably migrated upward and weighed heavily from time to time on our well-paid, if under-exercised, shoulders. On the other hand, this realization offered an incredibly hopeful perspective as something more, something immediate, something completely within our control that was available to remedy any shortcomings of the team.

If we saw something screwed up somewhere or noticed some good fruit dying on the vine, we could immediately find and fix the problem. To inspire other team members to go get that fruit before it died, we would gather and visibly devour tantalizing fruit that had gone unpicked in our own neck of the woods.

If we wanted any property to materialize on the Level I team, we would have to incorporate that property into our own behavior. This change in behavior was conceptually simple, but challenging to implement. In any case, keeping this basic framework in mind exposed many novel approaches to team problems. When we first applied this perspective, so many new possibilities opened up at such a rapid pace that we were unable to keep up with them. Although many little tests and a few big ones did yield the desired results, we saw so many new solutions to problems that had plagued us for years that we hardly knew where to begin. We quickly realized that we couldn't possibly conduct sufficient experiments to develop a full understanding of precisely how useful the formula was; to discover where it failed; or to see where the behavior it inspired might lead. We wanted to explore its dynamics and map its etiology in the systems we believed it governed—that is, check it out all the way.

Unfortunately, the experimental opportunities in a commercial software development effort are necessarily limited. A major obstacle is the simple passage of calendar time. A large commercial software project can take months or years. The possibilities we were seeing appeared so valuable, however, that even a few months seemed far too long for each cycle if we were to learn everything possible. With millions of dollars at stake on a single development effort, radical experimentation seemed risky. The number of variables with which we could tinker was low. Together, the sluggishness of "real-world" calendar time and the responsibilities of prudent business practices worked against the idea of implementing the sustained, radical, and rapid experimentation that we envisioned. Still, we thought big breakthroughs in team dynamics were possible—breakthroughs that could make collaboration simpler and more effective for any team.

To study this material in depth, we had to complete a development cycle in a much shorter time. Life itself was too short to go through enough development cycles. Even a very busy, unusually stable, and highly focused development manager could—if he stayed with the task for a long time—expect to oversee 10 to 20 projects in one professional lifetime. Many of these projects would use essentially the same teams, reducing the diversity of team sources that would enrich the manager's education and hasten experimental progress.

In early 1996, to accelerate the rate and breadth of our experiments, we went out on our own and established a laboratory devoted to the study and teaching of teamwork. The ultimate existence of The Core protocols became a virtual certainty when we decided how we would operate the new lab, which we named "Software Development BootCamp." The principal experiment conducted would be a recurrent product development simulation, lasting five days and nights with a new team each time. It would take place every month or so. The developers would complete four steps:

1. Form a team.
2. Envision a product.
3. Agree on how it would be made.
4. Design and build it.

At the end of the week, the teams would have to deliver their products on time, or stay longer to do so, or not, as they chose.

We knew that we could successfully conduct such a product development effort, even leading it personally, if needed. We had done just that for many years, earning our living in a variety of environments. We had sufficient information, tips, techniques, and useful practices to transmit high value to most students. We could teach them practices that could ensure the successful outcome of their own product development efforts, now or later, simulated or not.

We had already gained, organized, and articulated considerable knowledge from our experiences in leading or otherwise contributing to dozens of development efforts, most of which proved quite successful. This body of knowledge would serve as the starting point for the first BootCamp teams. Even if we learned nothing during BootCamp, we still would have plenty to offer.

BootCamp has allowed us to effectively compress a software development cycle into a five-day experience. In five days, students learn what would normally require a long development cycle. The intense BootCamp experience includes all of the failures and triumphs that occur with normal team formation; the creation of a team-shared vision; and the design, implementation, and delivery of a product. The days in each BootCamp are packed with accelerated team dynamics; what usually takes a year or more is created in a few long days and nights of exceptionally deep engagement.

The many new insights from BootCamp emerged at a vastly increased clip. The learning pace was accelerated by our experience of working intimately with some 60 different software development teams. We first helped to create the team, and then their products. We experienced complete development cycles with incredible frequency and velocity—one or two times per month at peak periods. Working with teams of every kind and composition, and working before and after BootCamp, we applied what we learned to our own teamwork.

One additional factor led to the creation of The Core protocols, and originated in our standard assignment to the students. Each team would have to build a product in one week. But what product would the BootCamp teams make?

At one level, BootCamp is conceptually simple: We assemble a group of software developers. Sometimes the students are members of a preexisting team. Sometimes they represent as many types of developers as possible: corporate employees, entrepreneurs, computer scientists, software testers, writers, editors, graphic artists, coders, managers, executives, program and project managers, and producers. Often, there will be nondevelopers in attendance: nurses, teachers, homebodies, consultants, and press members. We give each new team-in-waiting a single assignment:

*Design, implement, and deliver a course that teaches you everything you need to know to ship great software on time, every time.*

This assignment has remained unchanged since the first Boot-Camp. It seemed to us that it would be useful to look at team dynamics from the real-time point of view of a team actually working in a state of effective teamwork. Teams exhibiting the most desirable teamwork were best able to solve the riddles of such teamwork.

The decision to devote the BootCamp teams' efforts to resolving the issues of bringing teams to the effective state they were enjoying was a productive innovation. Teams in a newly gained high-performance state produce extraordinary results. When they examine the conditions and elements of their own high performance, as it occurs, the quality of insight is substantial.

Almost every BootCamp team has experienced the following flash of insight: If teamwork itself could be made more efficient and direct, then the team members would be able to find the solutions to the big problems that vexed them. This knowledge could then be leveraged to enhance their other endeavors.

High-performance teams typically acquire their reputations by accomplishing the specific goals they set for themselves. For example, a great basketball team wins many basketball games. The players are not remembered for their contributions to the art and science of team enhancement, but for putting balls through hoops. Achieving a team's original goal is a task not directly related to explicitly uncovering the dynamics of team formation. In the case of the Boot-Camp teams, the presenting task became the discovery, refinement, and codification of practices that would always lead to the formation of great teams.

As one BootCamp led to the next, we began capturing the best practices employed by the teams, and we encoded these behaviors to make them easily transmissible. These lessons from the Boot-Camp experiences gradually evolved into The Core protocols. When a team applies The Core protocols consistently, it will produce superior results.

The booting process stimulated by The Core protocols can be ongoing, yielding more efficient and capable groups. The lesson that the booting process continues in a general way is reinforced vividly when we see every new BootCamp team learn more, do more, and add more to the richness and the reproducibility of the "multipersonal" patterns and protocols that lie at the heart of The Core.

And that's our story—how we watched The Core protocols emerge.

# THE ELEMENTS OF THE CORE

We have encoded information regarding team behaviors that in our experience will invariably increase any team's desirable results. We have organized the information in a small group of textual structures that make up The Core.

## THE FOUR CORE STRUCTURES

1. Patterns
2. Antipatterns
3. Definitions
4. Protocols

To the potential adopter, The Core protocols are the most significant of these four classes of information. The Core patterns and antipatterns articulate the reasons behind many of the choices we have made as designers of The Core protocols, but The Core protocols are the elements that actually specify—in a detailed, formal way—our recommended personal and team behaviors. The Core protocols have been developed and experimented with through many iterations, and have been used by many people over significant periods of time. We are confident that their consistent and correct application will yield very good results. Even if all the ideas in The Core patterns and antipatterns are mortally flawed, use of The Core protocols will still produce the best results of any set of practices we've seen or tried. If we do not understand why they work, we do understand *that* they work.

Additionally, it should be noted that the common understanding and practical acceptance of some terms included in The Core definitions are required in order to properly apply some of The Core protocols. To the extent that this is so, those Core definitions must necessarily be given equal weight to The Core protocols.

## *Patterns*

A pattern is a standardized way of efficiently communicating the solution to a problem in a context; a pattern should generate something and tell you how to generate that something. Patterns promise particular results and consequences if you apply them. A pattern for a dress, for example, will support you in creating the dress it promises but limit the wearer's options. Use of The Core patterns has repeatedly generated teams that perform better than the teams originally expected of themselves.

The word "pattern" has come to have a special meaning for software developers. The idea of patterns in software descends from a special use of the term first articulated by Christopher Alexander, thinker and architect, in the 1970s.[1] He created a structure for documenting patterns and collections of patterns called "pattern languages." These pattern languages were used to encode and communicate important ideas about the practice and purpose of architecture.

Patterns are a means of transmitting general solutions to common problems. The special software or architectural sense of the word "pattern" is not really all that different from the usual use of the word. If you have a pattern, especially one that has been consistently successful in its application, you don't have the thing itself,

---

1. See, for example, Christopher Alexander, et al., *A Pattern Language* (Oxford University Press, 1977) and Alexander, *The Timeless Way* (Oxford University Press, 1979).

but you do have a head start in making the thing, or learning enough to make it or use it. For this reason, patterns have come to be widely written about and discussed as a communications mechanism in the software field.

The classic definition of a pattern of this type is "A solution to a problem in a context." People being what they are, there is some dispute about the definition of software patterns. Generally, software patterns are abstract solutions to recurrent technical problems faced by programmers. They are a way for a programmer to understand and acquire a language for discussing problems. This can lead to the accumulation of intelligence. Theoretically, patterns enable the re-use of the best thinking done to date, and allow a pattern consumer to access the body of solutions available.

We define patterns as software for your head. Our pattern-based software, like other applications of the pattern concepts, provides solutions to common problems. The patterns in The Core contain information, procedures, and constraints that you can "load" into your mind. Once loaded or learned, you can apply them. Your team-mates can do the same, and then all can share in what we believe is a rich source of psychological, linguistic, and behavioral resources. Apply these patterns however and whenever you care to.

The Core patterns apply to the shaping of a group's thinking, and the making and execution of its decisions. Our goal in supplying patterns of this type is

*We want to create a world wherein a group's behaviors consistently achieve that group's predetermined goals.*

### *Antipatterns*

These are patterns that describe common solutions that yield unde-sirable results. In effect, they are false patterns, patterns that reliably fail. For every antipattern in The Core, we present a pattern or a protocol (or both) that has provided a satisfactory solution to the problem many times.

"One-eighty" is the somewhat whimsical name we have given to a special type of phenomenon we have observed more often than we expected. A one-eighty is an idea that expresses conventional wisdom, but it yields undesirable results and does so in the most abysmal way conceivable. A one-eighty is so wrong-headed that, if instead of following the idea in question, a person performed steps precisely opposite to those specified or suggested, he would actually achieve the ostensible goal of the one-eighty. In other words: Conventional wisdom is often real wisdom, but encoded as the opposite folly.

## *Definitions*

Most software systems have their own definitions of special terms. Generally, the system authors define these terms. Naturally, the definitions of such terms are local in scope.

The words used in The Core are found in everyday English. To reduce complications caused by the availability of the same words for everyday use and their specific application and meaning in the context of The Core, we supply a lexicon of Core definitions.

- The purpose of the lexicon is to specify the exact meaning of what might otherwise be overloaded words or phrases. These may or may not have general usage beyond The Core, but, if they do, we define them locally because we found that their application typically lacked precision.

- The definitions are designed to increase the results of your team, not necessarily to provide any real truth-value beyond the scope of the team life. The Core's definitions are not dictionary definitions. They are tokens in a system.

- The definitions are somewhat arbitrary and must be accepted for the system to function. For the purpose of applying The Core, they are best seen as straightforward but local axioms, arbitrary little chunks of meaning. Just "givens."

- These definitions provide the linguistic material required to construct and use The Core. The definitions are just a part of the rules of the game. They are special constraints that can channel substantial power to and from the team playing the game.

Wherever possible, we have tried to use words that do have some generally accepted meaning close to what we are trying to convey in our application of the term. We dislike making up new words. This way, anybody can get a sense of what is being discussed by a Core team without recourse to the lexicon.

## *Protocols*

Almost all team activity is untouched by The Core. The Core protocols are meant to ensure that a few important results-oriented behaviors will be attained by a given team with a

- Previously unavailable degree of reliability
- Higher than usual degree of efficiency
- More uniform distribution of accountability

Any team can use The Core protocols to achieve these goals. The rest of the time, team life goes on, as the team desires.

When adopted, Core protocols will provide teams with a reliable means to efficiently achieve at least the following:

1. Group interpersonal connection with an increased level of access to one another

2. Collective, unanimous decision making and related accountability distribution

3. Team and personal alignment

4. Achievement of a shared vision, including

   - Long-term or far vision

   - Short-term or version-oriented vision

   - Personal commitment to personal and team goals

   - Team commitment to personal and team goals

Many teams have never experienced these achievements. The Core protocols turn them into everyday activities.

The Core protocols do not predefine or limit[2] the content transmitted between connecting parties. Instead, the protocols provide the opportunity to transmit and receive the content deemed important by the parties.

The protocols in The Core are conceptually simple, memorable, and practical. We have found each one to be extremely effective; many teams have used them, and they quickly become second nature for the teams. While we have no desire to formalize normal team interplay, we do provide sufficient structure so that teams can enjoy particular kinds of interplay that are as consistently high quality, highly reliable, and as results oriented as a team might desire.

―――――――――――――――――――――――――――――――――――――――

2. Beyond supporting the normal limits expected in an environment allowing civilized discourse, at any rate.

*Offer what you have,*

*disclosing what you feel and think,*

*connecting only with those who do likewise.*

# I

# Check In

DISCLOSURE, CONNECTION,
AND THE VARIABILITY
OF PRESENCE

---

*"I'm in."*

*Imagine a team at the beginning of a new project.*

*Pretend this team is having a meeting. A kickoff meeting for a new product team members have been asked to build. And you—because of your experience with so many teams over so many years here; because you've been to so many kick-offs; because you've seen what was the greatest that happened here, and the absolutely not-so-great so many times; because you have worked shoulder-to-cubicle with many of the people on this team; because you have fought for quality so noisily and so consistently, for so long, even though the victories were minor and infrequent; because you are a good thinker and a sensitive person; because you are now finally a bit more accepted by senior management; and because you have shown your loyalty, they feel, and show some promise as a more senior mentor—have been asked to observe this team at this meeting at the beginning of this new product creation effort.*

*It is a meeting more like other meetings than unlike them. For the most part, the atmosphere is like the dozens of other project starts: There's a drop of hope to go around, and a squirt of suspended disbelief (maybe this time things will actually go right), and a dollop or two of slippery new belief in the promise of the rare blank sheet, of the chance to do it right this time. Of course, there is the old bucket of dilute scars and cynical vapor being pumped into the air by that whining dehumidifier, and the great pool of dispassion is nearby, too (gets a lot of use). But there's some of it all, anyway, in the usual proportions.*

*Dampened by these ambient team fluids, the team members are discussing many things at this kick-off meeting: process, schedule, costs, risks, competition, time lines, and the like. Company politics. The expected disputes are here, contained within the acceptable bounds of conflict, but left mostly unresolved. Handled so-so, but as per usual. You readily discern the rivalries, the alliances. You can feel the newbies' poorly hidden excitement and fear, and you can smell the repressed hope of the cynics. Your mind drifts in and out of the meeting when the classic technical issues, the old standbys, resurface for another great gulp of communal airtime. Hello, old friends. We'll discuss you inconclusively once again, once again.*

*One thing gets you thinking. You notice that the vision behind the product is mentioned only in passing. You see that any discussions about purpose here are strictly pro forma, dispassionate. Technicalities and the usual resource constraints are the real bread and butter of the discussion, the things people care about, fight about. To the extent they care about anything, you think, they care mostly about the things that they believe stop them. They're creating some sort of blame scenario out of real and imagined deprivations— in advance. It's like shaking rattles at the evils beyond their control. Go away, bad gods. But they always win, don't they, if you believe in them at all. That's why they're there. To win.*

*My, but you're feeling anthropological today, aren't you? Is it maybe the presence of the cynics nee idealists? Does it touch you somehow?*

*Whatever. The scarcity of vision does strike you as interesting, even though it's not a major topic of conversation (or even a minor one, for that matter). You know that most of these team members would agree that "shared vision" is a vital thing for a team. Why, if you went around the room and asked who was for and who against a shared vision, almost all would vote for it. Some would hedge or go technical on you (define this, what do you mean by that, it depends). But none would vote no. And yet, despite this general conviction, no one seems committed to a particular shared vision, or attempts to achieve one on this team. Of course, catching a shared vision, that's a tough problem. Who knows where lightning will strike? Who has mapped the rainbow's end? You note that there are a few who absolutely believe that a shared vision is the vital ingredient for a successful team. Still, no one speaks up about this obvious vacancy.*

*Instead, while you drift in and out, they plod on through the usual meeting follies, cracking a few minor jokes, interrupting without reason, talking overlong and repetitively, sporadically fighting for control, while somehow meandering through a poorly conceived and prematurely written agenda. Yet all the while the people on this team are somehow numbing themselves to a frightening lack of vision of where it is they are going. You wonder, why doesn't anyone speak up? Don't they care? You are willing to bet dollars to dog biscuits that plenty of perfectly good beliefs and values are lying dormant within the members of this team—beliefs and values that would make all the difference, if only they were put into practice.*

*But, because you are acting as a kind of mentor or coach, and are really troubled by this curious vision oblivion, you decide that the obvious first step is to get them going on a shared vision.*

*This* would *help. Short-term, anyway. Now that you've decided how to help, you can barely restrain yourself from saying something that might awaken their somnolent vision-building potential. But you say nothing now, and not only because of the difficulty of fighting the others for precious airtime, and of suborning the agenda, but because you intuit that jumping in with that straightforward and inarguable direction (get a vision, people!) might be a long-term mistake. You are having a growing belief that there just may be bigger, tastier fish for you to fry here. No sense settling for little crappies, you think, when some big ole lunker bass might be about.*

*You are increasing your degree of presence.*

*The problem, you think, is not merely that they ought to acquire a shared vision. Clearly, they need one, and they aren't about to get one, not with their present behavior, anyway. And yet, your intuition whispers that the lack of a shared vision is* not *the most important issue to address. So, trying that on, you think some more. What was that about fish to fry? Teach a man to fish, etc. Yes, that's it.*

*You know that some of these team members* do *believe in having a common purpose. You know the whole team would really catch fire if team members just had this one big, energizing, lightning-striking, all-solving vision! But here, on this team, almost unbelievably, not one person will even say anything about this AWOL vision.*

*You wonder why would they lie and betray their beliefs. A little more of your dwindling supply of innocence goes poof. There must be* some *explana-*

*tion. Maybe the lack of shared vision is the symptom here, not the problem. The problem with this team is that not one damned person on it is speaking the truth. They don't really lie, not much; they just focus on the smaller stuff, because the bigger stuff is too scary. So they don't tell the truth. Not all of it, anyway. Hell, not even the pieces of it they have.*

*So now what? You lean back and think. Well, your first impulse—to get them going on a shared vision—was wrong. And the second impulse to get someone to say something about the Case of the Missing Vision, or even better, get someone to do something about it, this impulse is also wrong. After all, these people are smart: They know they lack a compelling vision. They don't need that tidbit from an advisor, or even from one of their own. Who really wants more meetings and retreats in which people don't speak the truth, even if the topic is vision? More going through the motions won't help.*

*Then what? What would be most helpful? You reason, the most helpful thing you could do would be to encourage someone—just one—to examine his[1] own personal failure to speak the truth at this meeting.*

*Now you've got your guidance. Anyone smart enough to ask for it gets it. It would be simple but difficult at the same time. You would tell him that he should think, feel, and engage more deeply, and really participate as if it mattered, as if he cared, as if his time counted. You would advise him to examine what he believes in right now, what's happening in his own heart and mind, and to honestly assess his engagement with his work, values, and team. And then, he would want to seriously question his evident willingness to tolerate— hell, endorse—wrong action. Does he act on his beliefs? Or does he just like to believe in them?*

*That sounds about right. You wonder what impact this question might have had on teams where you and your teammates expended large amounts*

---

1. We have surrendered to the inadequacy of our greater history and our linguistic development. For reasons that are no doubt lamentable, we have no personal pronoun that encompasses both male and female. To maintain strict neutrality in extended discussion about individuals, we were not willing to subject the reader to endless clumsy reminders of his ancient and contemporary tribal failures to consider anyone but himself as English evolved. Now and then, when it is a short passage, we attempt to maintain gender neutrality. However, more often than not, we choose to use the masculine gender when picking on a metaphoric individual. In so doing, we believe we are more punitive of the masculine than honoring, for it does seem that our metaphoric guy is always requiring correction or exhortation to simply do the right thing. Doing the right thing is a practice that his linguistically disenfranchised colleagues, thankfully, often find easier.

*of effort for only mediocre results. If just one person on this team who believed in something that the team was neglecting, something important (like, say, the necessity of a team having a shared vision)—if just one person who knew he was doing the wrong thing and yet let himself go on doing it; if he would just answer this question: Why is he willing to accept less than the best possible results, even though he is the one investing his time and effort in this project?*

*If he answered that and also really saw how this self-betrayal wasted his time, then he couldn't say he was "too busy at work" to the family anymore. He'd just have to say he was "too wasteful" or "too cowardly" the next time his little girl wanted him to play pretend with her on a Saturday. If he answered that, you figure he'd probably nearly soften up enough to actually engage with the others.*

*But wait. That's not the important thing, the talking with others. That's a trap, a diversion, like fighting for quality instead of creating it. It's what he* does *about it, not just what he says about it. They have to balance; what he says has to mostly be like how he acts. But, geez, if he just shared his true thoughts and feelings with the rest of them without preaching or dictating; if he could just tell them what he actually believes about the vision problem, say, and could describe how he hasn't consistently acted on his beliefs in a way that makes any difference, then he could tell them what he is going to do. He could say, "I'm not ever going forward with another project on a team without a genuine shared vision." Or, even better, he could say, "I'm going to work on this vision, starting at x time and place, and I'm going to keep working, with whoever wants to work on it with me until I clearly know where we're taking this product. Will you help?"*

*Well, hell, if he did all that, you would consider him to be all the way checked in. Hmmm. What's more, you think maybe, just maybe, that scenario might just do the trick for the whole damn team. Tell you what, you'd bet your bottom dollar that his teammates will at least respond with their fullest, focused attention. That's just what people do whenever someone reveals himself a bit. If he's talking and acting with just the least little bit of enlightenment, something new, they're going to listen up and watch closely. As long as the person says what he says and does what he does with thoughtfulness and truth.*

*But if it is true, you'd predict that the team, just by witnessing a more honest, genuinely new engagement level, will then be much more likely to act on questions of shared vision (which, you remind yourself, is the top-level symptom). At least, you figure, they'll be more likely to act on things they care about, anyway, and that would be all to the good. Moreover, everybody who watched this thing unfold from just one person will have been really informed, and maybe even inspired, by the difference made by his acceptance of personal accountability for how he has been spending his own life. Really, not only for his own results, but for the results of all.*

*You half listen to the team struggling to cram everything in the agenda in the last few minutes. Maybe the others would also begin to experiment with the new power they are seeing and feeling (and there is tremendous power in accepting individual responsibility for achieving results together). If your guidance would help one or more of them to engage more deeply, and not to waste any time and never to do anything dumb on purpose, why, you'd have made a huge difference. Hell, the dumb quota can always be met by doing things you thought were smart to begin with. You don't have to do anything dumb on purpose to meet the quota.*

*You imagine that a newly awakened team member would see a whole bunch of things, maybe all at once; the problem is not a case of a team without a shared vision, a case of just another stupid project, or another example of bad management or poor leadership. No, when he thinks it all the way through, he'll see that the trouble is not "too few people," or "not enough time," or some other cockamamie story about how the mediocrity was out of his control. The crux of the thing is that he, personally, has been accepting less than he wants, and less than he deserves. What's more, he has been doing so without making any genuine creative effort to get what he requires to efficiently create what he wants. He'll see that the problem is his own lack of integrity and his shallow engagement. The problem is rooted somewhere near his deficient caring about his own life. To persist as it has, the problem requires his repression of passion, it mandates that he fail to accept his own wisdom, and it seduces him into daily acts of cowardice that promulgate rather than abolish the general foolishness of which he is such an important part.*

*But should just this one person truly check in, you think, the whole team will be moved to a better ground. Even if team members backslide, and all do, they won't forget this vivid instance of accountable behavior and the simple, unambiguous actions that supported it.*

*One self-respecting person, you reflect, with even a modest degree of personal engagement, is all it takes to start this team on the path toward much greater achievement. No permission is required for the pursuit of greatness, no consensus to improve your own results. All the orgs and re-orgs in the whole damn corporate universe, all the resources consumed and processes proceeding can't stop one honest person from making sure he spends his time wisely. And that's all that is needed to get the ball rolling.*

*Why not believe, you think. Pretend. OK. So from this one moment of surpassing individual and dawning team clarity, this whole group will quicken, will revive. Of course, team members will need some new supportive structures; they'll require whatever information there is about highly effective connection and collaboration. In particular, they'll damn well want more moments of clarity, and will be willing to adopt whatever practices create just the right conditions for genuine checking in.*

*They can't hold it, probably. And would they spread it around? You have a spike of unease, but then you reassure yourself that the team you are envisioning would of course look for any behavior patterns that would achieve its goals. If there weren't any, team members would just figure a way to create them. And put them in a book.*

*But first, one of them must check all the way in. Just one. Who? All this, after one of them has decided that his life, time, and creative output really do matter. But not before.*

*Interrupting your reverie, your nascent vision, the meeting suddenly stops as people scatter and depart, ceasing to meet rather than finishing their work. Finishing is way different from ceasing, you muse. As you gather yourself, one of the team newbies, together with the team's most infamous cynic, approach you. You bet they want your take on things. Your help.*

# ONE

# The Elements of Check In

## OVERCOMING DISTANCE

Whether the members of a team are dispersed across the world or crammed shoulder-to-shoulder in rows of cubicles, distance is always the central issue among collaborators. The remedy for distance is presence.

Of course, it is easier to spot distance-related difficulties in a geographically dispersed team, and people are more likely to attribute team problems to miles rather than minds; regardless of geography, the primary task with any team is that of surmounting distance. The distance that must be surmounted, though, is the psychological distance (or the "**headgap**"[1]) between people rather than the amount of physical space between their bodies.

*The remedy for distance is presence.*

*The distance that must be surmounted . . . is the psychological distance . . . between people rather than the amount of physical space between their bodies.*

---

1. The "headgap" assumes that basic costs are associated with applying your abilities. That is, some effort is involved in accessing and successfully applying your talents to a task. The headgap baseline is the cost for a person to apply his ability to an appropriate task. The headgap itself then is the increase in cost beyond the headgap baseline that a person would pay to apply the ability of another person. The cost of psychological distance or the headgap between two people is the additional cost required for Person A to apply an ability so that it is available to Person B as if it were B's own, plus the additional cost (beyond the baseline) for Person B to gain such availability. The headgap includes any costs of the interpersonal connection between A and B, the effort A and B must make to increase their availability to each other, and the effort B must make to apply A's quality. The headgap also incorporates the cost of erroneous transactions between A and B.

*Neither the highest nor
the lowest degrees of
presence are
achievable.*

*Because presence
trumps distance, and
distance is the enemy
of collaboration,
teams using CheckIn
will prevail.*

The **aggregate** headgap is the big cost of working in groups. This means that a psychologically close team that is physically remote is more desirable than the reverse. Team performance typically has less to do with the collaborators' physical proximity than with psychological, emotional, and intellectual proximity—that is, the individuals' degree of **engagement**[2] with one another and with their work. In The Core-adopting team, efficiently facilitating team members' **presence** is the function of the CheckIn pattern. Consistent adherence to this pattern creates a foundation for the team's greatness.

A team that uses the CheckIn pattern and its associated protocols will be more aware of team presence than teams that don't. A presence-sensitive team will be more likely to address and consequently surmount the challenges presented by its presence-related issues. Team members will be able to exploit the opportunities that emerge when their focused optimization of aggregate presence works. Presence-insensate teams will continue to address the wrong issues. Because presence trumps distance, and distance is the enemy of collaboration, teams using CheckIn will prevail.

## THE CHECK IN PROTOCOL

The CheckIn protocol provides two major components for establishing and developing high-performance collaboration: an enlistment procedure and an interpersonal connectivity process. The former (re)affirms each individual's commitment to a body of proven

————————

2. Degrees of individual presence are conceptual entities. You can encode whether or not your organism is in the room. Beyond that, personal presence cannot be measured with any precision. Neither the highest nor the lowest degrees of presence are achievable (though death is probably the nadir of presence). Still, it is equally obvious that you can personally vary the extent of your presence and the depth of your engagement more or less at will. So we need a vocabulary to discuss this phenomenon. The model of higher and lower degrees seems to work well enough for a start.

efficiency-enhancing behaviors. The latter provides individuals with an opportunity to efficiently reveal their personal states.

CheckIn begins with a rich, interactive roll call. This is its connective component. Conventionally, a roll call provides a way to determine who is physically present. With the CheckIn protocol, each team member can also disclose[3] the character and the disposition of his presence. While an ordinary roll call asks, "Who is present?", the CheckIn pattern also asks, "What's going on with you?"

Each individual CheckIn culminates in a brief statement (that is, "I'm in") that renews the individual's commitment to seek efficiency and to "play by the rules" of The Core.[4]

## THE CHECK OUT PROTOCOL

Occasionally, an individual will take a break from the intense levels of productive engagement required by The Core. The CheckOut protocol makes such breaks possible and minimizes any disruption to the rest of the team.

## THE PASSER PROTOCOL

The Passer protocol serves as a safety valve for the entirety of The Core protocols. It provides a means for any individual to decline to participate in a Core protocol or process without being questioned by the other team members.

---

3. Disclosure typically follows discovery. Each team member is routinely provided a good excuse to spend a moment discovering before disclosure, namely, that he is about to speak to his colleagues. His preparations before checking in are important moments of introspection and self-awareness. Also, the general attenuation to disclosures of each other's CheckIns helps align the group.

4. The rules are prescribed variously by each protocol. Generally, the group adopts the CheckIn commitments and/or a team constitution a priori. The "rules" are specific expressions of the guiding values behind The Core protocols. They grow out of an exclusive focus on achieving the most with the least expenditure of team time and other resources.

*Any team member can
pass on any activity
associated with The
Core protocols at any
time, for any reason,
without extra scrutiny.*

With few exceptions, any team member can pass on any activity associated with The Core protocols at any time, for any reason, without extra scrutiny.

# CONNECTION

Connection is a pattern that describes the process and benefits of mutual presence.

# PROBLEM BEHAVIORS

There are reasons that the higher degrees of individual presence aren't routinely found in teams that do not use The Core. The attitudes and behaviors we have seen repeatedly are captured in three presence-related antipatterns: TooEmotional, NoHurtFeelings, and WrongTolerance.

## TOO EMOTIONAL

When you encounter intense emotion at work, you often feel that someone is being too emotional. This condition usually arises when normal, everyday emotion, after being too long repressed, suddenly erupts. When emotions are processed in this delayed, bursty, and unpredictable way, the behavior that results often is, or seems, ineffective or **self-destructive**. The problem, though, is not that the person is too emotional. He is not emotional enough.

## NO HURT FEELINGS

This common antipattern describes the bad decisions and ineffective steps that people take to avoid telling one another the truth.

## WRONG TOLERANCE

*Behaviors that don't
work should not be
tolerated.*

Tolerance is not always a virtue. Behaviors that don't work should not be tolerated. But they are.

# PATTERNS SYNERGISTIC WITH CHECK IN

CheckIn depends on several other patterns also covered in Part I.

## TEAM = PRODUCT

The Team = Product pattern identifies and mediates group problems by comparing and contrasting the characteristics of the team with the characteristics of its products. Applying the Team = Product pattern supplies ample and effective team diagnostics.

## SELF-CARE

The Self-Care pattern describes the desirable effects that accrue to a team when each person on it is responsible for taking care of one person and one person only: himself.

*Each person . . . is responsible for taking care of one person and one person only: himself.*

## THINKING AND FEELING

The ThinkingandFeeling pattern describes the benefits and delineates the surprisingly challenging practice of thinking and feeling simultaneously.

## PRETEND

The Pretend pattern identifies the importance of experimenting with beliefs and performing thought experiments as a way to discover effectiveness.

## GREATNESS CYCLE

The GreatnessCycle pattern identifies a desirable group value system and describes in practical terms some of the behaviors that embody those values (smarts, presence, integrity, conflict, passion, and greatness). The sequence of GreatnessCycle is laid bare, and the pattern depicts how the application of one value leads to the next.

When smart individuals intensify their presence (a requisite characteristic of smartness), their resulting expressions of integrity lead to conflict. Conflict, in turn, will tend to line people up behind what they care about, which is, at heart, the definition of passion. The maturing of passion creates the conditions that allow for great results.

It is unlikely that a team will consistently attain excellence, and get its shot at greatness, without experiencing this cycle.

# Check In Patterns and Protocols

## PATTERN: CHECK IN

### PROBLEM

*Your results are unsatisfying.*

By definition, good results get you what you want. Satisfaction comes from the fulfillment of wants. So, if you are putting your time and effort toward getting the results you want, but keep getting results you don't want, you can either change the results or change what you want. You are probably misspending time and effort. What will really come in handy if you decide to stop wasting yourself this way is increased **awareness**; specifically, increased awareness of the ins and outs of how you generate undesired results. Increased awareness is the biggest danger to your whole system of developing unsatisfying results. Among other things, increased awareness reveals many more choices to you than does the old steady-as-she-goes awareness.

    Increased awareness can even be sort of magical. Take now, for example. This very moment. Accept as **true**—just for the moment—

*If you . . . keep getting results you don't want, you can either change the results or change what you want.*

*Increased awareness is the biggest danger to your whole system of developing unsatisfying results.*

*Many people struggle with letting go of false beliefs, conceptual bookmarks that explain unsatisfying results.*

that you *can* choose whether or not to persist with your "unsatisfactory results strategy." Now things have changed for you. Perhaps the biggest change is this: If you now decide *not* to stop generating unsatisfying results, you're in a bit of a pickle. You can no longer really *have* results that are unsatisfying, because you are pursuing them by choice. They are what you want, and therefore they satisfy your wants. To continue generating more of what you don't want under these new conditions, you either will have to cook up a completely new story or *decrease* your awareness.

Assuming you prefer to hold onto new awareness (or at least a pretense of awareness, which smells the same), you have changed, and your results must too. To intentionally eliminate unsatisfying results is straightforward but challenging, because you must first know what you want. Many people struggle with letting go of **false beliefs**, conceptual bookmarks that explain unsatisfying results. Examples include

- Feeling that other people, or conflicting commitments, or unyielding conditions, or foolish institutional policies, or *some* prohibitive set of obstacles, block you from getting what you want. To progress, any false beliefs must be set aside (they can always be exhumed, if needed).

- Pursuing things that may be desirable to have, but you believe you *can't* have them. What you can't have is of no interest, and energy spent on it must cease. Chasing something you believe you can't catch is a great generator/maintainer of unsatisfactory results.

- Wanting something that is *less* than what you already have. This is, in effect, a subset of your already satisfied wants, which possess their own set of awareness-related problems.

More ideas and practices are outlined in Part III, "Aligning," to help you deal with these sorts of issues. Once you *are* aware of what you want, you will pour fewer resources into acquiring something else. Instead, your resources will flow into getting what you want. Moreover, because you actually *want* these results, you will be increasingly engaged and more generally results-oriented. One additional benefit coming from this: Because caring about something is basically equivalent to being passionate about it, you will experience more **passion**. You will be passionate again.

CheckIn's job in all this is to provide a persistent, robust, self-correcting structure that does the following:

- Helps you continuously increase your awareness, your presence, and **engagement** levels;
- Helps you to efficiently seek help from and offer help to others pursuing wants the same as or aligned with yours.

Others will want to help you, especially if they share your passion for the results you want. More than just *wanting* to help, the people on your team actually *can* help you. They—like you—have enormous unused potential that becomes much more available as awareness and engagement levels climb. Here lie the untapped resources. Your colleagues will also help you sustain your awareness of just what it was you wanted; they will inspire you to want it even more, now that you want it for them, too. Together you will fill in the details as you go about getting it. CheckIn makes it easier to increase the amount, the frequency, and the depth of your interpersonal connection, and thereby the exchange of help, ideas, and other forms of support.

*Here lie the untapped resources.*

Continuously increasing your degree of personal presence requires increasingly **efficient behavior**. Your degree of presence correlates with your degree of efficiency. Regardless of their level of personal presence, however, people still squander their time. Adding more people to the mix compounds the problem. The number and intensity of temptations to waste time seem to grow with the number of people involved.

*Your degree of presence correlates with your degree of efficiency.*

If your presence is reliably increasing, any time wasting must come from either trouble with your goal, your efficiency, or both. Lack of clarity about your goal, and/or problems with your commitment to reaching it are the most common goal-related time eaters. These are addressed more completely in Parts II, III, and IV of this book.

*The number and intensity of temptations to waste time seem to grow with the number of people involved.*

*The belief that people suffer from some unstoppable raging time famine characterizes our era.*

*If you want more time, you have to figure out how to create it, and then do so.*

*It's a layer of ambiguity, made of human energy.*

With respect to efficiency, there are two fundamental sources of time erosion: (1) a lack of shared lucidity about how to develop increasingly efficient behavior, and the subsequent lackluster commitment to doing so; and (2) neglect of the vast potential of **interpersonal connection.**

The belief that people suffer from some unstoppable raging time famine characterizes our era. This hurtful belief comes from the generally accurate assessment that preservation of our personal resources is not even on the agenda. There will never be enough time when you aren't even working on creating any. If you want more time, you have to figure out how to create it, and then do so.

The everyday, nitty-gritty steps of actually achieving greater efficiency *via* connection are detailed below. They were collected at great cost, over many years of explicit experiment, trial, and error and with the forbearance and creative support of hundreds of participating team members from all over the world.

## EMOTION, WHERE THE USEFUL INFO HANGS

A large percentage of people believe that expressing emotion at work is inappropriate or unprofessional,[1] so they maintain an emotional façade, usually presenting a diminished emotional affect. When emotions are expressed indirectly at work, the distance between people increases. Emotional self-repression reduces both team efficiency and product quality. When you hide behind any kind of façade, you are necessarily less present than you could be, and that intentional interjection of distance constrains engagement levels. It's a layer of ambiguity, made of human energy. Any awareness that you exercise is usually required to monitor the layers more completely and/or to build up the façade even more.

---

1. Though left untold here, the tale of how "professionalism" became associated—in common parlance, anyway—with a state of emotional antisepsis is both interesting and probably sexy.

The CheckIn pattern undermines all that. It increases your awareness of your emotions and helps you express them directly, efficiently, and productively in a team environment. This leads to more efficient communication of more important information with less effort.

The reason you adopt the CheckIn pattern is to benefit yourself. That is, *your profitable use of this pattern does not depend on the other team members doing likewise.* The benefits you realize include

- Increased self-awareness
- Greater capacity for engagement
- More time

The persistent self-awareness and efficient personal disclosure that CheckIn supports will also provide useful new powers and satisfactions.

Other benefits flow from CheckIn. While it is true that "you check in for you," your CheckIn practices affect other team members. Typically, some or all of them will join you in your use of the CheckIn protocol.[2] As a consequence of your *group* checking in, you will be working with people who are experiencing increasing self-awareness, showing greater capacity for engagement, and enjoying more time. Ideally, they will be gathering these benefits more extensively even than you are, which will make your experience even easier. Group CheckIns also provide important information that you might be missing about your colleagues, or worse, that you are empathetically sensing but interpreting incorrectly. The increased flow of important information, coupled with the reduced costs of applied misinformation, will substantially surpass the modest costs of adopting CheckIn.

---

2. "Checking in," as a procedure to inaugurate a gathering, is used widely in various psychotherapy and self-help settings. The Core's CheckIn is a variant of this practice; it defines what it means to "be in."

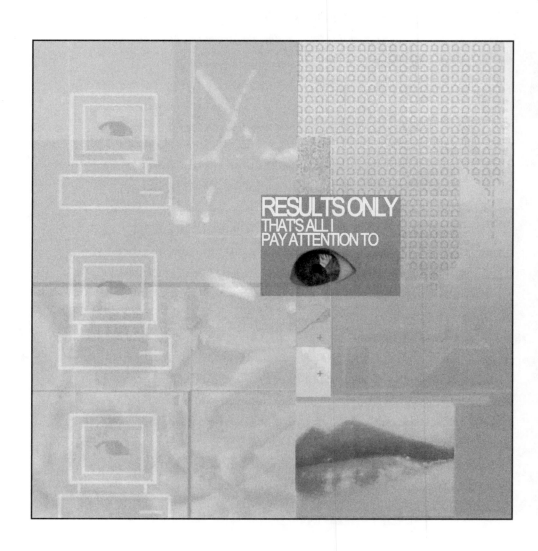

Initially, the adoption of CheckIn and the direct disclosure of emotion will trigger anxiety in some. This is most often due to various prejudices, mistaken beliefs, and the cultural biases of corporate life. Some of these problems are noted below:

- A false belief that you can hide your emotions from others, and that this is good
- Widely held bigotry about human emotions in the workplace
- Personal commitments to the existing indirect ways repressed emotions are dealt with at work
- General inexperience with intentional, cognitively managed emotional expression[3]
- Habitual neglect of the information in emotion—information that is often relevant to the effective execution of tasks

Adopting CheckIn is the first step along a team's path to a more effective and enjoyable life. It is the first thing to learn. It is also the last thing to be mastered.

## THE CHECK IN PROTOCOL

CheckIn represents a commitment to be present. A team's efficient behavior offers evidence of its presence. The CheckIn protocol[4] requires that you specifically commit to waste neither the team's resources nor your own with interpersonal bandwidth consumption that is valueless or diverting. When you check in, you re-express your *commitment* to operate within the constraints of The Core protocols.

*A team's efficient behavior offers evidence of its presence.*

---

3. This lack of sophistication is diminishing rapidly. Significant percentages of high-tech workers have had direct experience with psychotherapy and counseling.

4. If you pass, say, "I pass. I'm in." This statement means that you accept the commitments and decline to reveal your emotional state.

## The Specific "In-ness" Commitments

These behaviors, when used consistently in a team context and adopted in advance via a Decider session (discussed in Part II), seem to yield the best ideas most efficiently for team action. When you say, "I'm in" (see "Group Check In"), you commit to the following behaviors:

- You will listen and observe fully.

- You will offer to the team and accept from the team only rational, efficient behavior.

- If the team or its members stray from the CheckIn commitments, you will mention the deviation as soon as you are aware of it and recommend alternative action. If disagreement about your perception arises, you will efficiently propose appropriate alternative action and resolve the conflict using Decider.

- You will accept explicit emotional information as valuable.

- You will be aware of the ratio of time you spent effectively speaking to the time you spent listening.

- You will speak only and always when you

  - Have a relevant question.

  - Require more information about the current idea. In that case, you will frame requests for information succinctly and clearly.

  - You will ask no bogus questions—that is, questions that reveal your opinions rather than investigate another's thinking. An example of a good question is as follows: "Jasper, will you say more about [whatever]?"

  - Have a relevant proposal.

  - Have an official speaking role in a Decider.

  - Have immediate, relevant value to add.

  - Are responding to a request for information.

  - Are volunteering a supportive idea to the current speaker. You will ask the speaker if he wants your idea before stating it. The current speaker, of course, is free to accept, investigate, or reject your offer.

- Are performing a CheckOut or a CheckIn.

- Express an idea that is better than the current one (idea pre-amble). In exchange for the opportunity to present your idea, you commit to uphold your idea until one of the following is true: (1) your idea is shown to you to be unsuitable or ineffica-cious; (2) your idea is expanded in a way that includes or tran-scends its original value; or (3) your idea is resolved in a Decider process.

## *Personal Check In*

Anyone on the team can check in as, when, and if he desires. No permission is required. In the case of a personal CheckIn, no partici-pation beyond listening is required from other team members. When you want to check in, you say, "I'm going to check in." This activity takes precedence over any other Core activity except running a Decider session.

## *Group Check In*

Although the purpose of the CheckIn protocol is to facilitate the engagement of the person who checks in, it is more efficient if a general group CheckIn takes place. This situation brings the requirement that every team member will check in or pass (see "Pattern: Passer").

Usually, a group CheckIn takes place at the beginning of a meet-ing or other team gathering, after a break in a long team meeting, or when the group's activities or direction is confusing or conflict-laden. Group CheckIn also occurs at the beginning of telephone meetings, in any contact between individuals, or in electronic chats. To inaugurate a group CheckIn, simply suggest, "Let's check in." You, as the invoker of a group CheckIn, must check in first.

Execution of a group CheckIn proceeds as follows:

1. Start with the invoker. Each person takes a turn when he feels it is appropriate until everyone is "in" or has "passed."

2. Each person says, "I pass," or "I feel [sad and/or mad, and/or glad, and/or afraid]." (Optionally, each person might give a brief explanation of emotional state.)

3. Say, "I'm in." This statement seals your commitment as outlined in the CheckIn commitments.

4. The group responds, "Welcome." This statement acknowledges that they heard your CheckIn and accept your commitment to be "in."[5]

## Example

*Person checking in:* "I feel afraid and glad and sad. I feel afraid that this new project won't be exciting or that it won't turn out well. But I feel glad that we are starting a new project. Also, I feel sad that I'm not with my family today. And I'm in."

*Group:* "Welcome."

## Synopsis

*The expression of emotions is usually neglected on teams.*

The CheckIn protocol reminds you of your commitments to efficiency-seeking behavior and gives you a means of disclosing your emotional state, both for your own benefit and for the benefit of the team. The expression of emotions is usually neglected on teams. This omission causes problems, most of which stem from the irrepressibility of emotion combined with the de facto prohibition of its straightforward verbal expression. The CheckIn protocol provides a simple, structured way for you to do the following:

---

5. As with any protocol, positive and negative acknowledgments are essential to smooth functioning. They mark the ends and beginnings of things and serve as transition points. Saying "Welcome" at first feels artificial, but this feeling soon passes and the statement of welcome itself, though somewhat rote, leads to a genuine feeling of welcoming for both the person checking in and the team members who welcome that individual. The welcome is required as an element of the protocol to efficiently conduct the group CheckIn, because it creates rhythm. Experiments to eliminate the welcome (because of the initial fear that it's cheesy) have been uniformly unsatisfying. "Welcome" gives power to the welcomers by allowing them to establish, with certainty, the conclusion of someone's CheckIn.

- Reveal your emotional state.

- Receive vital information about the emotional state of other members of your team.

- Transcend the desire to avoid direct, emotional engagement.

- Reclaim information normally neglected or misinterpreted, and apply it to the achievement of personal and team goals.

- Eliminate waste that results from the maintenance of illusory team information—for example, that everyone is happy or presently involved to the same extent.

## *Core Emotional States*

CheckIn requires that all feelings be expressed in terms of four and only four emotional states:

- Mad
- Sad
- Glad
- Afraid

Although myriad other emotions exist, all can be expressed with acceptable fidelity in terms of mad, sad, glad, and afraid. This limitation does the following:

- Eliminates ambiguity about the naming of emotional states[6]

- Increases mutual understanding

- Supports the expression and acceptance of the traditionally "troublesome" emotional states like sad, afraid, and mad

- Encourages consistent surfacing of the most information-rich and self-disclosing emotions

- Overcomes anxiety about showing vulnerability

- Makes the CheckIn process simple and memorable

---

6. For example, exactly what is meant by the feelings "excited," "anxious," or "pumped"? How do we precisely define "annoyed" or "jazzed"?

If you are unsure which state(s) to reference in your CheckIn, simply pick one or more of the four legal states and check in as if you were in that state.[7] This strategy assumes that you do have an emotional state but find it difficult to identify this state. There are at least traces of each feeling in everyone at all times. Choosing an emotional state will help you focus on your actual state.

It is not legal to check in without referencing any of the four emotional states. Also, it is not legal to introduce emotions other than the four primitives.

## Check In Results

When CheckIn is applied with thoroughness and conviction, it accomplishes several things:

- It commits the team to specific results-oriented behaviors.

- It efficiently reveals individual emotional states in real time, reducing misunderstanding and troublesome misinterpretations.

- It establishes a high level and accelerated rate of personal transmission.

- It disarms participants, enhancing individual receptivity.

- It provides a routine structure for the team to become integrated by thinking, feeling, and acting simultaneously together.

- It minimizes **neurotic** team behavior by moving emotional resources directly into the game, where they can help.

- It increases team members' attention to one another and, hence, their presence.

---

7. The intention is not to deceive anyone but rather is in keeping with The Core's preference for action. If you make a mistake, it is a mistake of commission; that is, you were in a state of applying effort, not paralyzed with fear or confusion. Deeper investigation into the state of "not feeling anything" invariably reveals it as not true. One solution to the problem is to pick one of the four emotions "at random." This choice will yield an emotion that you were previously blocked on. That is, you were unable to feel the emotion, but it was there nonetheless.

- It discloses unperceived and/or unacknowledged team currents and patterns.

- It develops team maturity by explicitly accepting human realities.

- It invokes trust, thereby eliminating costly primary defenses.

- It helps team members understand one another and prevents them from becoming worried about one another's inexplicit but obvious emotions, and speculating on their sources.

### *When to Use Check In*

When should you use CheckIn?

- Check in at the beginning of any meeting. You can check in individually or call for a general CheckIn. If you call for a general CheckIn, you cannot pass and you must be the first person to check in.

- Check in whenever the team seems to you to be moving toward unproductive behavior.

- Check in whenever you feel the need.

### *Check In Guidelines*

- CheckIn creates maximal results if you express at least two feelings when checking in.

- Do not describe yourself as "a *little* mad/sad/afraid"[8] or use other qualifiers that diminish the importance of your feelings.

- Check in as deeply as possible (where "depth" can be thought of as the "degree of disclosure and extent of the feelings of vulnerability that result"); the depth of a team's CheckIn translates directly to the quality of the team's results.

---

8. Unless you are willing to check in as "a little glad," you shouldn't check in as "a little mad/sad/afraid."

*Your urge to confront or otherwise create drama . . . probably derives from the common (albeit unconscious) desire to divert energy away from achieving results.*

## *Check In Rules*

CheckIn is a time apart, and is governed by these constraints:

- No discussion is allowed during CheckIn—only welcome at the end of each CheckIn. Simply listen to each person, speak when it is your turn, and wait until everyone is done before speaking again. Listen and observe as deeply as possible. Gauge and note the congruency of your own emotional response to the CheckIn.

- Do not talk about your own CheckIn before or after CheckIn.

- Do not ask about, reference, or disclose another's CheckIn.

- Do not blame others for your emotions during CheckIn.

- Do not use CheckIn to talk about, yell at, get "pissed off" at, or confront another team member or anyone who is not present.

Unfortunately, the possibility of addressing or confronting other teammates in a CheckIn is sometimes a seductive one. A confrontational or dramatic CheckIn distracts from results. The emotional drama is much more interesting and can seem more important than anything else. If you want to discuss or resolve something with another team member, and you want to do it publicly, something is likely askew with your intention. Instead of obliviously crashing a CheckIn, first ask for help from a trusted friend or mentor. Your urge to confront or otherwise create drama during a CheckIn probably derives from the common (albeit unconscious) desire to divert energy *away* from achieving results. Waste of energy is the usual effect of acting on such an urge. Acting melodramatically is hardly ever about genuinely connecting with the other person. If, after consultation and deliberation, you still want something from the other person (including, perhaps, just being heard), then by all means talk to the individual; but do so in a way that does not distract the team.

# ADDITIONAL DISCUSSION OF CHECK IN

The CheckIn pattern is more than its protocol; it is an ongoing process for a Core-adopting team. CheckIn requires continuously applying team efforts to increase the presence of team members. It necessitates the formation of an additional layer of awareness and discussion centered on one another's level of engagement.

Authenticity, integrity, and consistency are the highest values associated with CheckIn. Increasing personal proximity is the foundation of The Core protocols and is the basis for The Core's style of teamwork.

Perhaps the default "checked-out" state common in today's workplace makes more sense when assembly-line workers perform the same task a thousand times per day. Though it's doubtful, maybe such a remote style is somehow beneficial to the individual when the employer's goal is mindless, repetitive effort. Or maybe it is more tolerable when such a style is combined with a strict caste system. However, on a team with imaginative and creative functions, this state inevitably leads to lateness, mediocrity, and ultimate failure. Few arguments can be made against being as present as possible when you are involved with the group development of intellectual property.

Institutions that depend on teams to think and create are plagued by a lack of personal presence. This problem is in part maintained by an ongoing cultural belief—namely, that "work lives" and "personal lives" are and should remain separate. Loosely stated, this widely held belief holds that you show your "true" self at home, but demonstrate another persona at work. This dichotomy—so goes the belief—is the "professional" way to behave.

One problem with such a belief is that intellectual property is drawn from the human intellect.[9] A given team member's intellect will manifest itself only to the degree that its owner is genuinely present. Human presence contains feelings.

Often, it is tolerable—even mandatory—for team members to "hide" their feelings. Of course, they can't fully hide them, and the cost of attempting to do so is high. Emotions, articulated or not, are the stuff of motivation. They predict and map behavior. They also

*Perhaps the default "checked-out" state common in today's workplace makes more sense when assembly-line workers perform the same task a thousand times per day.*

*A given team member's intellect will manifest itself only to the degree that its owner is genuinely present.*

---

9. Intellectual property is also born of the emotions, intuitions, conflicts, and concordances of the team members who make it.

*Feelings are usually repressed and spent to no purpose, like waste gas in an oil field, burning in a dramatic, purposeless flame.*

give form to incredibly valuable intuitions. The richest information available, feelings are usually repressed and spent to no purpose, like waste gas in an oil field, burning in a dramatic, purposeless flame.

CheckIn gives expression to an explicit group intention to achieve the most gains possible out of the feelings that arrive continuously. It rewards a team disproportionately to the effort involved.

## SOLUTION

*Publicly commit to rational behavior and efficiently disclose your feelings at work.*

The direct, authentic, and safe disclosure of emotion and the management of personal presence will radically increase interpersonal bandwidth, connectivity, and results.

## MULTIPLE LEVELS

The CheckIn pattern takes place simultaneously on different levels. Each individual checks in, thereby

- Bringing himself as fully as possible to the work;
- Connecting as efficiently as possible with teammates;
- Fully engaging his passion in the context of the team's work; and
- Creating a more meaningful, higher-bandwidth channel with the rest of the team.

At another level, the entire team checks in. Teams ordinarily exhibit varying levels of "in-ness" for their members. Their products also show the degree of human involvement in their creation. The checked-in team monitors and manages its presence.

## PRIMARY FUNCTION

Checking in starts or resets individuals, meetings, and entire teams.

# DIAGNOSTIC FUNCTION

The CheckIn protocol is an effective diagnostic tool. Whenever something doesn't feel right in a meeting or when behavior seems ineffective, you can simply refer to the CheckIn commitments. Invariably, at least one of those commitments is being broken. Asserting accountability for any observable broken commitments will increase the results of a meeting and/or take it to a new, more productive level[10] very quickly.

*When behavior seems ineffective, you can simply refer to the CheckIn commitments. Invariably, at least one of those commitments is being broken.*

# WHY ONLY FOUR FEELINGS?

The limit of four basic emotions keeps things simple and direct. Teams that have added other emotions to these four primitives have suffered ill effects.[11]

# COMMON CHECK IN EVASIONS

People may unconsciously evade the directness of the CheckIn protocol. For example, saying "I feel tired" during a CheckIn violates the protocol. If others tolerate this statement, an error condition prevails and results will be unpredictable.

Your fatigue probably can be expressed as an emotional state composed of two or three of The Core emotions. If so, "tiredness" in this case is a "complex" emotion, composed of more than one of the four simple emotions. Complex emotions can include a sequence of simple feelings over time.

For example, if you are "tired," you may be repressing anger—a very tiring effort. You may be suffering (mad and afraid) from a lack of connection with your own passion. You may be tired from excessive effort while experiencing sadness or anger regarding the team

---

10. Typically, this enhancement is referred to as "popping a level," as in the computer "pop" operation, which is often used to switch the current contents to the previously stored ("pushed") contents of a stack. For example, you pop a level when you switch the subject of discussion to *the immediate behavior of the people present while they were discussing the material.* When you "pop" from that topic, you focus on the discussion of the material rather than the material itself.

11. These undesirable results came primarily from the opportunities lost when information was watered down, summarized, or otherwise avoided.

conditions. You may be experiencing the sorrow of loneliness from your lack of closeness to other team members. And so on.

Seeing these phenomena in a useful way is important not only for your well-being but also for the health of the team. The limited palette of four emotional primitives makes it more difficult to persist in behavior patterns that you would rather leave behind.

## PROTOCOL CORRECTNESS AND ITS EFFECTS

Team members must not tolerate deviations from any Core protocol. Thus, in your "tired" state, you must still stick to the four Core emotions.[12] This somewhat minor effort accomplishes four goals:

1. It supports your cognitive development.
2. It helps you recognize your feelings.
3. It promotes your consideration of the stimuli that trigger your feelings.
4. It supports your well-being by helping you create a useful structure for your experience.

## THE DIVIDENDS PAID BY CHECK IN

CheckIn's features and the structure it provides allow its adopters to more effectively address their problems and to take advantage of greater opportunities. For example, if you feel "tired" and you see this state as simple fatigue, you would probably sleep to recover. Of course, you will soon be "tired" again. If you are angry and become "tired" when you repress your anger, checking in may make you aware of the migration of your anger to your "tiredness." With this new awareness, you can deal with the sources of your anger and its repression rather than simply addressing the secondary tiredness that is a symptom of the true problem.

---

12. When someone checks in illegally, by either ignoring the "I feel . . ." format or adding illegal emotions, it is expected that someone else will politely inquire, "So, do you feel glad, sad, mad, or afraid?"

# INCREASED IDENTIFICATION

Identification takes place in two dimensions. First, the practice of clearly expressing your emotions in simple, direct terms with your colleagues often catalyzes your identification of your underlying problems. Others will be able to help, but they can do so only when they know what is happening in your life. Commonly, identification of individual problems will happen for everyone upon the disclosure of general emotion. Second, you may discover that other teammates identify with your feelings, your problems, or both. People increase their identification with one another through shared difficulties. The commonality of feelings at certain times among team members will lead to effective group problem solving. Commonality of emotional states among team members will stimulate deeper thinking about shared underlying activities.

For example, you might check in as sad and then notice that most of your teammates also check in as sad. This realization could motivate you to address the underlying causes of your sadness. Because the sadness appears to be endemic, treating your own sadness might help the entire team.

*Because the sadness appears to be endemic, treating your own sadness might help the entire team.*

## A RESULTS/EFFORT SKETCH

It is helpful to examine the costs and benefits of legal versus illegal CheckIn. For example, when "tired" is the name of your state, you accrue smaller up-front costs than if you had followed the CheckIn protocol. Little mental activity was required to say, "I'm tired."[13] To get a fuller picture of the costs to you and your team when you check in as "tired," however, you must include the following:

- Your continuing ignorance of the reason for your tiredness

- Your repetition of the behavior that led to the tiredness

- Your teammates' ignorance of the cause of your tiredness and the consequent ineffectiveness of their connection with you

---

13. When oblivion is an acceptable mentality, the mental maintenance costs are cheap.

- Everyone's ignorance of team or product issues related to your tiredness

Checking in as "tired" is clearly a smaller initial investment than digging more deeply and mapping your state onto the four emotions. When you make that effort, the up-front costs will increase to include the following:

- Identifying that you are in a complex state[14]
- Reducing your state to emotional primitives
- Disclosing the primitive feelings to others in the language they commonly use and accept as legitimate (you may experience some initial costs in the effort to be courageous and truthful in your CheckIn)

If things go well, you will also experience more personal expense in terms of the additional thought expended to evaluate the cause of your true emotional state. These costs must be weighed against the following gains:

- Your deeper awareness of the emotional elements of your tiredness
- The diminished likelihood of your repeating the behavior that led to the tiredness
- Your teammates' awareness of the actual elements of your tiredness and the consequent extra effectiveness in their connection with you
- Everyone's consideration of possible team issues related to your tiredness

## OTHER COMMON EVASIONS

Two other emotions that are frequently substituted for the CheckIn emotions are "excited" and "nervous." Excitement is a mixture of gladness and fear, with the larger portion going to gladness. Sadness

---

14. A complex state consists of more than one emotion.

and anger may also creep into the "excited" state. Nervousness largely consists of fear, though anger makes more than an occasional contribution. The proportions of the four simple emotions that constitute one of these complex states[15] will vary, but the nuances will become clear only when the individual maps his complex state to a simple one.

## CHANGE AND FEELINGS

Groups are usually in motion, having both speed and direction. Feelings, when expressed publicly in a commonly understood language and updated sufficiently often, can guide a team in efficiently changing its course or velocity. Teams can change gracefully, in unison, in motion, just as a flock of birds might. Organizational change can potentially take place with both efficiency and precision. Ideally, a change of direction, velocity, organization, or any other feature of a group in motion will bring the group closer to its goal at lower cost. Feeling and thinking simultaneously represent the only way to accomplish this goal.

*Groups are usually in motion, having both speed and direction.*

## CHARACTERISTICS OF A CHECKED-IN TEAM

What should you expect when your team is checked in?[16]

- You feel feelings in a fluid way. That is, you can express your feelings clearly and then move on. You don't get "stuck" on a certain feeling.

- The expressed feelings yield useful information—energy that enables the team to make appropriate changes.

- Team members build on one another's ideas not only because it is policy, but also because the effort feels good.

---

15. Other complex states that fall into the class of common hybrid emotions include psyched, pumped, resentful, satisfied, full, and jealous.

16. This list is derived primarily from observing BootCamp teams and listening to their self-descriptions. Most BootCampers have experienced the final stages of BootCamp in these terms. At that point, they have reached a state of shared vision and feel fully checked in. BootCamp is really just a five-day journey to a fully checked-in state, providing a sample of what is possible.

- You laugh a lot.

- You ask teammates for help the moment you suspect you might be stuck.

- You finish teammates' sentences.[17]

- You need only a look to communicate a complete idea. Much of the time, you are aware of what other teammates are thinking.

- You can solve difficult problems in real time.

- You can make big changes with minimal discomfort.

- You are focused only on results.

- You are not afraid to let teammates feel things. You encourage one another to feel.

- You cry with one another.

- You feel like your work is an integral part of your life. It is indistinguishable from play. You work 24 hours per day and, at the same time, you never work. It is part of what you like about yourself. You eat and sleep work, and yet the job is not taxing. It is often fun and mostly meaningful.

- You feel that you can solve any problem that is presented.

- You tackle the biggest problems that you can imagine and solve them.

- You are willing to be patient and wait for a big idea if something seems like it will require too much effort.

- You only hire someone for the team who will push you to be greater.

- You don't solve problems by automatically requiring more time, money, or people.

- You have a constant flow of good ideas that you share with your teammates.

- You are always willing to drop your idea for a better one.

---

17. This sentence-finishing is a way of saying that you can anticipate where a teammate is headed because you are headed there with him. The speaker is just providing commentary for the team's trip.

# CHECK IN AT MEETINGS

CheckIn provides a way for you to increase your presence. How present you are is up to you. You can't pay attention if you are not attending. Showing up is "openers."

If you spend a good part of your work time doing things you'd prefer not to do, when you'd rather be producing specific results, you might want to consult your feelings. Your own desires and feelings about what you are doing can be an effective way to reach your most efficient behavior.

Sometimes, feeling angry about doing something that seems inefficient, or pro forma, is simply a healthy response to waste. If some of your tasks do not contribute to the desired result, they are not worth doing. Specs, schedules, plans, or presentations are not usually the result. Likewise, meetings, reviews, and administration are not the result. While these things can contribute to achieving the result, they often devolve into self-sustaining adjunct activities that contribute less than they cost. If you consistently perform tasks not related to producing the product or directly contributing to those producing it, you are probably doing something wrong. Your more fully engaged presence is surely needed somewhere. Not only can your feelings clue you in, but they can help sustain you in increasing your focus. Your anger—mapped into determination—will be required if you are to purge such wasteful expenditures from your life.

Most meetings are marginally effective, at best. If you complain about too many meetings and then continue attending them, you might want to check your integrity. If you do not feel inclined to change, protest, or revolt, then you are committed to waste and should stop complaining.

Don't attend many meetings where you don't use CheckIn. If you do check in, it means that you want to be there, and the other attendees must take you as you are. You may be sad, angry, glad, or in some more complex state. Yes, you'll be there, but teammates must let you all the way in. You have to stop dividing yourself; stop splitting. Stop being false just because you're in a conference room. Start actually engaging. For example, when you think an idea someone

*Showing up is "openers."*

*Specs, schedules, plans, or presentations are not usually the result.*

*If you complain about too many meetings and then continue attending them, you might want to check your integrity.*

*Stop being false just because you're in a conference room.*

states, or one a group adopts, is a poor one, use Investigator (see Part III). Either you don't understand it, or it *is* a poor idea. Stop everything, and find out why someone would say such a thing at this time. What was the purpose? What is the meaning of the contribution? Your teammates will have to live with your inquisitive engagement. You will be present, and you will engage them. You will see them. You will hear what they say. You will seek information about their emotional states, beliefs, plans, and skills. You will connect with other team members to the maximum extent possible. They will have to adjust to your strategy and its results or else not invite you—which would be fine.

That's checking in.

## BEING THERE

The process of developing high-tech products relies on team presence. This relationship is particularly crucial if you are aiming for great products. If you aren't present, you can't possibly be great.

## DON'T DO IT

*Don't let the mediocre monsters get you; they are just a diversion.*

You're a human being. Don't let the mediocre monsters get you; they are just a diversion. Check in. Bring your whole self to the job, including your emotional self. After all, that's the source of your creativity. Your creativity is bundled up in those repressed feelings, constrained by conflict you try to avoid, awaiting that seriousness of purpose you keep putting off. Your creativity can't be seen in that mess. Make it visible. Stir yourself up; stir up trouble. Conflict leads to passion, so you have no reason to fear it. Vitality is passionate. Care about how you spend your life.

# PATTERN: CHECK OUT

## PROBLEM

*When you can't be present, you stay in a meeting anyway, regardless of the cost of your false presence to yourself and your team.*

When the goal is truly achieving results, you must remove yourself from the environment when you cannot contribute. Convention suggests it is more important to be *physically* present than to be *actually* present, so most people will remain on the scene even when they can no longer contribute. When you cannot add to the process, however, you subtract from it.

Use CheckOut when you are aware that you cannot contribute at a rate you find acceptable. This behavior is important to you, because it is important to make your time count. It is important to the team, because you distract others from getting their results if your body is present but the rest of you isn't. The goal is that your physical presence means your actual presence.

*Convention suggests it is more important to be physically present than to be actually present, so most people will remain on the scene even when they can no longer contribute.*

## SOLUTION

*When you are not contributing, leave the environment without distracting your teammates.*

# THE CHECK OUT PROTOCOL

The execution of a CheckOut:

1. Say, "I'm checking out."
2. Immediately physically leave the group until you're ready to check in.

## Synopsis

*Others may become
alarmed by what they
perceive as your
abrupt disconnection;
but they'll survive any
momentary discomfort
and even prosper in
your absence.*

Use your time off in a way that will allow you to return refreshed and participate fully, even though you may not feel like using your time in that way. While there is no shame in checking out, your lack of contribution should inspire concern. Give it some thought. Also, you may experience discomfort when you check out, but it will soon be lost in the greater sense of relief that you feel in living out your commitments.

Others may become alarmed by what they perceive as your abrupt disconnection; but they'll survive any momentary discomfort and even prosper in your absence. Avoid the temptation to exploit their potential for alarm by making a show of your CheckOut (for example, dramatizing the viewpoint that *they* are driving you to check out).

## Check Out Results

CheckOut removes you from the group when you are not fully checked in, and it gives you the space and time to prepare yourself to return and be productive.

## When to Use Check Out

When you need time to take care of yourself in any way (e.g., to calm down, rest, or do what is necessary to return fully checked in). CheckOut gives you and your team the opportunity to be productive simultaneously when that is impossible if you remain.

CheckOut is also used when individuals need to take care of personal matters.

## Check Out Commitments

As part of adopting CheckOut, you make the following commitments:

- To admit your lack of productive engagement and physically leave

- To not check out to get attention

- To return as soon as you can be productively engaged again

- To return without unduly calling attention to your return

- To be clear with the team about your checking out (For instance, tell the entire team when you are checking out, not just one person. If you are checking out for more than an hour or so, let your teammates know when you will return.)

## Check Out Guidelines

CheckOut is an admission that you are unable to contribute at the present time. It is intended to help the team, not to manipulate it. This pattern is not intended for any of the following purposes:

- To express your anger
- To cause disruption
- To draw attention to yourself
- To create drama
- To trigger others' feelings

You can tell it's time to check out if the idea occurs to you. The rest of the team will be relieved of the maintenance costs of pretending that you are contributing. Seeing yourself as an occasional noncontributor is recognizing a truth about yourself and creating opportunities for others.

In our experience, when team members have trouble with CheckOut, a problem exists with the team. Not being clear about who is checked in and who is checked out indicates a lack of team connection.

When a person drifts away, whether remaining in the room or not, without telling the other team members, he is implicitly telling

*You can tell it's time to check out if the idea occurs to you.*

teammates that neither he nor the team matters. He is breaking the CheckIn commitments.

---

# PATTERN: PASSER

## PROBLEM

---

*You "go along" with group activities that
you don't believe in, increasing cynicism and your own sense
of powerlessness for yourself and your team.*

*Freedom is the center
of The Core.*

Freedom is the center of The Core. It is essential that all activities associated with it retain their volitional nature. This flexibility serves as the basis of accountability. If people do things because they feel that they are expected or in some way required to do so, they give themselves an accountability holiday. In The Core protocols, the right to pass—indeed, the obligation to pass when desired—is always available except as otherwise noted. The flip side of this right is that every individual will be held accountable for his Core-related actions.

Anyone using The Core can "pass" on any operation, with two exceptions:

1.  Team members may not pass on a Decider vote unless they were checked out before the proposal was made.
2.  If you call for a general CheckIn, you cannot pass and must check in first.

## SOLUTION

---

*Explicitly decline to participate when you don't want
to do something.*

At an appropriate time (presumably at the beginning of some process or protocol), say, "I pass." If you know you will pass on something, you are obliged to do so as soon as you are aware of your decision. Once something is started, you can still pass.

### *Example*

A CheckIn is occurring. You don't want to check in, so at an appropriate point (earlier is better) during the process, you signal the group by saying, "I pass. I'm in."

### *Synopsis*

Passing expresses your decision not to participate in an event—that is, to opt out of a process. Passing sets a margin of safety for everyone. It takes courage.

### *Passing Guidelines*

- Passing is always permissible except during a Decider vote.
- There is no discussion about a person's passing.
- To invoke your right to pass, you must say, "I pass." Silent passing is not allowed. Silence indicates that you are awaiting your turn.
- Inevitably others will be curious. Do not explain your passing.
- You can "unpass."[18]

### *Passer Results*

- It relaxes tension.
- It reduces resistance.
- It creates safety.

---

18. For example, you might "pass" before some activity gets started and then change your mind while it's in progress.

- It provides a way out.
- It generates wider acceptance of the protocols.
- It exercises self-care.
- It celebrates individual freedom.

### When to Use Passer

Do it when and if desired—even if you just want to see how it feels to pass.

### Passer Commitments

The following commitments are required with Passer:

- To take good care of yourself
- Not to judge, shame, hassle, or interrogate anyone who passes
- Not to judge, shame, hassle, or interrogate those who do not pass
- Not to explain why you are passing (no matter how great the urge)

*A temporary inclination to dramatics is always a good reason to check out.*

If you feel the need to "punish" the group, or you desire to use passing for some other reason than simply wanting to opt out of some activity, something more is likely afoot. You probably need to check out rather than pass. Like CheckOut, the Passer protocol should not be used for dramatic purposes. A temporary inclination to dramatics is always a good reason to check out.[19] The Core is intended to replace needlessly dramatic expression with more deliberate behavior.

## PATTERN: CONNECTION

### PROBLEM

*Others have desirable qualities that you lack,
and vice versa.*

---

19. A permanent inclination to dramatics is a good reason to launch an effective psychotherapy program.

*Connect before transmission; get close enough to others so
that all risk sharing desirable qualities.*

The same sloppy practices that degrade the emotional environment
(for example, the repression of feelings, tolerance of lack of thinking,
and frequent loss of intention) have other pernicious effects:

- Teams cannot decide anything.
- Shared vision is generally neglected.
- Useful feedback is seldom available.

These weaknesses—described in antipatterns throughout this book—
have a corrosive effect on team results and negatively affect team
durability. Sustained, high-performance, collaborative connection
among team members is impossible where such practices prevail.
Thus, **connection** is a *prerequisite* for the transmission and reception
of desirable qualities among teammates.

It is possible to connect with one another by adopting new,
intentionally designed behaviors. The idea of adoptable, designed
behavior may be new to readers. It may be difficult at first to even
imagine a new way of being together, much less to design one. What
would it be like? What could it be like?

*It may be difficult at
first to even imagine a
new way of being
together, much less to
design one.*

The difference between the lifestyle determined by the everyday antipatterns you typically encounter and the results-oriented
lifestyle of The Core is enormous. It is the difference between an
intentionally designed and optimized team culture and a loose collection of accepted practices that a team has accidentally inherited.
*It is the difference between dwelling in a cave you happened upon and living
in a house you designed.*

## CONNECTION AND RICH INFORMATION

Rich information is produced when a more open environment exists
among team members. For example, personal weaknesses are freely

*It costs the same amount of time for your listeners to listen whether you say something trivial or something profound.*

*Preventing discomfort seems to be the highest value in the default interface.*

discussed and team help is sought to remedy them. Personal gifts are acknowledged and accepted without fuss. Rich information carries more commitment, discloses more vulnerability, and clearly identifies more gifts and talents than does commonplace information. It carries more weight but does not consume more bits.[20] Each bit counts for more because the team culture requires more significance and less obscurity in each exchange.

It costs the same amount of time for your listeners to listen whether you say something trivial or something profound. If you say something important, you use your "bit allocation" more effectively. Of course, both listener and speaker must be prepared to deal with units of greater significance than "normal." This preparation, which resets expectations, establishes the higher bandwidth connection among the team members. *Higher interpersonal bandwidth is character-ized by more significance per utterance.*

In The Core, the additional significance derives from the per-sonal integrity behind the utterances. For example, you don't speak unless you have filtered your planned utterance through the CheckIn commitments.

Rich information is invariably produced when a team member expresses criticism in a way[21] that adds significant value to another's work. This value-generating capability is uncommon even though adding value is the normal, healthy thing to do.

Human-human inefficiencies must be handled before you can expect to routinely make the best class of connection and achieve the resulting hyperprogress. Most people spend their working hours in the default human-human interface environment, created by no one, but affected by everyone. The default interface provides only the most rudimentary, often self-defeating, interpersonal connection. Prevent-ing discomfort seems to be the highest value in the default interface. This is at the cost of achieving results. Being a part of this undesigned

---

20. By *bit*, we mean the smallest unit capable of carrying a single piece of information. Information is, in the classic Claude Shannon definition, the difference that makes a difference.

21. See Chapter Fifteen, "The Perfection Game Pattern."

interpersonal world, day after day, people simply don't connect, except by chance. *Chance*[22] *determines the most vital linkages.*

For your team to gain the capacity to perform remarkable interpersonal feats, you must implement (if not design) numerous new interpersonal practices, beginning with Connection. The problems addressed by the Connection pattern are easily stated:

- Initiate relationships with people and groups with whom you can have significant communication

- Ensure that you and other team members or groups can collaborate based on the continuous exchange of rich information

Once people are connected, the richer the information transmitted, the greater the team.

In The Core, a connection is made when two or more people explicitly decide to collaborate *intentionally*. They agree to disclose and receive information that, even at the start, is sufficiently rich to accelerate the process of collaboration. A connected team has the capacity to receive and transmit information according to mutually acceptable protocols. That is, it is positioned to communicate.

Most teams fail to connect because they don't define the vital preliminary tasks of Connection. They don't "test the line" to see what speeds are attainable. They don't invoke any communication protocols.

*Most teams fail to connect because they . . . don't "test the line" to see what speeds are attainable.*

You are connected when your team meets the following conditions:

1. Team members agree that the first goal is to establish a connection.
2. The state of connection has been explicitly acknowledged.
3. The effectiveness of the connection is constantly monitored.

Obviously, explicit connection will always precede attaining the highest rates of transmission and reception. In The Core, you don't

*In The Core, you don't bother to attempt communication without connection.*

---

22. Or "chemistry," "vibes," or some other quack notion or superstition that is neither examined nor explained. You might as well shake rattles and toss salt.

bother to attempt communication without connection. As all of The Core protocols heighten the probability of sustained connection, no single connection protocol exists. CheckIn, however, is the protocol used most often to initiate a connection.[23]

---

23. It is essential to periodically "pop a level" when working with a team and to scrutinize the state of connection and the effective rate of transmission prevailing. Generally, simply diverting the team's attention to this matter will cause the effective bit rate to jump to an acceptable level. The degree of innocuousness of the CheckIns is inversely related to the speed of transmissions that will follow. That is, deeper CheckIns mean faster connections.

# THREE

# Check In Antipatterns

---

## ANTIPATTERN:
## TOO EMOTIONAL

### PROBLEM

*You think that you or others are too emotional
at work.*

### SUPPOSED SOLUTION

*Constrain your emotions.
Help others do the same.*

Often, "conventional wisdom" either is so inefficient as to be functionally useless or is altogether wrong. The application of conventional wisdom usually does not lead to behavior that will achieve the desired results. This disconnection is especially likely in a world where the rate of change undercuts any value that conventional wisdom might have provided in slower-moving times.

*One-eighties are pathological, broadly accepted "truths" that prove to be—upon experimentation— incorrect by every measure.*

*"You are too emotional" is really a way of saying, "I am not emotional enough."*

*It is highly unlikely that any healthy, mature person suffers from superabundant feeling.*

People often adhere to ineffective policies and inefficient behavioral/cultural norms, despite the repeated failure of those policies and norms. Conventional wisdom so often turns out to be utter folly that we have created a name for the phenomenon: a one-eighty. We apply this term to common ideas that are not only incorrect, but maximally incorrect—that is, favorable results are virtually certain if the opposite idea is adopted. They are wrong by 180 degrees. One-eighties are pathological, broadly accepted "truths" that prove to be—upon experimentation—incorrect by every measure. These imposter truths are best viewed as virulent, mimetic viruses.[1]

"Too emotional" is a term often applied to explicitly emotional behavior or to people who behave emotionally. It is most often used incorrectly, and is a double one-eighty—it's wrong twice over. "You are too emotional" is really a way of saying, "I am not emotional enough." Both the subject ("you") and the diagnosis ("too emotional") are false, or at least support contrary interpretations. The true subject of the thought behind the sentence is not "you," but rather, the speaker. The diagnosis of "too emotional" is the opposite of the truth—the speaker's emotion is insufficient; your emotion isn't excessive.

The most obvious question to ask when you are the target (or are defending the target) of the declamation "You are too emotional" leaps out: Too emotional for what? It is highly unlikely that any healthy, mature person suffers from superabundant feeling.[2] Some disorders may cause "runaway" feelings. "Crimes of passion" call to mind the potential difficulties of emotional turbulence. In The Core context, however, the people involved typically remain within normal bounds, and strong emotion does not exclude vigorous thinking. On the contrary, it motivates the highest order of thinking. Generally,

---

1. A world replete with one-eighties is characterized by mnemonically attractive but high-folly-content phrases that masquerade as conventional wisdom. By the linguistic jujitsu of calling such travesties "one-eighties," bogus wise sayings—reflective of conventional beliefs—are converted to harmless and potentially useful aphorisms.

2. This sentence is not meant to argue for the absence of suffering. Obviously, much in our emotional palette is accompanied by discomfort, even suffering. The key idea is that the suffering is not pointless, but informative.

the stronger the emotion, the more essential it is that thinking take place, and the more vigorous the thinking should be.

"You are too emotional" really says more about the speaker than about the target. It is difficult to imagine that your emotions—no matter how strong—would cause more harm than gain.

## EMOTIONAL ENOUGH

One function of emotion is to quickly transmit a large volume of information to your cognitive faculty. Another is to reveal your personal state to others. Your emotions make your state readily visible: Your skin color changes; you unconsciously contort your facial expressions, tremble, gesticulate, laugh, or cry. You express your emotions in perceptible ways, and those near you can derive useful information about their own predicament.

Many emotions cause discomfort to the person who experiences them. In addition, one person's discomfort will often infect others; teammates often respond viscerally and empathically to your discomfort, and you tend to absorb their discomfort via some empathic channel. Empathy is useful, especially when the empathizer is aware of his responses as empathetic ones; nevertheless, empathetic discomfort may cause you to behave oddly. You will respond to your discomfort at another person's discomfort in ways that are not only self-destructive, but also harmful to those you would protect from discomfort. For example, you might very well leap into a situation, unprepared and uninvited, to preclude, prevent, or minimize another's possible discomfort.

*Empathetic discomfort may cause you to behave oddly.*

The emotions in The Core protocols (mad, sad, glad, and afraid) provide a sufficient palette to express and contain discomfort. It is easier to hear someone say, "I am angry" than to watch that person hurt himself and others by demonstrating otherwise unspoken anger.

## EMOTION PREVENTION

Early prevention is not more efficient than a tardy remedy in the case of emotion. The most common pathological team behavior used

*The absence of discomfort is not more important than the presence of the truth. Shielding others from the truth rescues no one, and condemns everyone.*

to avoid discomfort is called **rescue**. This term has its own one-eighty incarnation, as (1) no danger exists and (2) the rescue attempt causes more harm than the natural discomfort and any related empathic discomfort, so that (3) if any actual rescue is needed, it is to escape the good intentions of the would-be rescuers. Each of the four emotions can produce discomfort in others. Three (mad, sad, and afraid) are by nature uncomfortable, at least for the person who is feeling them, and usually for others, by extension.

Rescue is common and costly. It seems there is no limit to the effort that people will exert to deflect someone's anger, to defer potentially highly productive conflict, or to avoid "hurting someone's feelings." People absorb substantial inconveniences and go to great distances in vain attempts to escape the simple fact that where truth prevails, "hurt feelings" often arise. While minimization of discomfort associated with learning about oneself (or any topic) is a value worth supporting, the absence of discomfort is not more important than the presence of the truth. Genuine comfort is never increased by hiding the truth. Shielding others from the truth rescues no one, and condemns everyone. Wouldn't you rather know if your zipper is wide open before you give a speech? Wouldn't you rather experience the small embarrassment you feel when someone tells you about it, instead of feeling extreme embarrassment as you review the videotapes later?

The same principle applies to much larger matters than zippers. Sometimes entire organizations are created, maintained, and ultimately wasted in a company so that one executive can avoid confronting another who has failed, or is not performing as desired.[3] When someone visibly fails, everyone who cares to know it, does know it. This statement holds true for those in the hierarchy above and alongside the person who failed. Rather than "hurt the person's feelings," his boss may appoint the employee to a new position that salvages some pride.

---

3. Actually, vivid failure attracts rescue less than the more common lack of excellence or suitability.

In this case, the people getting "rescued" are mediocre managers who have failed to mature and often haven't a clue as to why they are unsuccessful, in part because nobody will talk honestly about their lackluster results. Furthermore, large numbers of people are often asked to follow the demonstrably incompetent manager. In fact, reorganizations commonly hinge on rescues. Moving mountains to "save face" is a "nice" way of (avoiding) dealing with real problems.

Not telling the truth may avoid short-term discomfort for someone, but more often it dooms the "rescued" party to an even larger disaster in the future. Saving face, in this context, means ultimately losing more face, and adds heaps of culpability to those people who didn't talk about the original, "avoided" truth. To be genuinely "nice," tell the truth to the person who needs to hear it. Even if you don't handle the session well, the truth is always the best thing to offer, if available.[4] If you were to tell the truth to the person who needs help rather than withhold the truth in an effort to rescue that person, you would find that the message you delivered would be much more precise and accurate.

*Reorganizations
commonly hinge on
rescues.*

## EMOTIONAL MATURITY

Being "too emotional" seems implausible, perhaps even impossible. Is "too emotional" an oxymoron? Not ThinkingandFeeling simultaneously, so that you cannot benefit from your feelings, is a genuine concern. While you may not be "too emotional," you may act without cognition. It is also true that you tend to want to act when you feel uncomfortable or observe another's discomfort. You want to "do something" to immediately relieve your own distress. Behavior without thought and intention, regardless of one's emotional state, is immature and usually costly. Avoiding unthinking action requires direct, substantial, and continuing attention.

---

4. On the other hand, telling a "truth" when there is no conceivable benefit and you merely produce discomfort is not recommended. See the discussion of IntentionCheck in Chapter Five.

*The extent to which you view yourself with increasingly accurate self-observation—in real time—is the degree to which you may claim to be mature.*

Maturity is really about the locus of one's identity. The extent to which you view yourself with increasingly accurate self-observation—in real time—is the degree to which you may claim to be mature. A mature identity considers more of its total experience than a less mature identity. In the emotional domain, this maturity includes the following:

- Experiencing your feelings
- Thinking about what you feel
- Monitoring the development of your relationship with your emotions
- Understanding the dynamics of your emotional idiosyncrasies and their effects on both you and other people
- Reflexive investigation into the meaning of episodes of emotional discomfort, rather than the more typical pursuit of "discomfort relief"
- Thoughtful assessment of any "sense of urgency" coinciding with your own or others' emotional discomfort
- Determination of intent before acting or speaking when faced with significant emotion

When these activities become habitual, you have probably become "emotional enough." Whether you can ever become "too emotional" is left as an exercise for the reader. Most likely, it is not the current problem. Rather than worry about the ersatz problem of excessive emotionality, mature team members will focus on the real meaning of, and issues related to, human emotion that arise on a connected team.

## ACTUAL SOLUTION

*Maximize your emotional abilities
and support them in others.*

Oddly, the biggest challenge to collaborative intimacy stems from defenses against the benefit of prolonged and increasing connection. The team crises that arise from this resistance occur early and persist indefinitely. When your emotions erupt, with neither clear intention nor mature self-observation, they function much like a baby's cry. You demand attention, but, unlike a baby, you lack the legitimacy conferred by the baby's utter dependency on others.

When your way of dealing with emotions disrupts team progress, then you are (at least) in a bad relationship with your feelings. The problem of "excessive" or bursty emotionality does not lie in the abundance or the richness of the feelings, but in their everyday denial.

Although emotions carry important information for the mature individual and team, they have little or no moral value. The way in which you respond to emotions determines the extent to which you benefit from them. Your responses are part of the habits that determine the value of your experience. Each of the four emotional conditions in The Core's palette brings essential information to light. This system provides more goodness to the team than the faux-rational palaver (that is, "let's discuss [or fight about] the architecture") that is often used for efficient emotional disclosure. Instead of limitless and irresoluble emotionally charged topics, why not subscribe to the effective discharge of emotions?

Obviously, the aggregate emotional information of a team is highly relevant to the team. This relevance applies not only at the time of an emotion, but also throughout the life cycle of that emotion on the team.[5] Any group includes several types of people: emotional leaders, who anticipate others' feelings with their own; empathic types, who feel what others are feeling; people who routinely project, by transmitting or attaching feelings to others; and the oblivious, the denying, and the obfuscating.

Often, your feelings are identical and/or occurring in synchrony with the emotions of other members of the team. This shared state gives rise to emotional wildfires, where a feeling leaps from person to person, out of control. Moreover, your emotional intensity often aligns with that of others, even when the specific feelings do not.

*When your emotions erupt, with neither clear intention nor mature self-observation, they function much like a baby's cry.*

*Instead of limitless and irresoluble emotionally charged topics, why not subscribe to the effective discharge of emotions?*

*This shared state gives rise to emotional wildfires, where a feeling leaps from person to person, out of control.*

---

5. Emotions do have a life cycle, which is especially vivid in a multipersonal environment. If you accept that the feelings of each person affect everyone on the team, then you must be open to the way in which emotions work, and to the fact that the process does not happen in zero time.

You will encounter dozens of strategies and phenomena on any team. Myriad types and kinds of human interpersonal emotional strategies exist—productive and benign, or costly and wasteful. A plethora of group emotional phenomena, such as wildfires and synchronicity, are possible. Obviously, feelings will wriggle through the emotional field created by the various forces emanating from the individuals in the group. The progress and resolution of each feeling takes time, and demands attention. Less obvious are the patterns that emerge in the way that a given team deals with the constant stream of feelings challenging its members.

Applying cognition to the strategies, phenomena, and patterns reduces these costs and the time required to deal with them. Mixing the feelings with intentional emotion processing facilitates cognition, leading to a mature, emotionally integrated team. There are only two requirements to begin:

- You must acknowledge the features of the emotional terrain.
- You must solicit support and information from others while navigating it.

If you don't investigate your experience together, the status quo will probably persist. If you do investigate it, profound change will inevitably come your way, because teams who read their own information will tend to exploit its richness. Even if their numbers are few at first, some teams will overcome their emotional superstitions, their irrational dread of expressing their feelings openly. These teams will win in the end.

*Most people have belittled and rejected the "touchy-feely."*

Most people are uncomfortable when their colleagues and friends admit what they are feeling together. Who would want to further investigate the meaning of the feelings experienced? Most people have belittled and rejected the "touchy-feely."[6,7] Often,

6. It is useful to reject exercises and quackery that is supposed to be touching and full of feeling, but isn't. Just because something is uncomfortable doesn't mean it is meritorious. Nor do failed efforts in support of connection condemn connection.

7. The only other team phenomenon that is so universal is the typical collaborative dysfunction. Perhaps a causal relationship exists between emotional bigotry and the extent of "people problems" encountered. Any group that collectively loathes and rejects the majority of the relevant information in its midst will have problems with group navigation.

*You cannot expect valuable intellectual property to flow from creatures that superstitiously fear and therefore shun the riches of their own information mechanisms.*

*You will still be scorched by blasts of heated feeling; you will still be bone-chilled by the occasional freeze of nerveless apathy.*

although perhaps they didn't mean to, they have also rejected touching and feeling along with it. The choice is whether or not to maintain such an immature posture indefinitely. Information-impoverished teams will obviously find it difficult to establish and maintain productive connections.

Just as a mature person will speak of feelings rather than simply react to them, mature teams will explicitly integrate Thinking and Feeling. They will apply intention to their actions. Their initial emotional reactions will provide information to be evaluated, catalogued, and applied as needed to achieve their collective goals.

The alternative—knee-jerk behavior—is little better than what you'd expect from other animals. You cannot expect valuable intellectual property to flow from creatures that superstitiously fear and therefore shun the riches of their own information mechanisms.

Don't worry about the perils of becoming "too emotional"; the opposite extreme is more dangerous. By accepting that emotions are useful, and by overcoming the habit of near-continuous emotional denial that has been virtually mandated by everyday conditions, your fear of revealing your feelings will lose power. Then you can acquire the greater awareness of your environment needed to explain your mysterious emotions. After you have cleared up the backlog, you may well see that there is ample space for a personal work environment led by pure intention.

You will still be scorched by blasts of heated feeling; you will still be bone-chilled by the occasional freeze of nerveless apathy. And you will give and receive information that produces discomfort. Added to the mix, however, will be a new sense of purpose and an increasing mastery of your environment.

# ANTIPATTERN: NO HURT FEELINGS

## PROBLEM

*You don't want to hurt the feelings of your teammates, so
you fail to add the value you have to the team's product.*

One challenge of being fully engaged is that some situations require
you to articulate perceptions that may cause discomfort in others.
Most people don't want to promote emotional distress. Typically,
they prefer that the people around them refrain from showing strong
emotions, regardless of the reason. People go to great lengths to
avoid saying or doing things that may "hurt someone's feelings" or
cause someone to be angry or upset.

## SUPPOSED SOLUTION

*If you can't find a way to tell a truth or perform an act of
leadership that doesn't upset people, don't do it.*

You can't really "cause" or "hurt" another's feelings.[8] A feeling,
as the consistent practice of CheckIn will reveal, is usually more of a
choice than a wholly involuntary event. That you *will* feel something
is typically involuntary; once cognition is awakened, however, much
of what is felt can be shaped by choice.[9] As a result of this fundamental emotional freedom, little is to be gained in analyzing or projecting

---

8. It is important to state clearly that NoHurtFeelings pertains to a specific class of emotional discomfort—emotional hurt that sometimes arises when the concerns of efficiency
and quality are addressed forthrightly and with candor. We are not supporting wanton
disregard of others' feelings or the causation of purposeless emotional pain.
9. It is sometimes difficult, however, to find the distinction between habitual and voluntary.

*Deciding how to behave based on your anticipation of another's feelings is folly.*

*The belief that you can hurt someone's feelings is based on a flawed idea, used to justify an ersatz "solution" you create when you want to avoid responsibility.*

the psycho-physiological mechanics of creating "hurt feelings" in someone else. Deciding how to behave based on your anticipation of another's feelings is folly.

"Hurt" feelings usually combine anger, sorrow, and fear in some way.[10] When you encounter hurt feelings, if you choose to view the emotions as being caused by someone other than the person experiencing them, you are making a disempowering choice.[11]

The belief that you can hurt someone's feelings is based on a flawed idea, used to justify an ersatz "solution" you create when you want to avoid responsibility. Much of the time, the typical person will try almost anything to avoid confronting another's naked, pained feelings. This is true no matter how roundabout, wacky, costly, and ultimately harmful to the other person the avoidance strategy proves. To prevent the unpleasant experience of seeing themselves as contributors to hurt feelings, people will commonly do the following:

- Avoid saying the truth
- Temporize and lie
- Dodge commitments
- Tolerate others' breaking commitments
- Fail to step in and get results
- Withhold vital support

At times, the avoidance becomes downright ludicrous, reminiscent of an "I Love Lucy" episode in which Lucy simply cannot come clean with Ricky about something and ends up spinning contorted tales and living out bizarre comic plotlines. To avoid uncomfortable feelings, you may do unnecessary or wasteful work that doesn't relate to getting the desired results, or you may knowingly tolerate diminished product or organizational quality.

---

10. There is often a feeling of gladness in the "hurt" party as well. It probably consists of relief that previously repressed truth is at last surfacing and being handled, thereby freeing the energy that had previously been allocated to its repression.

11. Precisely what a person will choose to feel in response to certain stimuli (for example, feeling anger when called a name), though it is not caused by the stimuli, is somewhat predictable. Because certain nearly universal emotional responses to various stimuli occur, it is easy to confuse causation with correlation.

Though it is a misnomer, many refer to the underlying dynamics of this antipattern as *conflict avoidance*. Actually, the term "conflict avoidance" is itself a one-eighty. Conflicts aren't avoided by avoiding the feelings that determine or arise from them. On the contrary, the unresolved conflict continues to smolder, greatly complicated by new layers of indirection. The conflict elements themselves may migrate, appearing (in disguise) in behavior, mistakes, bad decisions, and product deficiencies. In fact, conflict-avoidant people are actually clinging to the conflicts they fear. The conflict-avoidant might better be called the "resolution avoidant."

Some initial discomfort almost always is part of the direct, unambiguous communication that is powerful enough to resolve conflict. Among its other virtues, the practice of speaking directly resolves and avoids conflict. Trying to dodge a moment of resolution, out of a fear of hurting someone's feelings, ultimately causes much more sorrow, pain, stress, and loss than the alternatives. Resolution Avoidance[12] is not a well-intentioned sensitivity but a type of neurotic cowardice. It is not concerned with the other person, though it seeks that appearance. Rather, it is an expression of the urge to self-destruct.

As for the hurt feelings you may be afraid of "causing" in other people, their pain most likely reflects just the latest perturbation of old psychic wounds. The sensitivity that is aroused[13] is designed in response to, or to protect, that earlier wound. Whatever the etiology of another's hurt feelings, however, the negative effects are felt in the present: To avoid contact with this discomfort, you avoid genuinely useful contact with the person. This avoidance represents a

*The conflict-avoidant might better be called the "resolution-avoidant."*

*Resolution Avoidance is not a well-intentioned sensitivity but a type of neurotic cowardice.*

---

12. ResolutionAvoidance is really an antipattern intended to explain stresses caused internally when one attaches them to a repressed conflict. These stresses are chronic and only loosely attached to the avoided conflict. Even if the presenting conflict does surface and become resolved, the stresses will remain with the avoider. They will then attach to new conflict situations with a similar constellation of features. Conflict episodes manufactured by these ongoing stresses are generally perceived by their bearer as wholly new and different stresses; in reality, all that has been accomplished from one conflict to the next is the renewed sustenance of an undesirable internal equilibrium.

13. You can usually tell precisely what will hurt someone else's feelings before the fact. He has, by some means, signaled you, ahead of time, regarding the location and class of his sensitivities.

vain attempt to prevent feelings that would arise in the other individual regardless of your behavior.[14]

## ACTUAL SOLUTION

*Focus on team results, not team members' feelings.*

Instead of avoiding feelings, recognize that feelings are important aspects of team functioning. Appreciate demonstrations of true feeling, but act with integrity despite them. Ultimately, your consistent show of integrity will help create an environment where the best possible feelings prevail.

*Minimize manipulation. Focus on results. Practice kindness. Avoid any effort that diminishes your experience of the feelings of others.*

# ANTIPATTERN: WRONG TOLERANCE

## PROBLEM

*You tolerate behaviors that don't work well.*

## SUPPOSED SOLUTION

*Learn to live with life in the "real world" or complain to others who can fix the problems.*

---

14. Moreover, the person's original hurt feelings are compounded many times over by the genuine injury caused by your workarounds. Thus, the person's habit of clinging to his antique wounds is renewed.

To "tolerate" means to permit something, or to allow another's action to pass without acting effectively to the contrary. If what you are tolerating is something good, tolerance is virtuous. Conversely, tolerating the undesirable is akin to creating it.

Whenever you perceive that a virtue is missing or that a vice is present, you either tolerate the situation or try to change it. If you cannot "fix" it, you can at least withdraw your participation. The problem with tolerating the absence of virtue or the existence of vice is that this choice summons them into your life.

You might tell yourself stories about the problem you perceive and your tolerance of it:

- That's just the way it is in the real world.
- Others will not listen even-handedly to your perceptions and advice.
- It's not your place to say truthful but difficult things.
- The problem lies in another department.
- You are not reading the situation correctly. You may not be able to discern beauty from ugliness or efficiency from waste, and your ignorance will be exposed. You'll be rejected or ridiculed.
- You will look dumb if you ask for help to resolve any uncertainty.

## ACTUAL SOLUTION

*Acknowledge that if you tolerate it, you insist on it. If you insist on something, you are its creator.*

Your most effective help to your team will not be limited to words. Preaching or complaining are not effective ways to create change. "We shouldn't . . . ," "We oughta . . . ," "We need to . . . ," "People think . . ."—all of these phrases, when unaccompanied by direct and immediate supportive action, signal insincerity and expose the speaker's lack of belief in direct and personal action.

*Tolerating the undesirable is akin to creating it.*

*The problem with tolerating the absence of virtue or the existence of vice is that this choice summons them into your life.*

*Personally modeling the behavior you desire in others is the most effective means to inspire change.*

Personally modeling the behavior you desire in others is the most effective means to inspire change.[15]

### Wrong Tolerance Corollary

The amount of destructive or wasteful behavior you tolerate is a good measure of (1) your own presence and (2) the amount of destruction or waste you desire.

---

15. Seeing someone do something effective or, even better, being the beneficiary of another's effective action makes an infinitely greater impression than listening to the person's words, no matter how stirring or beautiful (and they usually aren't). After many years of attempting to create useful protocols and patterns for interpersonal application, we have concluded that the "programming mode" of a human being (to the extent that one exists) is triggered only by another human's personal modeling.

# FOUR

# Other Patterns in the Check In Family

## PATTERN: TEAM = PRODUCT

### PROBLEM

*It's easy to identify symptoms but difficult to diagnose team problems and to take the appropriate steps for their remedy.*

Understanding and harnessing team dynamics presupposes that there exists a way to identify and categorize the state of a team. Effective team maintenance will require an institutional capability for treating dysfunctional teams. The institution and the teams must—at a minimum—be able to (1) diagnose a team relative to a normal developmental spectrum, and (2) routinely offer remedial measures to dysfunctional teams. While Team = Product won't provide all the answers, it is a sufficient beginning.

A floundering team promises ill fortune. It's easy to identify the superficial symptoms, such as late products, high turnover, and poor

*Effective team maintenance will require an institutional capability for treating dysfunctional teams.*

*A team's habit of late delivery is seldom remedied by asserting that the deliveries ought to be on time, no matter how emphatically the assertion is made.*

*If your team is process-heavy, your product will have excessive architecture.*

product quality. Identifying the causes underlying those symptoms can prove more challenging. Taking the right steps to purge the team of a particular malady is an even more elusive goal. For example, a team's habit of late delivery is seldom remedied by asserting that the deliveries ought to be on time, no matter how emphatically the assertion is made.

## SOLUTION

*Team = Product*

What's in the team will be in its product; what isn't, won't. And vice versa.

The formula Team = Product really stands alone, above all other guidelines and patterns associated with The Core protocols. In reality, it is the pattern/protocol generator of The Core patterns and protocols. Careful observation of a team creating a product plus straightforward analysis of the product created will reveal that the characteristics of the team are always fully expressed in the product. Others have noted this phenomenon.[1] People cannot help but express themselves in their work. Examples of Team = Product analysis: If your team adopts new ideas slowly, the product you produce will use senescent technology. If your team is brilliant, your software will be attractive and efficient. If your team is process-heavy, your product will have excessive architecture.

---

1. The most notable example is Conway's Law. In 1968, Mel Conway postulated that the structure of any information system is isomorphic to the structure of the organization that built it (letter to the editor, *Datamation*, April 1968); see also Coplien's pattern, *Conway's law, http://www1.belllabs.com/user/cope/Patterns/Process/section15.html.* Team = Product is possibly a more aggressive pattern with respect to relations between products and teams: It advocates diagnosing the team by scrutiny of the product and changing conditions of the team to optimize the product. Additionally, it extends the idea well beyond communication channels into every aspect of team life. Team = Product also addresses the question of management teams whose product is product development teams.

The exploitation of this parallelism requires that you first make the following assumptions:

- A direct correlation *always* exists between each characteristic of the team and each characteristic of the product.
- There is *no* way to avoid having the product express the values, interests, talents, and goals of those who make it.

## THE LATE TEAM

The knee-jerk reaction to lateness is often to "work harder," to castigate others, or to blindly slip the date another two months. These actions, however, don't address the underlying problems associated with product creation. They don't exploit the fact that Team = Product, the application of which can provide insights that will provide a way out of virtually any team problem.

If Team = Product, then you can always envision the untapped human potential on the team as a resource that is still missing. The lateness stems from not applying all the resources to the challenge. This approach does not typically suggest working harder, but rather thinking more, and/or communicating better, and/or connecting more deeply: whatever would draw out the untapped gifts and ideas that would make the difference. It certainly doesn't justify any kind of blame scenario; rather, it extends one's own accountability.

And, in any case, poor scheduling does not recommend more scheduling.

*This approach does not typically suggest working harder, but rather, thinking more. In any case, poor scheduling does not recommend more scheduling.*

## APPLICATION OF TEAM = PRODUCT

How can you use Team = Product? Consider a team making computer software. You might want to know how well a team thinks together. Examine the ideas in which team members have all chosen to invest—that is, their product. What possible sequences of thought and behavior might explain the choices in their product?

Alternatively, you can use Team = Product to gauge how trusting the members of the team are with one another, or how effective they are at dealing with creative conflicts. These elements are easy

*If any part of a product shines while other parts don't, a trust issue is invariably corroding the teamwork.*

*Much in the way that a physician or an alert parent can sometimes smell a particular disease on the breath of a child, awareness of the product will speak to you of the team's health.*

to perceive in finished software: If any part of a product shines while other parts don't, a trust issue is invariably corroding the teamwork. After all, the people who made the polished and pleasing part could have taught the others to make their parts shine. This procedure would probably even have saved time. Even better, the team might have been reorganized to spread more broadly the talent that could repair the weak areas. What about those who had the capabilities to produce the polished parts? Surely, they would have perceived the quality variance. To choose not to help the less effective members of their team was tantamount to hurting their own product, diminishing their own brilliance. Therefore, some element in the team ecology must have held even more sway for them than the terror of reduced market acceptance, or the misery of having brought forth ugliness alongside their beauty. Usually, the conflicts over quality that were there went unaddressed, or at least unresolved.

With any product that is only partly or intermittently good, the team creating it did not effectively surface and resolve its conflicts. Obviously, the team members did not trust one another. Their conflict was self-destructively channeled toward their own product, rather than dealt with rationally, among mature people who have decided together that the product of their effort should be as good as possible. The team could have seized on any of a myriad of solutions, but for some reason (see, for example, ResolutionAvoidance, NoHurtFeelings) they chose not to do so.

The wider the quality spectrum in a single product, the more degenerate the team creating it. If one part is truly great while the rest is awful, then pride, denial, fear, and intransigence in their various forms must surely be working their dark magic.

Once The Core premise, Team = Product, is accepted, simple diagnostic tools are easily identified. Much in the way that a physician or an alert parent can sometimes smell a particular disease on the breath of a child, awareness of the product will speak to you of the team's health, and your perceptions of the team will foretell the quality of the product.

# WHAT'S THE BLOCK?

The secret to exploiting the insights gained by comparing product and team is to find the countervailing force—the blocking force—in the team ecology that is holding team members in check. You must root out, name, and confront that awful element. Usually, it is a powerful force, almost a taboo. It must be potent, because it must overwhelm team members' needs for institutional approval, full market acceptance, and the joys of producing beauty and functionality.

You can be sure of one other thing when you are rooting out this malign force: It must hold sway over every single member of the team. Any one of them could have publicly stood up to the encroaching mediocrity, named it, and insisted that the team deal with it. Failing that, he could have then withdrawn his participation. Clearly, that behavior would have shifted the team agenda, at least somewhat. (See "Wrong Tolerance" in Chapter Three.)

*Any one of them could have publicly stood up to the encroaching mediocrity, named it, and insisted that the team deal with it.*

## *Team = Product Corollary: You Can't Put Something in Your Product that You Don't Possess*

Not only does the product reveal the team, and vice versa, but the product cannot express properties without those properties concurrently being expressed within the team. That is, Team = Product is more than a passive assessment tool. You are not helpless or doomed to express your inadequacy. You can inject positive action into the team, and have it show up in the product. This effort requires more than words and ostensible values, however.

Ask anyone on the team whether he values frequent integration of product components during the development phases, say, and you will doubtless receive an affirmative response. Unfortunately, saying you value something is insufficient to introduce that value into the product. Integration—both the word and the reality—comes from integrity. To transmit a virtue via your team into its correlative in your product requires virtuous action during the process of creating the product. Moreover, for a virtue to become incorporated in the

*No fairy dust will magically transform your product into the more desirable thing you envision. In the end, there is only you and your application of virtue.*

product, the virtuous actions must be of greater magnitude than the team's resistance to that virtue.

No fairy dust will magically transform your product into the more desirable thing you envision. In the end, there is only you and your application of virtue.

# PATTERN: SELF-CARE

## PROBLEM

*You take care of others
and expect others to take care of you.*

A common team malady is a fragmented sense of who takes care of whom. NoHurtFeelings is one symptom of this team sickness. Respect for "turf" is another symptom. In a healthy team, each individual takes care of himself, exercises good self-care, and respects[2] the ability of every other individual to do the same.

## SOLUTION

*Take care of yourself.*

Caring for and about yourself touches everything on your team. While good self-care is not the only element of a healthy team, its presence alone is sufficient to generate these team characteristics:

- The truth is not hidden or suppressed.
  - When people think they are taking care of one another, they tend to "cover up" the truth (see "Antipattern: No Hurt Feelings" in Chapter Three).

---

2. That is, he expects and requires it.

- A person taking care of himself will not compromise his integrity.

• Rescue impulses are properly redirected into underlying self-care actions.

  - When you feel the urge to rescue someone, stop and tend to the feelings that encourage your desire to "protect" others.

• Each person does what he needs to be maximally present at work.

  - Physical exhaustion is remedied.

  - Long stretches of isolation are not tolerated.

  - Personal neglect of responsibilities is not supported.

• Only results are valued.

  - The number of hours you work is not interesting. That is, long hours are not rewarded nor are short hours punished.

  - Any activity likely to increase results is more appropriately valued, no matter how unconventional or commonplace.

• Team members who do not consistently get results leave or are asked to leave.

  - Individual performance is not obscured by rescuing; it is visible.

  - There is sufficient aggregate integrity to act on performance problems.

  - Performance remediation is correctly seen as support.

  - People who are asked to leave the team are cut off from the team's support of their neglect of their own care.

• Whoever sees a problem becomes the owner of it.

  - You care enough about yourself to resolve what annoys or concerns you.

• All ideas are welcome in the environment, no matter their origin.

  - No concept of turf influences the primacy of an idea.

  - An inferior idea is not supported as an ostensible act of inclusion.

  - There is always action on the best idea.

# CARING FOR YOUR IDEAS IS
# CARING FOR YOURSELF

If you care for yourself, you eliminate the costs of your care from others. Moreover, an increased contribution of ideas is the best way to care for yourself and others at the same time. A big part of caring for yourself is, therefore, understanding and nurturing your creative faculty by taking care of your ideas. The CheckIn commitments supply the necessary infrastructure for taking good care of your ideas, because they commit you to the following actions:

- Stating your ideas in real time
- Standing by them
- Only surrendering to their improvement or their replacement when you are convinced something better has materialized
- Directly acting on them and leading others to do the same

*Stop censoring yourself.*

Self-care requires ongoing self-disclosure. Because you care, say what you think and feel is the truth, especially when no one else is saying it. State your idea when it is the best idea of which you are aware. Stop censoring yourself. Fighting for airspace in which to broadcast your thoughts in meetings should be a thing of the past if your team is properly running Core protocols.

*If you care about yourself, your team, and your product, then expressing your ideas becomes a no-lose proposition: You either learn or directly contribute.*

When you are in a dispassionate state (that is, you don't care), you are more likely to repress your ideas and neglect your sensibility. Often, you fear that you will be seen as stupid or wrong, and you don't care to take that risk. But if you really care about yourself, and, hence, the outcome of your work, you are more likely to risk revealing yourself. In a Core-adopting environment, when you suggest an idea that is based on mistaken information or ignorance, someone will teach you. If you offer a useful idea, your team is committed to adopting it and improving it with you if possible. If you care about yourself, your team, and your product, then expressing your ideas becomes a no-lose proposition: You either learn or directly contribute.

# PATTERN:
# THINKING AND FEELING

## PROBLEM

*You act on feelings without thinking,*
*or act while ignoring feelings.*

Because tolerance for the subtleties of intuitive information is
extremely low, there is little awareness about and virtually no practice of the effective integration of ThinkingandFeeling, whether
individually or on teams.

## SOLUTION

*Check both your ThinkingandFeeling and the*
*ThinkingandFeeling of others before acting.*

The information that emerges when thoughts and feelings are
integrated is not typically used by teams. Surfacing this rich
material—by explicit discussion and analysis—is a high-priority
activity for any team that cares about the outcome of its efforts.

Non-verbalized emotion and disconnected thought will ultimately
emerge in the form of acts of aggression against the self, the product,
and the team. Given the usual bigotry about the explicit management of emotion, a kind of pseudo-rational discourse becomes the
only approved way to vent. As an example, consider the venting that
takes place when two software developers (or camps of developers)
argue fruitlessly about two different—and often more or less equal—
technical strategies. In such cases, the lack of a proper discourse
technique can lead to highly manipulative behavior. Since the
straightforward expression of the largest part of the human informa-

*As a consequence, what passes for reasoned team discourse is actually a travesty of it.*

*These events amount to bad performance art.*

*The way to bring down the curtain on lame theatrics is simply to question the intention behind them.*

tion generation machinery—for example, feelings, imaginings, intuition, aesthetic responses, and the relationship milieus that give rise to them—is virtually taboo, all these things find distorted expression in the context of more accepted topics and voices. As a consequence, what passes for reasoned team discourse is actually a travesty of it.

## DISJOINTED FEELING AND THINKING

Practically speaking, how can this disjointedness be identified and expunged? Examples abound. Someone "throws a fit." Someone resists a proposed change with extraordinary heat. Two developers dig in their heels in opposition about some technical issues. A clique of cynics holds everyone else back from accepting a valuable contribution. A few team members create a dramatic spectacle in a meeting to further a lost cause.

These events amount to bad performance art.

They are sufficiently compelling to distract a group from getting the desired results, but insufficiently rich to inspire the required focus and alignment. In the best case, the actors involved are feeling without thinking. If the actors thought about the issue (whatever it happened to be) and their feelings, they would understand that the group's time and energy are far too precious to waste on personal theatrics. What complicates matters is that such dramatic presentations usually appear to relate to the topic of the job at hand. Often, the actors will invoke key terms and buzzwords (such as "integrity" or "passion") in ostensible support of their cause. Because the team usually devolves into discussing the players and the issues involved in the drama rather than creating the product together, and because bystanders tiptoe around the presenting issue in the future, for fear of an encore, progress slows.

Good performance art has different effects. It knows it is art; it has intention. The way to bring down the curtain on lame theatrics is simply to question the intention behind them (see the discussion of IntentionCheck in Chapter Six): What does the actor hope to accomplish right now, you might ask, with the performance? The answers to this question are more amusing than the performance itself, and they also take much less time and psychic energy to obtain than would otherwise spent.

The related problem is thinking without feeling. Often, this state of semiconsciousness takes the form of a ghastly quiet support of a banal idea. In groups, otherwise animated people may passively "go along" with ideas that they know are not the best ones. Typically, these uninspiring ideas meet general expectations for the most likely type of idea that ought to be adopted at this point. They are conventional ideas. Conventional ideas gather support (albeit passive-aggressive) for a variety of reasons:

- The idea comes from the boss.
- It is the "turf" of the person who is proposing the idea.
- That's how things have been done before.
- It's how you have read or heard that things should go.
- It's how you believe that "adults" or "professionals" might do things.

Clearly, these reasons are poor justifications for going along with something. The act of going along creates latent feelings of anger and fear that later produce disjointedness. Typically, you know when you are going along. You can *feel* the quality hit.

To proceed as if you endorsed a lame idea is to reject your own feelings. It requires you to shut down the sensations that could guide you toward improved results. If you were to clear out the passive, apathetic fog that engulfs you at such a time, then you might acknowledge—even if only to yourself—your anger at your own "going along." You would then have to change your thinking to align it with your feelings. You'd have to feel angry and use that anger to promote a better idea. This is thinking and feeling at the same time.

In the end, the source of the ideas doesn't matter. What does matter is that you implement the best ideas. Don't go along with an idea just because an authority figure said it or because you're afraid of the extent of your own originality. Accept the energy and motivation

*Typically, you know when you are going along. You can* feel *the quality hit.*

*If you were to clear out the passive, apathetic fog that engulfs you at such a time, then you might acknowledge—even if only to yourself—your anger at your own "going along."*

*Don't go along with an idea just because an authority figure said it or because you're afraid of the extent of your own originality.*

provided by your feelings, think about them, and apply your thoughts and feelings to improving results.

## PATTERN: PRETEND

### PROBLEM

*You reject new alternative beliefs before you understand them.*

### SOLUTION

*Don't resist a new idea. Instead, pretend that it is valuable and experiment with it, until you understand it.*

*He bellows at the professor, pointing his finger accusingly, "That is ridiculous! Periodic, schmeriodic! Put everything in a little table. Control it. It's a cult!"*

People can get stuck thinking and behaving in ways that don't work very well. When it comes to an idea that implies changing behavior patterns, most individuals prefer to argue before understanding it.

For example, most students wouldn't consider arguing with a college professor about the value of an idea that they are paying him to tell them. Picture this scenario:

*A first-year chemistry student leaps to his feet when the subject of the periodic table is first introduced. He bellows at the professor, pointing his finger accusingly, "That is ridiculous! Periodic, schmeriodic! Put everything in a little table. Control it. It's a cult! Organizer! Fascist!"*

He storms out of the classroom.

The effects of his unreasoned tirade ripple throughout the classroom. Several of the other students immediately take his side, accusing the professor of being unsympathetic to those who don't believe in organizing ideas. Why didn't he express both sides of the issue? The hapless professor is shouted down. Bunches of erstwhile students conspire at break time and leave in concert. They go to the dean, who, of course, is dean because at least in part he knows how to appease many diverse constituents simultaneously. The story continues. . . .

This scenario is clearly a fantasy. It is a fact of human nature, however, that the same student who is the suppliant learner when it comes to the periodic table will prove very eager to argue about any idea that implies (or may ultimately imply, should he come to understand it) his behavior might be more effective than it is at present.[3] It's as if he wouldn't want more results from his effort. The student's initial reaction to the newness or boldness of an idea suggesting personal change is the same impulse that led other humans to burn the proponents of new ideas at the stake, or to excommunicate them.

As a child, your ability to pretend was limitless and always available. As a person who could pretend, likely you were at your peak. Remember how easy it was to become someone different from minute to minute, changing personas with every breath? You could act as if you were in one scene, and then yet another dramatic situation, all day long. Like the ability to ride a bike, the ability to summon instantly a new pretend reality remains an available skill. This skill is useful, and perhaps even vital, for learning how to create a great team. When presented with an even remotely credible new idea about group and individual behaviors, simply pretend that it is true. At least, do so for a while. Assign a time limit, if desired. You can always change your mind later. There is always sufficient time to discard ideas that prove useless. The best time to do so is generally after you understand them, however—not before.

Pretend that the ideas in this book are true long enough to understand them, before either throwing them out or adopting them.

*The student's initial reaction to the newness or boldness of an idea suggesting personal change is the same impulse that led other humans to burn the proponents of new ideas at the stake.*

*There is always sufficient time to discard ideas that prove useless. The best time to do so is generally after you understand them, however—not before.*

---

3. Because of this nearly universal phenomenon, we make an agreement with students at the beginning of our BootCamp program that they will "pretend" that the new ideas presented are true, *just for the duration of BootCamp.* Rather than argue with our ideas, the BootCampers agree to try them out until the end of BootCamp. At that point they are, of course, free to keep the new ideas or throw them out. But by that time they have been educated.

If you do so, you will be more likely to gain the maximum benefit for your time and money.

---

# PATTERN: THE GREATNESS CYCLE

## PROBLEM

---

*Mediocrity.*

## SOLUTION

---

*Smartness leads to greatness, via presence, integrity, conflict, and passion.*

Greatness is conceived in your intention to achieve at an appropriate scale;[4] it is born in the application of integrity; it flourishes in your navigation of conflict; and it matures in the vitality of your passion.

The GreatnessCycle is an important group behavior cycle. It is simple to understand, but difficult to practice. Its phases are as follows:

*Smart people will exploit the fact that the deeper one's presence in any given moment, the more valuable the moment.*

1. *Smart people are present no matter what they are doing.* It is smart to avoid wasting time. It is even smarter to enhance the value of your time as much as possible. If you can improve this value but fail to do so, it suggests that you are not smart. Smart people will exploit the fact that the deeper one's presence in any given moment, the more valuable the moment. Smartness leads to presence.

---

4. Although this must be determined by each person for himself, it does seem that an appropriate achievement scale for any human must be such that he produces more than was expended by his total consumption.

2. *Presence leads to integrity.* Presence is driven away by the violation of integrity. Even tolerating the lack of integrity in others is a personal diminishment. In either case, to accept a lack of integrity, you must split yourself in two: into an aspect with integrity, and into the remaining aspect of yourself that shows some type of presence. By accepting or practicing a lack of integrity, you leave the better part of your presence behind. Sustained presence inevitably leads to the emergence of integrity. A lack of integrity and the fullness of personal presence are mutually exclusive. That is, a high level of presence is always accompanied by a comparable level of integrity.

3. *Integrity leads to conflict.* Smart, engaged people behaving with integrity will inevitably encounter differences with others. This situation arises because they cannot agree with something they don't accept and cannot forgo speaking when it is required of them. Individual integrity doesn't automatically bind together individuals, but those persons will deal forthrightly with the differences that arise. To do less—whether to avoid a conflict, to gloss over it, or to deal with it surreptitiously—is to lack integrity. The maintenance of integrity leads to conflict.

4. *Conflict leads to passion.* If you care enough to weather the direct, honest conflict with your colleagues that flows from your practice of integrity, then you must care a great deal indeed. The emotions you feel when issues you care about are threatened will intensify into passion. Conflict is catalyzed by caring, and summons passion.

5. *Passion leads to greatness.* Passionate living provides the power to do great things. Though it neither mandates nor guarantees it, passion always attends greatness.

## PHASE 1: SMARTNESS

The people who are "smart" greatly outnumber the people who have the other essential attributes required to create great intellectual property. Nevertheless, it is always most desirable, or smartest, for teams to have the right *mixture* of qualities. Moreover, any team consisting of

*Any team consisting of truly smart people will not remain focused exclusively on "smartness" as the only team virtue required for success.*

truly smart people will not remain focused exclusively on "smartness" as the only team virtue required for success. Smartness, by definition, knows better than that; if it doesn't, it's not smart, but pseudo-smart.

Applied intelligence, which characterizes the truly smart, does the following:

- It always helps.
- It is the "seed virtue" for a team.
- It always plays a vital role in any substantial group success.

## What Is Smartness?

*To be smart, a person must apply his understanding.*

What characterizes "smartness"? The Core lexicon defines being **smart** as "applying what is understood to attaining what is desirable." The smartest people are those who develop and apply the most relevant understanding. That is, to be smart, a person must apply his understanding.

The posture of learning and investigating characterizes the smartest among us. Conversely, the posture of knowingness is antithetical to smartness. People who insist on their expertise rather than demonstrating it, or those who cite their education instead of building on it, are not behaving in a smart way. True experts continue to seek out more education and tend to the development of more expertise. They apply their beliefs rather than value their credentials. They are first to see the inadequacy of their education and first to recognize the limitless extent of the expertise they lack.

*In a world of dramatically increasing availability of information, the connected triumph over the knowledgeable.*

People who already know "the most" are probably at the highest risk: The duration and the value of what they know shrink in proportion to the rate of the dissemination of information. In a world of dramatically increasing availability of information, the connected triumph over the knowledgeable.

## Smart People Look for Smarter People

A behavior pattern that characterizes "smartness" is the practice of searching for others who meet the following criteria:

- They know more or learn faster than you do.
- They know how to learn.

- They know how to go about the efficient exchange of relevant information with others.

## PHASE 2: PRESENCE

Employee engagement can be visualized in (at least) two dimensions: depth and duration. In the past, people were paid for the time they spent carrying out the tasks for which they were hired—that is, for the duration of their engagement. This legacy lingers on today. Even in the twenty-first century, people on salaries are expected to work all day, every day, for at least nine-tenths of a year in the United States.

### *Depth*

Increasingly, an employee's degree of engagement is the heart of his contribution of value. When human minds are the factory floor, traditional productivity studies of quality, yield, and efficiency must focus on employees' depth of engagement: how to deepen it, speed up access to it, remove engagement blockages, and insert engagement catalysts.

The value of your contribution is less a function of the time spent at the enterprise than of the degree of intellectual engagement with the enterprise. But how can you assess this degree of engagement? In the unlikely event that you devise some technique for numerically establishing your level of engagement, how can you then tackle the problem of logging your varying engagement level over time? By developing new time clocks that record on engagement punch cards?

Likewise, how can you measure your degree of presence? You might imagine a self-disclosing employee engagement worksheet that assigns a number from the engagement scale. It's too easy to destroy the integrity of that idea. For example, how often would the employee fill out the form? Every half-hour? Whenever he "feels" a change in engagement level?

Ultimately, you have to track the level of engagement by the results obtained.

*When human minds are the factory floor, traditional productivity studies of quality, yield, and efficiency must focus on employees' depth of engagement.*

*Engagement*

Engagement can be observed in one's receptivity, focus, high valuation of efficiency, and connection to others. Of course, high-quality presence is intermittent, even with the most present individuals.

Are there phases in engagement? Focused attention alternating with unfocused dreamlike states? Could the ebb and flow of these phases be central to optimal engagement? Or is that just hooey? "I may look like I'm disengaged, boss, but I'm just following my presence waves."

How do you account for creativity and inspiration? Don't they result from high levels of engagement? What about the person who appears disengaged, but, at the optimal moment, suddenly awakens, expresses a brilliant idea, and then resumes his narcoleptic trance? When the individual's idea is implemented, it saves tremendous amounts of money, reduces effort and cost, and allows the product to ship on time. For the rest of the year, however, the worker does nothing. Nevertheless, his single idea made the difference between prosperity and poverty for the team.

Is it possible to contribute even more than the steadiest contributors by applying a momentary massive engagement level? Perhaps this question is the wrong one to ask. Is the quiescent, seemingly disengaged, listen-and-observe state actually the most important part of very high levels of engagement? If you could somehow get more frequent contributions from the problem solver, would you want them if the cost were the loss of the genius idea-generator within him?

In intellectual property creation, how can you ever know when someone is working, anyway? There are no reliable external signs. An employee may be banging away on a keyboard, sweating, thinking, frowning, or smiling. He may seem to be working ferociously, when he's actually playing games.

Imagine that another employee is lying on his office floor, with his head on a pillow and his eyes closed. Is he asleep or solving a problem? For that matter, can sleep solve the problem?

*In intellectual property creation, how can you ever know when someone is working, anyway? There are no reliable external signs.*

*True results
orientation requires
that you conceptually
demolish the Puritan
work ethic.*

For these and many other reasons, you really can't measure engagement. You can, and must, hold yourself and others accountable for their results. On the one hand, the steady contributor with daily results may be the easiest to monitor. The practice of holding people accountable requires that you not care if someone shows no visible effort whatsoever, but the results must be there. True results orientation requires that you conceptually demolish the Puritan work ethic. You can assign no greater value to the daily producer than you do to the invisible contributor, except when their results differ.

## PHASE 3: INTEGRITY

Virtually all of the other requisite qualities on a team are virtues that stem from integrity. According to The Core lexicon, **integrity** is "the unity of thought, word, and deed." Although that definition may seem abstract, personal integrity is itself an abstract thing. Integrity can be presumed when someone does what he has previously promised to do,[5] or *behaves* as if he believed in what was said previously. If your actions and words align consistently, you will be judged by others to have integrity. For all practical purposes, if you act as if you have integrity, then you do have integrity.

### Integrity Is Applied

*Apparently, the rarity
of personal integrity
has led to a massive
amount of "integrity
insecurity."*

Integrity is nothing if it is not applied, and its application is a potent, though rare, event. Acts of integrity (and apparently the quality itself) are much more uncommon than is generally believed. It is unusual to find integrity, even occasionally. Apparently, the rarity of personal integrity has led to a massive amount of "integrity insecurity." A vast (though somewhat rote and largely unconscious) body of obfuscation has sprouted up around the question of personal integrity.

---

5. Presumably, in doing what you've said you'll do, you are also doing what you think you ought to do. What you think can't be seen apart from your actions, however, so it's not generally interesting as any kind of integrity indicator. Even what you say is interesting only insofar as it provides something that can be balanced against what you actually do.

## Integrity Rarity Syndrome

Life is full of the oh-so-predictable, endlessly sustained, but ultimately hollow protestations of personal integrity ("Are you questioning my integrity!?"). A moment's introspection will remind you of the very sporadic nature of your integrity. Your reactions to someone questioning your integrity really amount to a universal syndrome— the "integrity rarity syndrome," which is really a culturally mandated conspiracy of mutually supporting one another's lies. This complex network leads to the pretense that everybody consistently acts with integrity, when actually no one does.

## Question Integrity

As an example of integrity-related practices, consider the act of "questioning someone's integrity." This practice has somehow become taboo—a reprehensible, horrific act of aggression. To discuss possible integrity lapses attracts a "them's fightin' words" kind of response, which is both brutal and primitive. Whatever statement one might make, or whatever question one might ask on the topic of another's integrity, will elicit responses such as, "Are you calling me a liar?" or "Are you questioning my integrity?" Your question or remark is a "bad" thing for you to have said, hitting below the belt, uncalled for, unfit for discussion, and so forth. You quickly get the message that you're not to support people in their practice of integrity, at least not by discussing it with them.[6]

To further illustrate the point, imagine that someone is wearing ill-matched clothes. He looks ridiculous. You are his friend and want him to look as attractive as possible. As a show of your support for him, you might reasonably say, "Hey, is it me, or does that shirt clash with those pants?" Even though this is a touchy topic, you would not expect your friend to erupt in outrage at your effrontery. "What?" he bellows accusingly, "Are you questioning my taste!? This is uncalled for. I am a person of high fashion sense. No one questions my sense

*This complex network leads to the pretense that everybody consistently acts with integrity, when actually no one does.*

*You quickly get the message that you're not to support people in their practice of integrity, at least not by discussing it with them.*

---

6. And how else would you support it? Praying about it? Wishing?

of style! You may say whatever you like about me, but don't ever, ever question whether my clothes match! You're the one with the clothes that always clash!"

Should you hazard to make impugning statements or ask challenging questions in spite of the taboo that exists around them, you can count on provoking hair-raising, knee-jerk, fighting-word challenges and questions. The question at that juncture is how you respond to the defensive onslaught. If you depend on the general pretense that everyone has integrity, you can only say something like, "No, of course not. I didn't mean *that*."

Witnesses to this exchange will know (in their nonsupportive, though entirely cooperative conspiracy of silence) that for you to deny the obvious implications of your own remarks or questions and back down in the face of the reactionary hostility is, quite simply, a surrender to ResolutionAvoidance. Your back-pedaling denial is the lie that conquers your initially truthful approach: Of course you were "questioning his integrity"! By denying it now, you undermine your own integrity, and the conspiracy prospers and grows.

Your false reassurance may include a certain, small (though nonredemptive) honesty. The threatened and threatening responses you elicited, however, constituted an extreme overreaction to your words. They are designed to instantly shut down all productive discussion of the constant integrity lapses that all people suffer. They are a ritualized cultural response to an assault presumed to be lurking in your remarks. Whatever your friend's responses to your "questioning his integrity," they were certainly not reflective of an actual sense of your friend being truly violated by your remark.

There are few new developments here. In another age, for men, an insult to one's (usually remote) mother or sweetheart virtually required a duel to the death in response. The only differences from the modern-day example are the lack of balky pistols and a misty dawn in the park. In your back-pedaling your (clearly slender) claim to at least a little bit of honesty is that you were *not*, in fact, judging your friend to be guilty of whatever it is that he atavistically fears. Instead, you were merely questioning his integrity.

*The only differences from the modern-day example are the lack of balky pistols and a misty dawn in the park.*

Questioning integrity, beginning with one's own and expanding from there, is the most sensible and supportive strategy imaginable in a world where the amount of personal integrity is dwarfed by the amount of refined plutonium. This fact is obvious upon reflection. Just a dollop of integrity in even one person, when sparingly applied, stirs up all kinds of troublesome, though good, things for any group to which that person is connected. Any sort of integrity is noteworthy and becomes something you can discuss over meals, make notes on, and find inspiring indefinitely. You notice it. Thus, there's virtually no time at which it's not appropriate to question integrity—and especially your own.

Integrity is often what people really mean when they babble on about empowerment. What you really want to know when you're contemplating empowerment is, "Does being empowered mean that I tell the truth?"

Your team smarts, when present in force, will readily see the need for consistent acts of integrity. Such acts usually require courage. **Courage** entails making wise choices while feeling fear. The feelings of fear never go away. Because integrity is visible in the unity of acts and words, you must not only say brave things, but also actually do them.[7] Often, the brave things required of you are the very things you've been taught not to do, such as making critical remarks about another's idea to his face or explaining the superiority of your own idea. Although this goal can be achieved in a nonegotistical way, it does go against the typical indoctrination template strictures that you should avoid "being critical," never "boast," and at all costs do not "be prideful."[8]

When you persist in your search for integrity and triumph over the uniformly resistant indoctrination template you suffered, your reward will be conflict.

*Just a dollop of integrity in even one person, when sparingly applied, stirs up all kinds of troublesome, though good, things for any group to which that person is connected.*

*Because integrity is visible in the unity of acts and words, you must not only say brave things, but also actually do them.*

---

7. Sometimes, of course, the saying *is* the doing.

8. Pride may goeth before a fall, but it also goeth before a reduction in bug count.

# PHASE 4: CONFLICT.

When conflict is born of a team's devotion to integrity, it is the welcome harbinger of the presence of the GreatnessCycle. If you act with integrity on your team, you will inevitably encounter some resistance; if you did not, your team would be great already.

Conflict is difficult. The means to resolving every human conflict is, alas, not a part of The Core protocols—at least, not this version. Nevertheless, a behavior pattern can significantly reduce the costs of conflict on a team. This behavior is related to another key pattern in The Core, Alignment (see Chapter Nine).

### Ask for What You Want

People avoid conflict (or resolution) because of the many twisted cultural rituals that are played out when it occurs. People who come into conflict with you may be unpleasant. They might yell, scream, or otherwise sabotage the effort, perhaps even become violent, and yet resolve nothing. They might like you even less than they already do. Who wouldn't want to avoid that kind of stressful waste?

*During a dispute, you can eliminate most of the noise and waste by staying focused on what you want.*

Applying the GreatnessCycle pattern includes embracing your ability to act in a mature way in the face of conflict. During a dispute, you can eliminate most of the noise and waste by staying focused on what you want. For example, you could spend energy and time telling a coworker that he is mean-spirited and inconsiderate because he makes sarcastic remarks about you. This action is unlikely to get the desired results, however. You are much more likely to gain what you desire from others by asking for it. For example, of a particularly ironic colleague, you might ask, "Will you not use sarcasm when you speak to me?"

*Expect to have to ask for what you want several times. Expect to have to remind someone about an agreement several times.*

It is common to contribute needlessly to conflict by presuming that, because someone granted your request once, he will never have to be asked or reminded again. In reality, you are unlikely to adopt new patterns of behavior without mistakes. Consistent repetition of the new behavior and consistent constraint of the undesirable behavior will be required.

### Reduce the Cost of Conflict

You will always reduce the cost of conflict and promote self-preservation (yours as well as that of others) by following these guidelines:

- Require that others behave respectfully toward you. If or when they don't, disassociate from them, at least until they are willing to agree to behave respectfully.

- Clearly and repeatedly ask for what you want, especially in conflict-charged relationships.

- Hold others accountable for any agreements they have made and insist that they provide what you have asked for.

- Invite (and, even more difficult, accept in real time) the mature support of your colleagues as you struggle to make your own desired changes.

### Find Out What Your Opponent Wants

When you have exhaustively requested what you want in a conflict situation, hold the other person accountable for clearly answering the question as well. That is, ask your opponent, "What do you want?" Many people have trouble answering this question and will attempt to change the subject. Do not get drawn off the topic. The single most efficient step to take in resolving any conflict is to obtain a clear statement from each party expressing what he wants. In most cases, everyone can get what he desires.

Even if one participant is unwilling to give the other what he wants, stating that fact clearly can itself resolve the conflict, leaving nothing to fight about. One person wants $X$; the other wants $Y$. Both are unwilling to give the opponent what he wants. The conflict itself is not irresoluble; it is just that no exchange is likely. Once this fact is accepted, the noise will abate. Armed with that information, each party can independently choose a future course.

*The single most efficient step to take in resolving any conflict is to obtain a clear statement from each party expressing what he wants.*

Saying what you want and understanding what your opponent wants will reliably minimize the pain and toxicity of everyday conflict.

## PHASE 5: PASSION

Smartness finally brings us to passion. Like vision, passion is something that virtually everyone wants.[9] Unfortunately, very few people seem to actually figure out what passion (or vision) is, how it works, and how to get and use more of it. Passion causes you to behave as if you cared deeply about the object of the action.

In The Core, **passion** is an experience characterized by an intensified and sustainable incarnation of one of the four feelings, plus a well-motivated, intentional response to this feeling. Table 4.1 describes the passionate instances of the four Core emotions.

In the passionate case, mad becomes transformed into a determination to do the most effective thing, drawing motivation from righteous anger. Sad enlarges to sorrow, shows vulnerability, and elicits connection. It accepts grief. Glad ripens to joy, spawning rejuvenation, creativity, and infectious fun. Afraid reaches all the way to courage. Courage, of course, is not the absence of fear. The passionate variant of afraid resolves into a bravery that incorporates fear and invokes behavior of unshakable integrity.

*Sublime emotion plus mature action equals passion.*

This simple mapping of emotions can help make passionate living become more accessible. Passion, after all, includes emotion. It is also a larger and grander state that integrates the mature response: Sublime emotion plus mature action equals passion.[10] The specific dimension of maturity that surfaces in the experience of passion is less important than the fact that maturity does emerge. For example, while sad might map to grief in one environment, in another environment it might map to a deeper sense of the super-

---

9. Of all values on the many teams with which we have worked, passion was the virtue desired above all other virtues.

10. Passion is *not* excessive emotion. "Crimes of passion" derive from the breakdown of passionate capacity, just as rage is the absence of emotion. Violence is the ultimate passivity, the extremity of not caring.

Table 4.1  *Passionate Instances of The Core Emotions*

| Mad | Righteous anger | Determination |
| --- | --- | --- |
| Sad | Sorrow, grief | Consolation, vulnerability, connection |
| Glad | Joy | Rejuvenation, creation, fun |
| Afraid | Courage | Integrity |

natural. While the two are related, important and persistent differences exist between emotions and passions:

- Passion is largely free of neurosis; feelings are often inextricably bound in neurotic behavior. For example, you can be mad while manipulating others or sad in a whining, costly way. Conversely, a passionate righteous anger is pure, motivational, and direct, and a passionate sorrow shows an extreme (and extremely attractive) vulnerability. Others don't seek to eliminate your sorrow, but they often want to quash your sadness or rescue you from its continuance. As another example, joy transcends gladness in its power, transmissibility, and creative results. Glad feels good, but it can be utterly blind, without positive results, giddy, and wholly superficial. Passion, however, seeks good results and is itself a positive good. In contrast, emotions are a critically important but value-neutral source of information.

- Passion persists even when the passionate emotion subsides.

- Passion always produces positive change in those it touches. Emotions produce information for cognitive receptors, which *can be used* to promote positive change but is often just transient sensation.

- Passion doesn't overwhelm the judgment of its receiver. Emotions are often slow to integrate with rational thought.

- Passion has a larger choice component than emotion. That is, you must care about something before passion swells. Emotions, though influenced and at times shaped by choice, are not as dependent on it.

Passion arises in engaged people. Thus, team members must care about a project to become fully engaged with it. The more you care about a project, the greater your hopes and fears surrounding it.

In addition, passion awakens the dreamer within. It renews hope for the immanence (or the ultimacy) of great results. It also stimulates fear of poor or inadequate results.

*Although each passionate victory will be ecstatic, the ecstasy may be fleeting—so infinite is the cause, so limitless the number of victories yet to be had.*

If you care, more of your presence is required. More of you must be in—all the way in. The truly passionate are so deeply involved that each disappointment is excruciating, long lasting, and memorable. Although each passionate victory will be ecstatic, the ecstasy may be fleeting—so infinite is the cause, so limitless the number of victories yet to be had.

The profound caring of passionate engagement and the results that it brings will give you the power to achieve sufficient connection with others. The high-bandwidth connection of those sharing a cause enables them to create something great together. Passion insists that you pay more attention to yourself, as well as to the people, ideas, processes, and activities on which your efficient progress depends as you move together in the desired direction.

*Passion inevitably radiates, and the passionate you is the radiant center.*

You can't avoid caring about yourself while caring immensely about something external. Passion inevitably radiates, and the passionate you is the radiant center.

Remember: Smartness leads to presence; integrity leads to conflict; conflict leads to passion; and greatness belongs to the passionate.

## GREATNESS

In the context of the new team conflict brought on by more vigorous general integrity, emotions become stirred up. As a result of maintaining your integrity, you will necessarily feel strong passions about what you are saying and doing. That is, you will have to care.

In turn, your teammates will encounter their own passions. These elements—the general integrity and passion forged in conflict—serve as the raw ingredients of greatness. When a team is alive with passion, then and only then does it have the required maturity and power to work on what really matters. Greatness comes from that work.

## Greatness and Genius

Greatness is more easily identified in its practice than through theory. Civilization has sporadically been vastly enriched by the appearance of geniuses throughout history. A few recent examples will suffice to prove this point:

*Charles Darwin* was among the first scientists/philosophers to see how all living things reached their present states. Thanks to his insight, all creatures are now seen as connected and adaptable. Because of Darwin, the beautiful fluidity of species was first beheld. The world and its inhabitants are now viewed as changing entities, robust with evolutionary processes: from the geologic to the historical to the biological. Darwin made it possible for humans to see themselves as natural.

*Sigmund Freud* was the father of psychology, the discoverer of the unconscious, and the original pioneer who examined the drives and unheralded motivations of human behavior. Because of Freud, it is commonplace to analyze why humans behave the way they do, to assign meaning to what is going on beneath the surface, and to nobly attempt to influence human behavior for the better. By adding an entire layer to cognition, Freud made humans deeper.

*Albert Einstein*, like Freud, gave humanity a new dimension in which to forage. With numbers and particles, he enlarged human life and revolutionized human perception of the universe.

These three people are considered great because the world was forever altered after they expressed themselves. They shared

*When a team is alive with passion, then and only then does it have the required maturity and power to work on what really matters.*

*By adding an entire layer to cognition, Freud made humans deeper.*

*You could consider such geniuses as mutants, who are able to perceive life with virtuoso breadth and depth.*

*It is difficult to argue that the world would not be better off with more geniuses per century.*

*We might increase the genius count by actually realizing the combinatorial potential of "multipersonal" entities.*

their gifts with us, as fully as can be imagined. Each of their main contributions created an entirely new worldview. Apparently, they saw more than others (or believed more of what they saw) and faithfully reported their perceptions, though the reporting proved personally expensive. Each had to suffer the reactions that arose from his having threatened—and ultimately overturned—the established order.

Unfortunately, only a handful of these great contributors appear in each century. You could consider such geniuses as mutants, who are able to perceive life with virtuoso breadth and depth. Moreover, they act upon their perceptual gifts. They somehow escape the worst of the self-destructive and nondisclosing tendencies common to the rest of us.

It is difficult to argue that the world would not be better off with more geniuses per century. Unfortunately, the odds against any one person realizing this level of achievement are long indeed— billions to one. Because civilization's progression has, to a large measure, depended on the emergence of genius, the rate of progress is limited by the chance that another great person will appear.

What should the rest of us do? Wait for the next genius?[11] What if teams decided to be geniuses? What if they combined their favorable attributes and applied them consistently? We might increase the genius count by actually realizing the combinatorial potential of "multipersonal" entities, and by acting as if every team ought to be a genius of comparable magnitude and effect to Darwin, Freud, or Einstein. This transformation is feasible and desirable, and it is one of the underlying premises of The Core protocols. So why isn't it found in today's world?

## Upping the Genius Count

A persistent and baffling mystery of human intelligence and the collaborative creation of intellectual property[12] limits the potential of collaborative achievement. This mystery can be stated as follows:

---

11. While "waiting for the next genius" is not a recommended course of action, seeking out, recognizing, and fully supporting any practicing genius who happens to be on the scene has historically been needed as well.

12. Which, after all, is the type of property typically associated with genius.

*Why can't n + 1 people working together create at least as much intellectual property as n people working on the same problem?*

In other words, why can't humans consistently aggregate their personal abilities? It seems as if this equation ought to work. Desirable qualities *ought* to accumulate in proportion to the number of quality contributors. Furthermore, the multiplication of intelligences (and not their mere summation) may turn out to be the normal—though clearly not the common—outcome of a devoted group or team.

Even if a multiplicative effect is not what happens, why isn't the simple accumulation of intelligence from groups of people explicitly desiring it straightforward? Surely, the money invested in software development alone (to say nothing of the investments in entertainment, science, journalism, and all other collaborative IP production activities) would warrant uncovering the underlying group dynamics that could explain the failure to achieve this goal.

Shouldn't there at least be no *loss* in personal intelligence throughput because one joins a collaboration? If you faithfully express the information you possess, say the ideas that come, and apply your knowledge and other intellectual resources, isn't it reasonable to expect that this effort would be the theoretical minimum intellectual output on your team? And yet, on average, people will experience personal diminishment if the team's product is even slightly less than would be wrought by the summation of its individuals' capabilities. Part of the reason for the per capita diminishment is the cost of the exponentially increasing number of connections required. Everybody must connect with everybody else, and there are usually no noticeable bandwidth gains with each additional person.

### Interpersonal Costs

Interpersonal communication generally entails the disclosure of one's own intellectual property and the receipt of others' intellectual property. Unfortunately, open trade in IP within and among teams commonly causes troubles even as it achieves results. Sometimes, the costs of these troubles approach or even exceed the value of the results.

*Shouldn't there at least be no* loss *in personal intelligence throughput because one joins a collaboration?*

*Unfortunately, open trade in IP within and among teams commonly causes troubles even as it achieves results.*

*A team can thereby aggregate the intellects and elevate the nobility of the group as a whole to create a greatness of effect comparable to, or even surpassing, the individual genius.*

Conversely, something very powerful, even transforming, does happen when team members make an explicit, unanimous commitment to connect with one another, and to use their interconnection to receive and transmit one another's intellectual property.

The mechanics of the disclosure and receipt of one another's IP with predictability, efficiency, and reliability is provided by The Core protocols. The Core provides a structure within which collaboration can more effectively combine the individual intelligences of a team's members. In addition to the genius-grade volume of accumulated personal assets of such a team, total effort will be reduced, many negative attributes are likely to be cancelled, and more of the total individual potential will be realized.

The Core protocols can be used to minimize the headgap among team members. A team can thereby aggregate the intellects and elevate the nobility of the group as a whole to create a greatness of effect comparable to, or even surpassing, the individual genius.

## Back-of-the-Envelope Genius-Fabrication Arithmetic

Although the genius is smart, is he or she three times smarter than the average person? Five times smarter? Although such questions are not really answerable, posing them does serve a purpose. Even after accounting for the headgap and other burdens arising out of a group organization, participating at a genius level may be more available. Some number of people must surely have at least as much of the personal properties of a genius needed to produce the same beneficial effect for civilization.

Fill in values for *x* and *y*:

*A genius is* x *times as* y *as a normal human.*
where x = *an integer*
and y = *one or more of* smart, courageous, gifted, effective, productive, driven, *or other attributes that may come to mind as characteristic of genius*

Now, the question to consider is whether *n* nongenius people would be able to replicate the genius effort by exhaustively

- Applying their intention,

- Acting smart together,

- Increasing their personal presence,

- Establishing and maintaining their integrity,

- Navigating and resolving conflict,

- Working with their passions,

- Nullifying collaboratively many of the disconnecting individual impulses, and

- Establishing a milieu wherein the best ideas generally prevail.

These $n$ people ought to able to achieve the functional equivalent of a genius state. Could there then be 100 geniuses/teams per century instead of the handful to which humans are accustomed? Or 1,000? Or 10,000? Could there even be just one extra genius-equivalent?

*Could there then be 100 geniuses/teams per century instead of the handful to which humans are accustomed? Or 1,000? Or 10,000?*

*Choose as one.*

# II

# Decider

UNANIMITY AS VALUE

AGGREGATOR

*"Yes."*

*Frankly, the whole thing has surprised you, though it shouldn't have. The team was actually receptive to your message regarding the increase of presence, the care of self. You talked with the two team members (the newbie and the cynic) long into the night. Sitting, shoes off, feet on table, inside the white-boarded walls of that conference room, you three talked for hours. As the setting sun delivered the latest version of its daily surrender, you spoke thoughtfully of the chain of thoughts you had had at the earlier meeting.*

*While you were speaking, somewhere along the line, you realized that this very moment might actually be your moment to check all the way in yourself. So, while the room evolved from ambers to golds, and then to reds, pinks, and purples, you did just that. Checked all the way in. The rest of the building hushed, like a grade school after the kids have gone home; the sound of your voice morphed into "a friends at a campfire" kind of voice; and, after you were done with your initial disclosures, each of you disclosed your greater stories, your larger feelings, your deeper hopes. The moon, the stars, and one flickering parking lot light were all the light in the conference room now; but no one switched on the room's fluorescents. Somehow, that evening things came together among you three: the intimacy afforded by the softening darkness and the stillness of the workplace, the longish silences that attend a true campfire mode discussion, the shoes off, the truth you were telling, your fresh point of view—probably all helped the three of you connect.*

*They took your message to heart. Made it their own and played it back. Now it was different, better, and you signed on to to their improvements.*

*The next day, at a hastily arranged team meeting, two people (not just one, but two) checked all the way in. The newbie, full of hope and willing to directly name and express the fear and hope, even teared up a bit when he referred to "the long road" he had traveled to get to this first product. The cynic finally dropped his rage and blew the coals of his genuine anger into the bright flame of passion. And the way he drew his personal line, his "here and now," finally showed his idealism a bit. At last, ideals again. Dramatic stuff. Enough to lend credence to the possibility of a real team shift. Enough, in fact, to draw in his surprised co-cynics.*

*Several team members have now decided to quit wasting time. They are experimenting with disclosing their feelings and saying their thoughts and ideas more directly and more efficiently—they have talked about and decided to intentionally maximize their presence at work. To give it a shot. Others didn't care to do that. This didn't stop those who wanted to. Things are progressing.*

*Although many seem initially uncomfortable applying this* Checkin *protocol, you note how that plays out in the face of the radically improved connection, the more authentic teamwork that results from it. The several meetings that have since taken place—even the ad hoc ones, even the ones with "outsiders" in attendance—began with the* Checkin *protocol. This seems to renew each person's interest in real results. It helps focus the team's emotional energy. Team members rapidly gain (or regain) deeper levels of connection by their* Checkin *disclosures. Increasingly, you can see that teammates are actually more checked in—in spirit as well as according to the formal use of the protocol. Many of them have taken* Checkin *home to their families. They report that their children love it.*

*Gradually, the utility of* Checkin *takes hold. Before it could really do so, you now realize, the team members had to experience more pronounced feelings together, had to see that their more structured expression of them worked, had to discover firsthand the utility of treating strong emotions with respect, had to hit pay dirt when they mined them. Seems like they had to experience a few heated moments to see for themselves that their new, straightforward management of emotions provided better access to collaborative engagement.*

*As other elements of protocols they're adopting come on line, you're willing to bet that the necessity of* Checkin *becomes even more clear, probably bringing those who mostly pass now to a more engaged spot.*

*Here's how you think it evolved: As the number of the "new" teams'
decisions mounted, their individual ideas and wants emerged more, and an
escalating sense of promise came to predominate. In sorting all this out, the
team's use of CheckIn was increasingly seen as the indispensable tool it is.
Its use was then fully accepted by the team and its adoption normalized.*

*You envision the normalization: Throughout a workday, each person
will periodically check in, usually at various meetings. He discloses his state,
accepts that from others, and may spend a moment or two finding out for
himself whether he is as present, as engaged, as he wants to be. If something is
needed to increase his presence to an appropriately productive level, he uses
CheckOut to get it, or he directly asks the team for help.*

*This team is more aware of the variability in the presence of each mem-
ber. You're certain of that. Teammates are growing more facile at CheckIns
and more comfortable with CheckOuts. Members let the rest of the team
know when they check out. When they return, they simply say, "I'm checking
back in." (They may or may not go through the emotional disclosure part of
the CheckIn protocol. You wonder if this is right.) On the whole, CheckIn et
al. seem to lay a foundation of trust. You can see the overall expectations
rising: Team members trust that their peers will be present only when they
can contribute and when they are able to uphold the CheckIn commitments.
They also can let go a bit, and trust that each person feels responsible for
maximizing his own contributions. Wasteful, bogus caretaking and "rescuing" are noticed and occasionally called out.*

*When a team member doesn't want to participate in a particular
activity, he just passes. Nobody gets to squawk, or give him the third degree.
Nothing. This also increases trust—both now and in the future. You sense
that passing is really important, that it underlines the primacy of the individual. Team members—scared to death of anything like group think or
committee designs—actually see in practice that any loss of individual
autonomy is also a team loss. They begin to appreciate that no one can claim
to be "forced" to do anything or "pressured" into something that he would
not have otherwise done, and that each person is responsible for the activities
in which he participates. This recognition increases the clarity of the emerging
practice of personal accountability.*

*The foundation of trust, the blossoming awareness of emotional cur-
rents, and the clear evidence of individual autonomy create a team environ-*

*ment that feels more ripe for action. And there's a bit of a holdup there, you see. This team—though ready to think and to choose as one, to make its own decisions—is kind of hung up on the politics of power and the org chart. Now that they're checked in, the power seems to originate more from them than from the hierarchy. They have to resolve this.*

# FIVE

# The Elements of Decider

*"I think there's a problem with your intention here."*

*"Intention? Huh? You mean, what was my intention in saying what I did?"*

*"Yes."*

*"Well, I didn't really have any particular intention."*

*"Right. That's the problem."*

Decider promises two things to groups who adopt it:

1. Their decision making will aggregate team resources and apply them to making choices collaboratively.

2. Their decision making will create a clear system of individual accountability for team results.

Decider's central feature is its protocol. In turn, the Decider protocol's most distinctive characteristic is that *all team decisions must be unanimous.*[1] It is a by-product of unanimous team support that

---

1. Unanimity is a much less radical requirement than it might seem at first. Since the making of high-IP products fundamentally requires the intellectual support of everybody involved anyway, explicit unanimity is more an efficiency measure than any shift in the reality of organizational power politics. If the optimal behavior of the people who must live with a decision is the goal, their unanimous support for that decision is at once both the highest possible and the least acceptable amount of support required.

---

*The regular excuses
and exculpatory
stories often used to
rationalize ongoing
half-heartedness or
failure are neutralized
up front by the team's
simple requirement:*
unanimity before
action.

dissemination of decision accountability takes place, without thinning it down or clumping it up. By explicitly "signing up" each team member in support of every team decision, Decider delivers on both its purposes.

The accountability derives from the right of any team member to make a proposal that is resolved immediately, combined with each team member's capability to effectively veto any team proposal. Individuals who don't agree with a proposed plan of action must merely vote "no." *A single, persistent "no" vote from any team member will kill a proposal, no matter how many others support it.*

A Decider world is airtight with respect to accountability and empowerment leaks. Typical commitment-phobic tendencies are purged from the team as its decisions are made. The regular excuses and exculpatory stories[2] often used to rationalize ongoing half-heartedness or failure are neutralized up front by the team's simple requirement: *unanimity before action.*

Common self-defeating behaviors have always been theoretically unacceptable, but are often tolerated. In a Decider-driven team, such self-destructive patterns will be more visible, so they can be explicitly rejected in the most useful (and hence supportive) way. All team members can make proposals (indeed, are *required to* when they believe they have the best idea), and *all* are required to support those that pass. Going forward only with explicit commitments from all to behave so as to achieve the team's purposes provides tremendous leverage.

This vivid and total accountability stands in stark contrast to the more common circumstance: No one is quite sure who decided which steps the team would take. With unanimity-based self-governance, virtually all team failures can be clearly traced to particular breakdowns of personal integrity.[3] Moreover, because individual and communal integrity lapses can be easily traced to their point of

---

2. These tales are told (in part) to evade accountability in the event of failure or unexpected difficulties. Such stories are typically about how events beyond the storyteller's control caused the failure or difficulties.

3. Usually, the lapses are when someone votes "yes" but means "no," or when someone votes "yes," means "yes," but acts as if he meant "no."

origin, their frequency is reduced. Common potential excuses[4] are eliminated at the voting stage when Decider is the driving decision-making process.

The Decider group decision-making process includes two components:

- The Decider protocol structures the initial steps that a team takes toward a unanimously supported decision. Given a proposal, it will yield either an adopted plan or a rejected proposal.

- Many times, however, there is an intermediate stage prior to full acceptance or rejection. An initial Decider vote results in a majority-supported proposal, but not a unanimously supported one. The Resolution protocol is then used to either upgrade the level of team support to unanimity, or kill the proposal altogether.

# OTHER DECISION-RELATED ELEMENTS

Beyond using Decider and Resolution, maximizing the effectiveness of team decisions and team decision making will depend on the team's understanding and application of another important Core pattern (EcologyofIdeas) as well as the consistent use of an additional Core protocol (IntentionCheck).

## THE ECOLOGY OF IDEAS PATTERN

The team mentality is sustained by a constant stream of fresh ideas flowing from individual team members. The rate of flow, as well as the depth and quality of the ideas, determines the vitality of the team mentality. These factors are a function of the connectedness of the team members. When the connections are good, the ideas act

---

4. These excuses include the usual after-the-fact explanations of failure attributed to "uncontrollable" circumstances.

synergistically rather than as a collection of individual contributions. Personal attachment to ideas of mixed lineage is less important here than in more compartmentalized environments. Indeed, every idea worthy of being considered is properly articulated by someone. Every articulated idea is released into a more nourishing milieu, rather than championed into a hostile one. Ultimately, each idea must compete with and connect to other ideas, and it must establish its own place in the team's mental ecology.

As a consequence, the qualities of the ideas themselves must suffice to animate and propel the ideas forward. Their own vitality must ensure their realization and development: in the minds that think them, in the memories they leave, and especially in the objects produced by the team after encountering the idea. An idea's persistence in the creatively rich environment of a mature team will be determined by its degree of attractiveness, and its accessibility to the multiple curious minds on the team.

If a team desires to develop the most robust team mentality, its members will study EcologyofIdeas, and then create their own implementation of it.

## THE INTENTION CHECK PROTOCOL

The IntentionCheck protocol helps you assess the quality of your intentions before speaking, deciding, or acting on them. To a lesser extent, it can help you assess the intention of others by weighing their words and actions.

## ANTIPATTERNS

The degree of success in adopting Decider is also contingent on the team's avoidance of several antipatterns. Decision-making and accountability issues will, if not addressed by all members, lead to ineffective behavior. Most teams working without The Core will already be trapped in some of these antipatterns.

*Every articulated idea is released into a more nourishing milieu, rather than championed into a hostile one.*

*An idea's persistence in the creatively rich environment of a mature team will be determined by its degree of attractiveness, and its accessibility to the multiple curious minds on the team.*

# RESOLUTION AVOIDANCE

ResolutionAvoidance occurs when you create or prolong conflict, believing that you can avoid it. People who think of themselves as "conflict avoidant" are often "resolution avoidant."

# OBLIVIOUS ACTION

ObliviousAction occurs when you act or speak while your higher cognitive faculties are "looking the other way." These cognitive faculties might have guided you to better results. In some ways, ObliviousAction is the opposite of intentionality.

# TURF

Turf is a common anti-strategy that precludes the benefits from EcologyofIdeas. If your respect of role ownership causes you to forgo ideas, reject leadership, or avoid desirable things, you are turf-building.

# BOSS WON'T YIELD

This antipattern arises when an authority figure attempts to slow or stop a team from getting results because he doesn't understand or accept their methods or vision, or because he doesn't understand the actual power dynamics.

# SIX

# Decider Patterns and Protocols

---

## PATTERN: DECIDER

---

### PROBLEM

---

*Your team's decision process does not provide each team member with an explicit say, or provide a means to hold members accountable for the result.*

### TEAMS MUST INCORPORATE FREE WILL OR LOSE VALUE

Choices demonstrate free will and are one sign of sentient presence. People have free will. Take it away, reduce it, pretend that they don't have it, or allow them to pretend they don't, and they are greatly diminished. A team can never surpass the limits of its individual members unless it exploits or even increases the exercise of their free will. An individual can never become a part of—nor really identify with—a team that requires the subversion of his free will as a precondition of membership. Such subversion paradoxically nullifies

*A team can never surpass the limits of its individual members unless it exploits or even increases the exercise of their free will.*

his ability to truly join. This is why The Core protocols include **CheckOut** and **Passer**.

Making decisions is a way for a team to create (and apply) group intention and to identify, incorporate, and mobilize free will. "Deciding as one" requires (at least presumptively) that a team do the following:

- Gather and apply its accumulated information
- Reveal its desirable qualities
- Inhibit its undesirable qualities
- Specify its subsequent behavior

## TEAMS THAT DON'T DECIDE ARE HOPELESS

Even though many teams struggle along without an explicitly defined, full-blooded, decision-making apparatus, their quality of life is still largely determined by the quality of the choices[1] they make. The greater the attention, intention, creativity, thought, and focus put into those choices, the more enriched team life becomes, and the more enriching the team's product.[2] Without an explicit decision-making process, the team won't know its own choices until behavior reveals them. Unless the team uniformly holds members accountable for the results of their decisions, they will not work as one toward the improvement of their choices. The situation cannot improve; group learning is precluded.

*You can't improve team practices as long as the team's choices remain indistinct.*

You can't improve team practices as long as the team's choices remain indistinct. Of course, these choices proceed with or without improvement—whether conditions are murky or revealing. Every meeting, and each creative act, expresses a team choice. In murkyville, the choices are incoherent, and their potential for accountability is wasted.

---

1. In the context of The Core protocols, a *choice* is not a *decision* unless it creates explicit obligations for specific future behavior of those making it.

2. Enriched lives produce more abundance than do unenriched lives. The production of surplus is one way to measure the quality of any life, including that of a team.

# TEAM DECISIONS AGGREGATE TEAM QUALITIES

**Decisions** are choices that are especially vivid and/or important. They are often recorded, and any decision is expressed by the subsequent behavior of those making it.

When a team decides, it chooses to do, or not to do, something. Unfortunately, on many teams, team members are often left in an untenable position of ignorance regarding their own decisions. They don't know

- What they've decided,
- When they decided it,
- What obligations the decision confers, or
- What transactions constitute the decision.

Such teams lack a cognitive function. Naturally, the lack of precision and the low level of clarity surrounding such dysfunction greatly complicate team behavior. If a team has no cognition about the fundamental elements of a "team decision," can the team members be said to have decided at all?

This type of quiescent-to-passive decision making creates a vacuum in the power system of an IP-producing team. While typical product development teams actually have all of the political and creative power required, they suffer from their lack of ex officio group acceptance of power. This absence muddies the formation of an acceptable accountability structure for the team.

Furthermore, the quality of the behavior resulting from a decision seldom improves on the quality of the decision that determined it. The transition from decision to action is lossy.

## DECISIONS AWAKEN

As a consequence of the imprecise and undemanding decision-making machinery available to a team, teams often suffer from a lack of "team awakening"—that is, the realization of team identity. Team awakening will occur when a team experiences group cognition: All members perceive themselves simultaneously choosing

*The quality of the behavior resulting from a decision seldom improves on the quality of the decision that determined it.*

*A team without group cognition is inevitably lackluster and unenlivened.*

the same course of action. Like one being, they realize that they can choose to act as one.

Even without this experience of applied team "free will," things might appear healthy. The choices might seem to be aligned, the required information might seem to be properly exchanged among team members, and a team memory might exist. Nevertheless, a team without group cognition is inevitably lackluster and unenlivened. Unfortunately, such team members have not made the transition from a group of affiliated individuals to larger group self-awareness. No quickening or vivification of the new, larger team identity has taken place. As a result, all go without the cognitive joy that happens when the team-as-team decides something. Team decisions require that the team identity become operative, that it choose, and that it act.

## OTHER EFFECTS OF NOT DECIDING

The failure to make decisions has a variety of other ramifications for a team:

- There is limited loyalty to a team that has limited coherence: Why permanently devote yourself to a temporary confluence of interests?

- Without any group cognitive function, the group is deprived of the steady flow of "aha" moments, the refreshing bursts of energy that occur when team members become simultaneously aware of important new ideas.

- Lacking the team self-awareness that is created by making decisions together, teammates can neither align nor share vision.

## COMMON DECISION-MAKING TECHNIQUES

Observations of contemporary group decision making reveal profound and mostly unnecessary problems.

- *Decision making is conceptually promiscuous.* The values behind decision-making behaviors are an eclectic mix, a hodgepodge of autocratic impulses and majority-rule democracy, colored by local mores. The greater cultural forces of peer pressure, respect for authority, and fear of joblessness ensure compliance.

- *Behaviors are not implemented in a standard way.* Decision making varies from one locale to the next, even within the same institution. Which decision-making elements are emphasized and which are ignored is determined by chance, local management, and the character of the individuals and teams involved.

- *Decision making is connected to the hierarchical levels of individual financial power.* The most significant organizing element of contemporary decision-making practices in institutions larger than just a few people is the concept of finality, as in, "Who has final authority for items exceeding $100,000?" Your authorized spending level or your institution's decision on whether your signature is binding determines whether you are consulted or your approval is solicited by others prior to spending resources.

When contemporary decision-making styles are described informally, certain concepts repeatedly come up, along with particular words that somehow highlight the various decision-making elements and processes they use. They fall into two categories: those that are democratically oriented, and those that are autocratically oriented. Democratic decision making is characterized by these behaviors:

- Securing (management/staff) buy-in
- Following a consensus style
- Socializing an idea
- Building consensus
- Creating support

Autocratic decision making relies on different precepts:

- Someone's gotta decide.
- The buck stops somewhere.
- It's not a democracy.

*The most significant organizing element of contemporary decision-making practices in institutions larger than just a few people is the concept of finality, as in, "Who has final authority for items exceeding $100,000?"*

*The still-formidable energy of the "buck-stops-here-boss-decides" style continues to heavily influence contemporary group decision-making styles.*

*The boss-as-judge doesn't usually receive information regarding the underlying issues causing the conflict.*

*The idea that someone is "in charge" is familiar and somehow comforting, and it maintains great currency, even though it is increasingly fantastical.*

Behind these clichés are commitments to power and accountability distribution structures. When you use this terminology, you are endorsing a particular voting structure.

The first set of characteristics suggests a democratic or group-oriented ideal. Each of them derives much of its value from a common impulse for "majority rule." Openness, inclusion, and communal agreement are suggested by these characteristics. The second set of phrases is based on an autocratic or individualistic ideal, which emphasizes individual accountability and personal authority.

In most cases, the majority-rule bias plays an important role in everyday decision making. At the same time, majority rule is constrained by active autocratic ideals. The still-formidable energy of the "buck-stops-here-boss-decides" style continues to heavily influence contemporary group decision-making styles.

Autocratic decisions are routinely sought when sustained conflict emerges between two players on a team, or between two teams. The boss is cast as judge in these spats. That is, two or more testy combatants demand immediate judgment. The questions addressed by the boss in these cases are often articulated in grossly oversimplified terms. In reality, the issues are simply disguised rearrangements of the less acceptable "him or me, boss" ultimatum. The boss-as-judge doesn't usually receive information regarding the underlying issues causing the conflict. Instead, he will be confronted with two or three equally noxious "solutions" to a problem he hasn't studied in depth.

Additionally, organizations look toward the autocrat in situations requiring significant changes. The idea that someone is "in charge" is familiar and somehow comforting, and it maintains great currency, even though it is increasingly fantastical.

Autocratic techniques are also widely used when people at higher organizational levels seize the initiative.

The various decision styles supply or fail to supply, catalyze or prevent, the unity that is ideal for great collaborative efforts. Marginally explicit decision systems cannot yield the broad accountability required of great teams. If a group is to routinely transcend its previous limits, continuously attain higher levels of achievement, and constantly create things of lasting value, then that team's full complement of human intelligence must be completely engaged in its decision processes. Furthermore, each participant must bear the full weight of accountability for the group's explicit choices. Half-hearted, fuzzy decision-making processes typically leave outliers[3] out of and do not bring supporters into a chain of accountability.

Many decision-making techniques and practices exist, and the complete analysis of these processes is well beyond the scope of this text. Nevertheless, you should recognize three common ways of making decisions or achieving "consensus" in any institution that includes teams or collections of teams:

- No outward resistors
- Formal or informal majority rule
- Decisions dictated by a higher level in a hierarchy

These methods have significant weaknesses for collaboratively building the best possible IP-based products.

### No Outward Resistors

This "consensus-style" decision-making process usually leaves no record of who did or did not agree with what. Obviously, no systematic resolution of lingering, unsurfaced conflicts occurs. An absence of visible resistors does not indicate widespread support, nor is it predictive of consistently good results, in part because of the imprecise accountability for the decision.

Humans are capable of complex conscious and subconscious acts of sabotage, which often manifest themselves according to the following cycle:

- Someone dissents from the plan of record (that is, one or more of the collection of decisions). If the dissenter lacks the initiative or courage to deal with his objections directly, he may deal with them indirectly, often in ways that reduce the team's overall effectiveness.

*Each participant must bear the full weight of accountability for the group's explicit choices.*

*An absence of visible resistors does not indicate widespread support, nor is it predictive of consistently good results.*

---

3. People who are not (at the moment) supportive of a plan that the majority of the team supports.

- Even if the dissenter[4] has benign purposes, it is difficult for people to believe one way and act another over a sustained period of time. At best, a passive dissenter will exhibit intermittent half-heartedness; at worst, he will infect others with cynicism or spawn other varieties of team-negating behaviors.

- Often, resistance masquerades as technical or process complications. Even one resistor can single-handedly grind a project to a halt while the rest of the team complains or waits.

*Ignoring or otherwise tolerating resistance amounts to insisting on it.*

Resistance must be exposed first before the team can deal with it. A loosely structured "consensus-style" policy—"go forward if there are no outward resistors"—simply doesn't work. There is no mechanism for exposing and resolving the basis of the resistance prior to the otherwise inevitable sabotage. Instead, the resistance goes underground, where it siphons power from the team in proportion to the amount of energy that goes into ignoring it. If you're not putting energy into seeing the problem, then you're putting energy into ignoring it. Ignoring or otherwise tolerating resistance amounts to insisting on it.

*In IP development, even if resistance is somehow evaded or repressed everywhere else, it will be seen in the finished product.*

In IP development, even if resistance is somehow evaded or repressed everywhere else, it will be seen in the finished product. The effect of one resistant person on an IP-based product can be disproportionately large.

*What manifests as resistance after a proposal is adopted often manifests as wisdom before a proposal is adopted.*

Unanimity is achieved by surfacing resistance and dealing with the issues that cause it. As this work must take place anyway, sooner is much better than later. What manifests as resistance *after* a **proposal** is adopted often manifests as wisdom *before* a proposal is adopted.[5]

### Majority Rule

A strategy using majority rule is ineffective in IP development for the very same reasons that "no outward resistors" fails. That is, dissenters who are in the minority will be either vocal or silent resistors. The

---

4. That dissent is silent is, in and of itself, grounds for suspicion regarding the quality of a dissenter's intention.

5. The neurosis of not expressing one's wisdom when it can make a difference morphs into the more obvious neurosis of passive resistance.

issues that trigger their resistance are best dealt with in the open. Ignoring the inevitable minority resistance will only invite rebellion and sabotage.

### The Boss Decides

However well disguised, dictating decisions from on high doesn't work, because it runs afoul of the same aspects of human nature and of the collaborative development of IP-based products. In this case, the power vacuum in the decision-making engine is often symbolically "filled" by the immediate boss or, worse, by some even more remote boss.[6]

When the boss "rules," the team defers accountability for officially "deciding" to the boss. This system is not a show of respect, but rather the unconscious perpetuation of a system of "blame preparedness." The boss knows at some level that he is dependent on the team and is typically only "deciding" what the most respected members of the team advise. The team, where the power, brains, and passions originate, ends up less accountable for results than a somewhat disconnected boss.

*This system is not a show of respect, but rather the unconscious perpetuation of a system of "blame preparedness."*

This system would be analogous to the contemporary British monarchy proclaiming governmental policy *and* being held accountable for the results; but the development team's case is more pernicious. There is a concerted effort not to acknowledge the actual power of the team in a forthright way. Although many people in the IP development arena are completely aware of the disguised power distribution, many are not. The unaware become confused and don't know where to go for what: Who really decides? The aware, on the other hand, become cynical.

*The unaware become confused and don't know where to go for what: Who really decides? The aware, on the other hand, become cynical.*

---

6. Of course, the power vacuum cannot be truly filled by the boss, because he often has no genuine power in the matter. While it is theoretically possible for the boss to fire, punish, or even to reward, these capabilities are not as useful in today's economy as they might once have been. Even in a rocky economy, IP product developers have good chances of landing high-paying, creative jobs. Unfortunately, new jobs almost never provide relief from the fundamental, hamstringing effect of the unsolved interpersonal challenges in IP development.

A leader's true job is to ensure that the team acknowledges its own power, steps forward to achieve self-determined results, and assumes accountability for its decisions. The effective boss provides the team with the technology to achieve group cognition and to make itself go.

The Decider protocol provides a structure for the exercise of a team's cognitive faculty, from which decisions and accountability flow.

## SOLUTION

*Use a reliable, unanimity-driven decision process*
*with your team.*

The Decider protocol has been developed over several years, with much practice, thanks to the contributions of many teams who needed to decide and finish things on time. Decisions made using Decider are generally

- Creative,
- Timely,
- Fully supported, and
- Carried through.

## THE DECIDER PROTOCOL

The Decider protocol involves five steps:

1. The **proposer** says, "I propose. . . ."
2. The proposer offers a concise, actionable proposal.
   - No more than one issue is resolved per proposal.
   - The behavior expected of the voters if the proposal is accepted is clearly specified.
3. The proposer says, "1-2-3."
4. All team members vote simultaneously in one of three ways:
   - "Yes" voters raise their arms or give a thumbs-up.
   - "No" voters point their arms down or give a thumbs-down.

— "Support-it" voters raise their arms midway or show a hand flat.

5.  Once the vote is taken, use the Decider tally procedure:

    — If the combination of "no" voters (called *outliers*) and "support-it" voters is too great (approximately 30 percent or more, as determined by the proposer), the proposer drops the proposal.

    — If any of the "no" voters states his absolute opposition to the proposal, the proposal is dead.

    — If there are just a few "no" voters, the proposer uses the Resolution protocol to resolve things with the outliers (the "no" voters).

    — Otherwise, the proposal passes.

    Table 6.1 summarizes this protocol as pseudocode.

Table 6.1.  *Decider Vote Tally as Pseudocode*

---

1.  If (too many (no votes) or (too many (support-it (votes)))) {
        the proposal is dead
        Decider ends
        }

---

2.  If (unanimous (yes or support-it)) {
        the proposal passes
        Decider ends
        }

---

3.  If (a no voter states he will "not get in no matter what") {
        the proposal is dead
        Decider ends
        }

---

4.  else {
        Resolution protocol is pursued for each no voter
        Decider ends
        }

---

## *Guidelines*

1. The proposer is responsible for tallying.

2. No one speaks during Decider except the proposer

   – When stating the proposal or

   – When using Resolution

   Or the "no" voter

   – When using Resolution or

   – When declaring his absolute "no" state.

3. "Yes" or "support-it" voters cannot speak during Resolution.

4. Voters requiring more information must vote "no" to stop the proposal before seeking information.

5. Voters do not state why they voted as they did.

6. What constitutes "too many" of a given category of votes (for example, too many "no" votes or too many "no" votes plus "support-it" votes) is determined solely by the proposer. Typically, three or four "no" votes out of ten total votes are considered "too many" to pursue to Resolution. A majority of "support-it" votes suggests a very weak proposal.

7. Passing is not allowed on a Decider proposal. You must vote if you are present.

8. Unanimous "yes" votes or "yes" votes mixed with some "support-it" votes are the only configurations that cause a proposal to be adopted as a part of the team's **plan of record.**

9. Each team member is accountable for personally carrying out behaviors specified in a Decider decision, and no member has more or less accountability than any other. Each is also accountable for insisting that the behavior specified in the proposal is carried out by the other team members.

10. After a proposal passes, a team member who was not present during the vote is responsible for acquiring information about what transpired,[7] and will also be held accountable for the deci-

sion. If the person prefers not to be accountable (that is, he would have voted "no" if present), he now must make a new proposal as soon as possible. In the meantime, the individual is bound by the decision just as if he had voted "yes."

11. When a "no" voter states that he "won't get in no matter what" (that is, an "absolute no" vote), it means that there is no condition that the voter can imagine that would change his vote.

12. It is traditional, though not mandatory, for an "absolute no" voter to make a new proposal following the death of the proposal killed with his vote.

## *Voting*

Given a proposal, the Decider protocol provides three possible voting strategies:

- Yes
- No
- Support-it

"Support-it" is a "yes" vote with an attitude. It can be translated as, "I can live with this proposal. I believe that it is probably the best way for us to proceed now. I support it, even though I have some reservations. While I don't believe I can lead the implementation of this proposal, I do commit not to sabotage it."

The goal is to collaborate with openness and efficiency so that the best thinking of all team members is incorporated into the team's subsequent behavior. As any "no" vote prevents action until it is switched, there is no cause for apprehension over wrong team actions. For the team just adopting Decider, there may be widespread discomfort over the fullness of accountability for all team decisions.

---

7. It is a waste of time and energy for team members to sit through a rehashing of a Decider process they already experienced. In general, you should use team time only for extremely important transactions. In this case, pull someone out of the room and have that one person update you on what transpired.

## *Decider Outcomes*

Three outcomes are possible:

- *Affirmative decision.* Immediate and universal acceptance of the proposal occurs.

- *Efficient negotiation with conflicts exposed and the proposal resolved.* Finer proposals are created while the team's inclusion effort proceeds.

- *Swift elimination of unsupported ideas.* Immediate, clear, and unremorseful rejection of an idea too many people think misguided.

## *Decider Commitments*

**Decider** requires the following commitments from team members:

- Actively support the decisions reached, with the behavior specified in them.

- Vote your true beliefs.

- Speak or don't speak as specified above.

- Hold others accountable for their decisions.

- Respect an "absolute no" voter. Do not pursue the voter or analyze his motives.

- Do not collect others' votes before making your own.

- Do not repeat failed proposals unless relevant circumstances have changed.

- Keep informed about **Decider** sessions run in your absence and resolve, via **Decider**, any lack of support you may have for decisions made when you were absent.

- Reveal immediately whether you are an "absolute no" voter when you vote "no."

# ANALYSIS OF DECIDER

A unanimity-based decision-making process is difficult to imagine for those who have not experienced it. To say the least, unanimity is not common in a culture brought up on majority rule. To expect or seek unanimity is seldom considered as a viable option. Not only is unanimity possible; it is readily attained and vastly more efficient than the alternatives. Results and execution are better because of the unqualified support from each team member and the clear and consistent accountability. The simplicity of achieving unanimity is a hallmark of a healthy team.[8]

Whether it has been widely experienced or even sought, unanimity is a desirable state for a group of collaborators. This state is not the unanimity of mindless cattle, without conflict or contest, but the unanimity of partners weighing alternatives together before deciding to act. A team that is capable of reaching absolute consensus on every group decision will demonstrate the following qualities.

*This state is not the unanimity of mindless cattle, without conflict or contest, but the unanimity of partners weighing alternatives together before deciding to act.*

### Increased Correctness

Because of the clear accountability that Decider provides and the elimination of excuses, team members tend to bring themselves more fully to the task at hand. Their intelligence, creativity, and other talents are more fully engaged. So much brainpower is applied to each problem that incorrect decisions are rare. Increased correctness results when the mature team resists its members' neurotic or distorted impulses. Typically, these impulses are less constrained in a solo effort. In summary, Decider brings more virtue, less vice, and better results.

### Timeliness

All teammates accept the group intention implicit in every successful Decider proposal. This cohesiveness produces aligned intention, a precursor of aligned behavior. Because everyone explicitly agrees on and commits to any schedules, timeliness is not just a possibility, but an intrinsic quality of the team.

---

8. If you are still shaking your head, set aside your skepticism for a minute and pretend that unanimity is possible. We were skeptical until we witnessed team after team shape a unanimity protocol.

## More Effective Accountability

*When they do vote
"no," it is a very
significant event.*

Every team member knows that he can stop the show. All teammates know they have the right to say "no," to be the sole outlier, and to stop any proposal dead in its tracks. As a consequence, what team members believe and think becomes more important in their own eyes, which helps them regard themselves with more respect. It also liberates them somewhat; they feel more like thinking about, improving, and tinkering with ideas until they truly accept and believe in them. When they do vote "no," it is a very significant event. Given this opportunity to provide lethal opposition to ideas, team members do so only when they believe that something is genuinely wrong with a proposal. This situation stands in stark contrast to the casual disbelief often seen in less empowered environments. Core teams are willing to be held accountable when they stop, as well as when they support, the motion of the team.

## Increased Purposefulness

Individuals do not work as effectively on something that they believe to be wrong or misguided as they do when they embrace the purpose behind the work. They also do not perform at their best when they feel an effort is hopeless. Using **Decider** circumvents such evils. Because people prefer more results for their efforts, they are more inclined to pursue more purposeful work when the less purposeful work is eliminated.

## Greater Ease

*No longer cruel and
withholding, the world
is seen as benign and
abundant.*

Unity eliminates many distractions; alignment anaesthetizes pain. A team unites and aligns when it chooses its behavior and then acts as one. Without distractions, in a purposeful manner, and in the ongoing state of unanimity, the team lives in a world that seems to offer more time, accepts more creativity, and provides more of virtually everything that team members desire. No longer cruel and withholding, the world is seen as benign and abundant. The team enjoys a greater sense of plenitude for many reasons, chief among them the effect of team members' concerted actions, which are conducted in a more beautiful state of union with others. Doing things together, properly and truly, is simply much more fun. Team members flourish in the security of knowing that, whenever necessary, they can forge even more unity, and they can achieve immediate and decisive creative action at will. This state makes everything much easier.

### Better Interteam Collaboration

Imagine that your group is in a state of **flow**,[9] that it is not the only team in such a state; but that other groups are also checked-in, deciding, aligned (see Chapter Nine) teams. In fact, the fully mature environment will include teams of teams, each collaborating team-to-team, all in a high-performance state. Your product and the services surrounding it will align with those from other teams from their inception. You will see an enormous reduction in the squabbling among teams, the draining, atavistic, ersatz sibling rivalry within companies, and the nullifying and chronic competition for resources previously believed to be scarce. Today, companies rarely try for full consensus on teams. This reluctance gives the teams who implement Decider or other methods for achieving unanimity an awesome advantage. They are the united and purposeful in a confused and chaotic world.

We have repeatedly witnessed an interesting scenario in companies where significant populations were using The Core or its predecessors: Disparate individuals spontaneously formed small teams, teams that had no predetermined function and no official status. These teams included people from the lowest levels to nearly the highest levels in the company. Team members came from prestige areas, as well as from the disciplines, and/or levels that were less respected or even poorly respected within their company. When such hierarchically and functionally diverse individuals combine to

*You will see an enormous reduction in the squabbling among teams, the draining, atavistic, ersatz sibling rivalry within companies, and the nullifying and chronic competition for resources previously believed to be scarce.*

9. To read more about flow, check out the following URLs:
http://www.apa.org/monitor/jul98/joy.html, and http://exploreit.net/mcole/thinkstop/flow1.htm.

form an ex officio team, powerful results have ensued. With their powers being won exclusively by their abilities and their desire to unite, such teams have tended to lead their companies from behind the scenes: making unofficial decisions and always working to support them with absolute unity of purpose, exchange of help, and loyalty to one another.

Any team genuinely using Connection can achieve the highest possible levels of influence. The members don't even have to work together directly. They can still act with unanimous support and react quickly as a single unit. Regardless of all other factors, a connected team is often the single most powerful entity in any organization, given the usual level of disunity.

## DECIDE BEFORE DISCUSSION

Usually, the team employing Decider reaches agreement without much discussion. Achieving this single-mindedness will greatly reduce the time consumed by typical low-bandwidth, half-duplex, physically based meetings.

## AGGREGATION

Decider provides a way to combine intellects. It works because the team agrees unanimously about good ideas and can quickly kill bad ideas. Decider also turns decision making into an intentional team activity. By using this protocol, the team says, "We are making a team decision right now. We will either become accountable to fulfill this proposal or decide not to act on it. There is no gray area." The team gains a type of super-consciousness that helps aggregate all of the individual team members' consciousnesses, and more.[10]

Of course, if group members' efforts are not united somehow, they will not reap all the rewards of working together. To the extent that a team can use each person's intellect toward the same end, it will achieve consistently great results with less effort. Establishing

*When such hierarchically and functionally diverse individuals combine to form an ex officio team, powerful results have ensued.*

*Regardless of all other factors, a connected team is often the single most powerful entity in any organization, given the usual level of disunity.*

---

10. The engaged observer will notice that combining two intellects for the purpose of achieving results always creates more results than the simple sum of the two individuals' results if they were working alone.

*Without being united, a team is a group of* n *intellects of 150 IQ running around, sometimes canceling one another out.*

*A common fear is that some "problem" team member will consistently kill good proposals by using the "won't get in" strategy.*

the precise ends around which to unite is a function that requires **Decider**.

Conversely, without being united, a team is a group of *n* intellects of 150 IQ running around, sometimes canceling one another out. When united in its choices, the team becomes a creature of at least $n \times 150$ IQ. **Decider** is an effective means of aggregating all intelligence and aligning all intellects.

## I WON'T GET IN

Outlying solo all the way through to proposal death requires enduring some discomfort. Such personally expensive and negative steadfastness must arise from a thoroughly motivated conviction. Absolute conviction can be built on solid thought, intuition, or experience, or it can emerge from a neurotic blindness. In the former case, the team is enriched by its courageous outlier. In the latter case, the team gains a vivid example of intransigence and an increased awareness of one source of its communal blindness. Appropriate action can then be taken. Either case yields extraordinary profit to the team and those who depend on it.

A common fear is that some "problem" team member will consistently kill good proposals by using the "won't get in" strategy.

Although this fear is a common one, we have never seen it happen—not once. If it did happen, the proposal killer could be asked about his motivation and prompted to change his mind. The issue could then be resolved by separating that team from its neurotic team member. Obviously, such an obstinate individual doesn't want to be on the team, because he disagrees with many decisions that the rest of team considers good. What happens instead, however, is that because of the extreme visibility of solo outlying, the clear accountability for stopping the show, the traditional assumption that a solo outlier will counter-propose with a better idea, and the unusual efficiency of his continuing "no" votes combine to eliminate the benefits (such as they are) of intransigence. People who are considered truly obstinate before **Decider** is adopted are correctly seen as great "showmen of resistance" after **Decider** becomes the team law.

Dec der is a Core protocol because it provides catalytic power to a team. It enables a team to move effectively, work together toward a common vision, and deliver products en route. Each individual must constantly make decisions on a team. With Decider, each team member must vote, so his wisdom is factored into all decisions the team members choose to make as one. This practice surfaces the latent conflicts that would otherwise chronically drag the team down.

Decider allows a team to make decisions quickly and effectively, usually taking much less time than even an individual would take to reach the same decision. There is no escape from team accountability for team results. The only way to move is to move forward. Decider will also trigger the adoption of other results-oriented protocols as problems are brought to the team's attention by the process of making decisions.

*Decider . . . surfaces the latent conflicts that would otherwise chronically drag the team down.*

## PATTERN: RESOLUTION

### PROBLEM

*You have difficulties reaching unanimous support for a Decider proposal.*

### SOLUTION

*Only talk about what it will take to get the outlier "in."*

Ask the outlier:

*What does he actually require to support the proposal?*

No other question or point is of immediate interest.

The Resolution protocol is quite efficient. It is designed to help a Decider outlier see and clearly state what he needs to support the proposal. It joins the Decider proposer and any Decider outliers (in sequence) in a structured discussion that will either gain support for the proposal from the outlier or abort the proposal. **Resolution** does not entail sophisticated, prolonged negotiations. Rather, its visibility and structure enable the outlier to effectively fulfill his needs based on a better understanding of his motives.

## THE RESOLUTION PROTOCOL

When a **Decider** vote yields a small minority of outliers, the proposer quickly leads the team, in a highly structured fashion, to deal with the outliers. The proposer's goal is straightforward and unabashedly promotes the proposal: to bring the outliers in at the least cost.

1.  The proposer asks each outlier to express his requirements for joining the team in support of the proposal: "What will it take to bring you in?"

2.  The outlier has only two possible legal responses:

    – He may state, at any time after the vote, but no later than when asked the above question by the proposer, that there is "no way" he will change his vote to "yes" or "support-it." This simple declaration means that the proposal is now officially dead, and the **Decider** and **Resolution** protocols end.

    – The outlier may state in a single, short, declarative sentence, precisely what it is he requires to be "in." In this way, he expresses a contingent commitment to see that the proposal is accepted and transformed into reality. If given what he requires, the outlier promises to drop all resistance to the proposal and to provide affirmation and support for it instead.

3.  As needed and as possible, the proposer makes an offer to the outlier. Two methods for incorporating changes into the original proposal while resolving any resulting perturbations to non-outliers' support are permitted:

    – If in the judgment of the proposer the adaptations to the proposal to accommodate the outlier's requirements are minor, the proposer may employ a simple, unofficial "eye-check" of the non-outliers to see if there is general acceptance to the changed proposal. If you are opposed to this implicit new proposal, or you require a formal restatement and a new vote, you must make your requirement known during this interval.

- If the required changes are more complex, the proposer must create and submit a new proposal that accounts for the outlier's requirements. The team reviews this proposal and conducts a new vote, and the Decider protocol begins anew.

4. "Yes" voters and "support-it" voters are not allowed to speak during Resolution. They have no complaint, and their listening adds quality to the resolution.

5. If outliers change their votes from "no" to "support-it" or "yes," then the decision to adopt the proposal is committed; it will be acted upon by the team. No further communication is required to achieve strong, unanimous consensus.

## Resolution Commitments

1. As an outlier, you must commit to answering the question, "What will it take to get you in?" with either an actionable modification of the proposal or a declaration of your "absolute no" status. Explaining why you don't like the proposal, for example, is off the subject.

2. As a proposer, you commit to ask outliers what it would take to get them in, each in turn. This is all you may ask.

3. As a proposer, you commit to reformulate the proposal as required.

4. As a "yes" or "support it" voter, you commit to absolute silence.

5. As a team member, you commit to insisting on the exact adherence to the Resolution protocol.

*Explaining why you don't like the proposal . . . is off the subject.*

## Resolution Results

Resolution leads to the following results:

- It creates efficient decision making.
- It distributes accountability.

- It exposes resistance.
- It identifies crucial elements blocking success.
- It facilitates the concrete expression of the group's united intention.

### When to Use Resolution

Use **Resolution** whenever a small percentage of the team votes "no" to your **Decider** proposal.

# PATTERN: WORK WITH INTENTION

## PROBLEM

*You don't know if your behavior will get you what you want.*

## SOLUTION

*Decide on your intention before acting or speaking.*

*When intention does not accompany behavior, excessive amounts of energy are wasted.*

Knowing precisely what you want often determines whether you will ultimately achieve it. The intensity of focus reported by those who are renowned for their achievements can be summoned only when behavior is informed with explicit intention. The united intention of its many members is as important a tool for a team as singleness of purpose can be for the individual. In both cases, when intention does not accompany behavior, excessive amounts of energy are wasted. Costs are much greater than strictly necessary, and results will be, at best, ambiguous. In fact, it would be surprising if the results of poorly intended efforts were not even more ambiguous than the ambiguous intention that spawned them.

Many methods and tools are available for creating a team that acts with intention:

- Prior to acting, ask yourself a few questions about your intentions:
  - What do I intend to achieve here?
  - What do I intend to achieve at the highest levels of abstraction and the farthest chronological reaches of my plan?[11]
  - Is my current action aligned with those intentions?
- Routinely disclose your intentions and solicit help in aligning your behavior with your intentions:

  *I am trying to behave with well-formed intentions. Here are my ideas about my situation. . . . I think I should act as follows. . . . What do you think? . . . Will you help me with that by . . . ?*

- Ensure that your team does not act without unanimously agreeing on what it intends to do.
- Ensure that your team does not act without unanimously agreeing on how it will act to achieve what it wants.
- Be willing to drop all assumptions and learned "rules" about how to behave at work. Be skeptical of all cultural norms. Many cultural norms are more accidental than they are supportive of intentionality.
- In one-on-one communication, if the discussion becomes boring or difficult, stop it and ask yourself what you intend to achieve and how you would act if you were showing integrity—and then act that way. If you are clear in that regard but continue to experience problems, ask the other person what he intends.
- In meetings of any size, if the discussion is lagging, boring, filled with unresolved conflict, or going in circles, stop and lead the team to determine its intention and subsequent behavior.

---

11. Plans are really just formalized intention, the details of which represent discrete steps in a single grand intention.

- After reading these ideas, come up with additional strategies by asking yourself, "If my team and I wanted to act with intention, what would we do?"

## VALUING INTENTION

A team that values intentional behavior creates the following:

- An environment in which intention and thinking before acting are highly valued

- An environment in which each member brings the full potential of his own intention to the team for the purpose of creating great products

- A respectful environment (i.e., productive intention is required during communications)

- An environment in which the wants of each individual are valued

- Products that deliver what is promised

- Marketing messages that engage the consumer

- A maximally efficient environment

Intention is a powerful tool. It is the solution to oblivion—that is, acting without thinking. The majority of actions performed on product teams today occur under conditions of partial oblivion. The power of intention can take the poor or mediocre team into the realm of greatness, by requiring that each individual bring his full potential to the team's endeavors.

## INTENTION IS POSITIVE PURPOSE

*Intention is a powerful tool. It is the solution to oblivion.*

Intention precedes our most effective actions. It brings results. Cognition precedes and accompanies intention; it provides access to intention. Humans—even those on IP development teams with an unusually high distractibility quotient—have the capacity to form and hold intention as a group.

Most waste disappears and obstacles are more readily surmounted when group intention is clarified. Group intention is assembled from the strands of individual intention. People who behave without intention cause the greatest waste of time, by doing and saying things that produce unintended consequences. You may have been told, "The road to hell is paved with good intentions." This saying has either lost its true meaning or it is and always was folly. A "good" intention is one that culminates in good results. It is difficult to believe that good results are a part of the trip to perdition (in the unlikely event that the road to hell is actually paved at all). On the contrary, we are much more likely to stub our toes on the uneven surfaces of obliviousness, poorly formed intentions, or on the very rare malevolent intention.

So good intentions yield good results, by definition. Think of the situations where you hear the following kinds of remarks:

- I didn't mean to say *that*.
- I didn't consider that you would take what I said that way.
- That possibility never occurred to me.
- He's overreacting to what I said.
- Well, I can see where you might think that, but . . .
- I didn't mean for that to happen.

Generally, you hear or offer this type of defense only after an undesirable event. The usual resolution of this situation is to consider—and ultimately accept—that the person who has been careless didn't *mean* to cause the undesirable eventuality. You then deduce that he is therefore less culpable than the person who did mean it.

Who cares whether some random disrupter did not intend the negative consequences of his words or actions? Is an analysis of this person's previously obscure thinking and demonstrably faulty reasoning even relevant to eliminating likely future repetitions? More to the point, what evils are now lurking about "unintended" in the disrupter even as he says that he didn't intend the previous problem? No doubt, if queried, the person would state that he didn't intend for his lack of clear intention to be supported and perpetuated. That, however, is the obvious effect of any acceptance of this defense on your part.

Does the disrupter's intentional innocence minimize your actual loss in any way? Don't the actions flow without respect to what the

*It is difficult to believe that good results are a part of the trip to perdition.*

*What evils are now lurking about "unintended" in the disrupter even as he says that he didn't intend the previous problem?*

*When you sip at the breast of Oblivion . . . you damn yourself three times over.*

*Why was your intention, assuming you intended anything at all, so weak that disaster followed every step of the way?*

*The consistent subordination of your divergent impulses and motives to your intention will get you what you want most expeditiously.*

culprit "thought"? There is no solace, no wisdom, no redemption, and ultimately no purpose in pursuing this line of inquiry. When you sip at the breast of Oblivion, which has long been a compelling source of mental refuge, you damn yourself three times over:

- You do not achieve your stated intention.
- You suffer the loss you've caused.
- You show your predilection for not thinking.

Whether negative consequences were unintended is not the question. Action without intention always means trouble. The question to pose is, "Why was your intention, assuming you intended anything at all, so weak that disaster followed every step of the way?"

A person who intends the mischief caused is actually more capable and more mature than the person who does not. There is no elaborate "oblivion defense" to dismantle prior to genuine engagement with the root cause of the culprit's negative energy flood. In the case of an intentional troublemaker, a more reasoned—and hence more human—problem is at play: Multiple intentions collided on execution. It happens all the time.

How can you achieve successful collaboration?

- Align your intention with your thoughts, feelings, and intuitions. (See Chapter Nine.)
- Align your intentions with each other and with your behavior.
- Hold one another accountable for this alignment.

The consistent subordination of your divergent impulses and motives to your intention will get you what you want most expeditiously. Of course, it will prove difficult to maintain awareness of your intention, especially at first. Eventually, a growing sensitivity to your intentionality will develop. It will enable you to create and maintain an increasingly aligned focus across all areas. Persistence in achieving and maintaining a high-bandwidth connection with your teammates (who, ideally, will all be struggling in comparable ways) will facilitate the most progress toward your goal.

In a sufficiently large group, at least one person will always remember the purpose in joining together. The odds of remember-

ing an intention increase with the number of people trying to
remember it.

# THE INTENTION CHECK PROTOCOL

IntentionCheck assesses the integrity of your own (and, to a lesser
extent, another's) intention. IntentionCheck evaluates conditions that
tend to skew or bias your effectiveness in dealing with a given issue
at the time you run the check.

## *Execution of Intention Check*

1. Ask yourself, "Is my current emotional state solid, turbulent, or
   intense?"

2. Ask yourself, "Is my current receptivity to new information
   high, medium, or low?"

3. Ask yourself, "Do I understand clearly what my current purpose
   is?" That is, "What result do I want?"

4. If your emotional state is not solid, and/or your receptivity is not
   good, or you are not clear about your purpose, then postpone
   your action, or use the CheckOut protocol to get the information
   needed to clear up your intention before acting or speaking.

## *Synopsis*

Checking your intention prior to going forward with significant
behaviors will improve the odds that your behavior will have the
desired results. The most common problem in being effective is the
low quality of intention. By invoking an IntentionCheck on yourself,
or inviting investigation of your intention, you will act less with more
results. This is the essence of efficiency.

## *When to Use Intention Check*

When should you use IntentionCheck?

- When ambiguity or uncertainty surrounds your motive

- When your behavior seems likely to discomfort others

- When your behavior will seem likely to slow others in achieving their goals
- When you are contemplating an interpersonally risky or ethically complex endeavor
- After you failed to use IntentionCheck
- When you have strong feelings about another person's behavior, are involved in it to some extent, and are about to engage with him
- When you are psychologically attached to a particular goal and believe others to be resistant to it

---

# PATTERN:
# ECOLOGY OF IDEAS

## PROBLEM

---

*You don't get the best ideas into the product.*

It is a common holdover from the previous era to value ideas because of the source. Bosses at the turn of the last century were authority figures; their ideas were implemented by workers. The tendency to maintain a system that awards extra points to an idea from the boss seems entirely vestigial in the business of ideas. The authoritarian model, although successful when measured against earlier standards for building material things, is inadequate for intellectual properties.

Workers who simply follow orders will not create great IP products because IP consists of ideas. There is no special need for repetitive motion or for the unthinking followers who repeat the same task over and over, as instructed by the boss. This type of behavior is, in fact, destructive to an IP team. Because Team = Product, teams that behave in this holdover fashion will create repetitive, uncreative, unthinking products—if they can create anything at all.

*Workers who simply follow orders will not create great IP products because IP consists of ideas.*

# SOLUTION

*Create a healthy EcologyofIdeas.*

Two of the most important aspects of a team that consistently performs great creative feats are as follows:

- The team must value ideas.
- The team must value true authority.

These team qualities are interdependent. A team that values ideas will value true authority, and vice versa, because true authority comes from ideas in action, not corporate organizational position.

To successfully implement a team structure, it is imperative to create an EcologyofIdeas. That is,

- The team must not place importance or a lack of importance on an idea because of its source.
- The team must intentionally seek to express the most ideas possible, and then pick the best to implement.
- The team must implement only the best ideas.
- The team must intentionally create an environment where it is safe to express all ideas.
- The team must view those who are sources of the consistently best ideas as authorities.

A team committed to creating great products on time will move from viewing authority as emanating from position to viewing authority as emanating from ideas and from the nurturing and championship of an ecology of ideas. In this way, a team can effectively get the maximum value out of each individual's intellect, aggregate it, and produce the highest-quality intellectual property. The best ideas must prevail.

When we speak of an "empowered" team, these characteristics are what we mean. An empowered team wants each member to fully express his ideas, especially the scary ones, so that it can choose the best ones and implement them.

*A team that values ideas will value true authority, and vice versa, because true authority comes from ideas in action, not corporate organizational position.*

# SEVEN

# Decider Antipatterns

## ANTIPATTERN: RESOLUTION AVOIDANCE

### PROBLEM

*You don't deal efficiently with conflict because you're afraid of it.*

### SUPPOSED SOLUTION

*Lay low. Don't cause problems. Avoid conflict.*

"Avoiding conflicts," as the phrase is commonly used, is a one-eighty strategy. That is, if you consider yourself a person who "avoids conflict," the chances are good that your behavior really has the opposite effect: You end up *attracting* conflict. You really can't avoid conflict. You can only avoid resolution. Hence, ResolutionAvoidance. By dodging situations wherein a conflict is likely to—or ought to—surface

*Unresolved problems grow. . . . They adopt new cuisines and grow fat living off the land: you.*

*They will party on, and your avoidance is the life of the party.*

*All the other problems will hear about this phenomenon. Naturally, they will want to live with you too.*

explicitly, and perhaps be resolved, you don't reduce the amount of conflict in your life; you gather and increase it.

Unresolved problems grow. Their appetites increase, and they extend their range. They adopt new cuisines and grow fat living off the land: you. They get more powerful. Sometimes, they multiply ferociously and mutate in ways that make them unrecognizable. But one thing your unresolved problems never, *ever* do: *They never grow to cost you less, or grow to cause you fewer difficulties than before.* Unresolved problems never diminish, and no problem ever dies of old age.

With your pattern of ResolutionAvoidance, you may finesse a few moments of discomfort here and there. You may successfully duck the anger and fear that would arise should your problems surface; but the problems themselves will simply declare a holiday. They will party on, and your avoidance is the life of the party. The additional screw ups and heartaches you and others suffer that stem from your problems' persistence will impose a fearsome tax on your resources.

It often helps to view a situation as a system. For example, in the present case, you can look at the elements of your Resolution Avoidance as a problem in some kind of physics. Think about the dynamics of the forces involved. How do forces interact here? Probably as they do elsewhere: In order not to experience (that is, to avoid) a thing that is actually present, you must apply more force to denying it than there is force behind its presence. The force you use is drawn from your personal stash, too. To maintain a falsehood in the presence of the truth, the force behind the falsehood surely has to be greater than the forces inherent in the truth.

Another system viewpoint to adopt is to imagine that your ResolutionAvoidance takes place in a rich though nonbiological ecology, evolutionarily active, with lots of little critters and creatures living off the windfall of your energy. One particular species of critter is called "problems." Look at your ResolutionAvoidance from the problems' point of view for a moment. The problems associated with you tend to endure indefinitely, and this endurance will be noticed. All the other problems will hear about this phenomenon. Naturally, they will want to live with you too (consider this: "Resolution" is another word for "death" in problem-speak).

What problem in its right mind wouldn't hustle on over to the happy hunting grounds you've got all set up there? In your world, problems gain immortality! They get to spend eternity with their creator. That's a fairly attractive proposition for problems, especially when all they have to do to live forever with (and off) their creator is to intimidate your better instincts and divert your more mature impulses. Typically, this is little more than zapping a quick fax to your imagination: If you resolve problems, you might have to endure the trial of feeling angry or scared for a few minutes while doing so, and you might actually *see* someone else feeling angry or scared, too.

## ACTUAL SOLUTION

---

*Seek resolution.*

Maturity offers a most robust principle for organizing your experience: *Achieve the most desirable results for yourself at all times.* If you are mature, certain behaviors and conditions follow. One of them is this: The fact that you happen to find yourself in a conflict offers no relief from the regimen of maturity. As ever, you must provide for yourself. There is just no substitute for your own continuity, and no gain quite as useful as a gain for you.

When you really break down the concept, conflicts don't have all that much substance in and of themselves. They are usually a condition of timing and perceived resource availability. A conflict occurs when simultaneous desires meet incompatible gratifications. Whether the apparently opposing desires beat within a single breast or throb in multiples is more about the scale of a conflict than the conflict, per se.

In one or many, conflicts will arise where interests differ, and where union is imperfect. That would be pretty much everywhere, always. Interests differ in *all* encounters; that's what *makes* them encounters. This everywhere-and-always divergence of interests is a

*The fact that you happen to find yourself in a conflict offers no relief from the regimen of maturity. As ever, you must provide for yourself.*

*Even though differences diverge everywhere and always, conflicts arise only in a small percentage of everywhere and occupy just a little of always.*

*Most often, people fight when they really believe there is insufficient supply of something vital, when they then subordinate their hope to the zero-sum game.*

*The millions of quiescent conflicts you navigate daily have long since been negotiated, mostly by others, and by degrees.*

good and vital thing, because it creates individuality. But even though differences diverge everywhere and always, conflicts arise only in a small percentage of everywhere and occupy just a little of always. But if conflict was *caused by* differences, you would have conflict everywhere and always.

Maybe, on some days, you feel that "conflict everywhere and always" is a phrase that just doesn't cover enough ground to describe the conflict in your life; but conflicts are not really ubiquitous, no matter how you feel in their presence. Conflicts come not from competing desires but from the scarcity of gratifications. The scarcity can be real or not (makes no difference); it can be scarcity right now, historic scarcity, or a scarcity foreseen into a bleak and distant future. It must be conceded by all; unfulfilled desires are a drag.

People fight over things, usually the things they think will gratify desire. Fights happen when other approaches fail to achieve resolution. Fights are not an escalation of conflict, but the devolution of it. Fighting is violent behavior. Most often, people fight when they really believe there is insufficient supply of something vital, when they then subordinate their hope to the zero-sum game, or when the mad grip of the Mutually Exclusive excludes every other idea. Then they believe they must fight. Intentions sink.

A fight begins when your intention shifts from providing for yourself to hurting the other guy, or vice versa. As the possibility of sufficiency recedes, intentions necessarily incorporate the stark dictates of the fight: attack and capture, defense against terror, thrust and parry, annihilation.

The person with ResolutionAvoidance is, at least on one level, afraid of "fighting." And what sane person isn't? Fighting is awful. In addition to a healthy fear of the fight, however, other less attractive impulses are at work. Unresolved problems conspire with old resentments and invite timeless rage to the party, just to scarf off a little bit more "living space" in the ecology. The person with Resolution Avoidance avoids not conflict but *negotiation*, and chooses not peace, but a quiet that all but guarantees the fight.

All encounters have terms, stated or not. The millions of quiescent conflicts you navigate daily have long since been negotiated, mostly by others, and by degrees. You and those you encounter have adapted in advance of the encounter, and the conflicts are pre-resolved; but some negotiations are yours to make or they won't be made. Sometimes, the lonely approach toward a conflict is a walk you must take, or that party of problems becomes a drunken brawl.

In conflict, as in all encounters with others, your awareness of what you want from the situation will help you gain it. The unattractive aspects you associate with the word "conflict" really belong to the fight: the dramatics of yelling and posturing, and the violence of people hurting one another. To minimize the amount of fighting in your life, you must, of course, seek resolution for the conflicts you know are within your life. But this is only the least dictate of maturity.

Long before your own awareness is yowling, "Problem! Problem!", and long before others confront you with what is a clear and vivid problem, you have better alternatives. Or earlier still, even before you start feeling uneasy about something or someone, you can act swiftly and be supportive. Or even before that, when you were gently whispering to yourself, "Is something going on there?" Or yet before that: This is the time to address what will become your problem.

At this earlier time, you are more curious, open, and receptive. Time is more abundant, interests are more interesting, and the puzzle is a benign challenge. What people want at this stage is utterly unlike the entrenched and raging demands that ungratified desires become later. Earlier, the resentments that will later flow torrentially could not even be realistically offered as predictions. Earlier, you can approach that person or those people in genuine amicability, perhaps a little afraid of the newness, and you can then embrace the abundant resolutions that show up whenever intimacy works its magic.

Earlier is cheaper and wiser. Earlier is more mature.

- Use the IntentionCheck protocol when you are involved in conflict that threatens to become a fight. Ask yourself if you are succumbing to hurtful behavior and the tactics of the fight, or if you are seeking more information to create resolution.

*Long before your own awareness is yowling, "Problem! Problem!" . . . you have better alternatives.*

- If your intention to achieve resolution falters during negotiations or discussion, check out until it stabilizes.

- Rigorously monitor how you allow others to treat you while you are attempting to resolve a problem. Do not personally use or tolerate others' use of frightening or cutting behavior (for example, yelling, berating, or any other physically or emotionally hurtful acts or words).

- Be aware of when you threaten or even partially intend to inflict pain on others and do something else instead, such as check out.

- If someone else is using hurtful behavior during a conflict, the conflict is a fight. Check out. Come back to the problem later.

- If others complain about your reactions, check out. When the time is right, ask for help from someone you trust.

- Make early resolution of proto-problems an explicit, ongoing goal.

## ANTIPATTERN: OBLIVION

### PROBLEM

*You act according to habit, customs, or business norms
instead of mature thought, informed intention, and
creativity. When the inevitable consequences cause harm, you
disavow responsibility for any unintended consequences.*

*Business culture has an even stronger bias toward rules and unintentional action than does the culture at large.*

Oblivion is the evil twin of WorkwithIntention. You are always doing one or the other when you speak or act.

Modern cultural and educational systems do not teach us how to act with intention. In addition, our culture supports actions based on rules determined by others. Business culture has an even stronger bias toward rules and unintentional action than does the culture at large.

# EXAMPLE

When a team decides to ship on time, it is mostly a wish: Team members wish someone else would make it happen. That is, the team fails to carry out timely shipment with intention. It will use decades-old methods for shipping without regard to the history of results. In fact, if the results history is lacking, the team will probably decide that the rules for shipping on time just weren't pursued with enough rigor.

In this case, team members never decide to ship on time—with intention. They never ask themselves, "If we want to ship on time, how should we behave?" They fail to set up mutual accountability and behave in the ways that could prepare them for success.

*When a team decides to ship on time, it is mostly a wish: Team members wish someone else would make it happen.*

## SUPPOSED SOLUTION

---

*When you don't get the desired results, say that you didn't mean for that to happen, blame others, or say it was out of your control.*

In business situations, employees serve several masters. There are "normal business practices" and "professional standards." Good ideas become accepted practice over time, and eventually become liability-limiters, comprising the globally expected minimum-quality behaviors for a given discipline. The range of these practices transcends that of the local institution.

Also, employees must adhere to the local manager's and/or the division's or the employing institution's guidelines and policies, or interpretations of same. These are drawn at least in part from the global standards, but have more teeth for the employee, because the manager and the company have immediate power over the employee. The employee will also follow the fashions and conform to the beliefs of his immediate colleagues. When possible, he might also listen to the dictates of his own personal efficiency, sense of taste, commitment to innovation, and creative urges.

*To demand that every rule or guideline be thought through anew before adhering to it is radical, maybe even heretical, and would be perceived as interrupting the team's flow.*

*And so here comes Fault, with its obnoxious buddy, Blame. They'll fill in the gap.*

Generally, the closer one follows the local managerial and institutional practices and guidelines, the safer—if not necessarily the more successful—one is. These guidelines come from some combination of past practice, stated policy, and precedent. In total, they are inexplicit, and they are assumed to be—if not always the most effective strategies—the way to do things "around here."

When a person feels uncomfortable with a rule, or thinks it is wasteful, he will likely feel inclined to squelch his doubt so as not to disturb the smooth functioning of the team. To demand that every rule or guideline be thought through anew before adhering to it is radical, maybe even heretical, and would be perceived as interrupting the team's flow. To question the thinking of a hierarchy might risk the employee's future and might equate to questioning the superior's competence. It might be considered offensive, or even mean, behavior.

Because corporate working structures have so much inertia, questioning norms is difficult and risky work. Whether true or not, the feeling will be that generations of workers and managers have followed these norms with success. There is no expectation of healthy skepticism. The cultures tend to make it somewhat risky to "speak out," and even more risky to act.

Team members have little educational or cultural support to think at the levels required to continuously create their own policies and rules. As a result, much action occurs without intention. The methods and outcomes are essentially passively inherited, and are seldom truly scrutinized and improved.

Because explicit intention is not expected from individuals and teams, when poor results arise, effective ways of assessing and alleviating problems are hard to come by. But something must be done, something must be said, something must be thought. And so here comes Fault, with its obnoxious buddy, Blame. They'll fill in the gap. Individuals blame individuals, teams blame individuals, teams blame teams, and bosses are always inviting subjects to blame.

The permutations go on, but you get the picture: Basically, everybody blames everybody. True accountability is never achieved, and the full human potential of the team is never realized. Worse, much of it is misspent on tweaking blame scenarios, people cycling through alternate bouts of personal guilt and shaming of others, constructing elaborate proofs of insufficient control, and the oblivious defense of Oblivion.

## ACTUAL SOLUTION

*Treat every problem you see as if you could actually do something about it, as if you were personally accountable.*

For shipping great, timely, IP-rich products, it is imperative that intentionality be a central design tool (see also "Pattern: Work with Intention" in Chapter Six). Because IP (e.g., software) is such a new arena for product development, and so much more is being learned than is known, the greatest gains come when team members are encouraged to think deeply *always* before acting. Unintended actions will lead to unintended results. Each mind, and each action coming from it, can have a tremendous impact on IP-rich products.

*The greatest gains come when team members are encouraged to think deeply always before acting.*

Being oblivious to the ill effects of your behavior in advance is really no better than consciously acting in a destructive way, and may even be worse. Saying, feeling, or hearing something like, "I didn't mean to (do, say) that," is a clear indicator of Oblivion's involvement. Such remarks or defenses should not be tolerated as an escape hatch. If you did or said something destructive, then you have a problem to address. It is important that you act with intention in the future, and not repeat the mistake. Others' commitments to you should include forgiveness for and learning support about your likely destructive missteps; but they should never award you extra points because you are destructive *and* thoughtless, or destructive *and* in denial.

*They should never award you extra points because you are destructive and thoughtless, or destructive and in denial.*

If you see a problem, it is likely part of your calling to do something about it. The safest and most useful approach to take with your perceptions is to *always assume that no one else has them but you.* Wishing that others would solve the problem wastes your potential as the objects of your perception and passion whither and die.

# ANTIPATTERN: TURF

## PROBLEM

*When getting results is difficult, you focus on
"role definition."*

*When facing the stress
of interacting with
neighboring castle
owners, you usually
become more explicit
about what you
"own."*

When things are uncertain or difficult, you often find safety in your predefined role. Your Turf is your castle, and you are master there. When facing the stress of interacting with neighboring castle owners, you usually become more explicit about what you "own." The more difficult the situation becomes, the more you take refuge in role definitions—both yours and theirs. You want to know what you're supposed to do, what they are supposed to do, and that everybody else knows.

Role definitions act as personal boundaries.[1] They define interfaces. Explicit roles carry the added support—and suffer the extra costs—of an assumed institutional blessing.

*"Bring on the
goodies," should be
your attitude. "Let the
superior ideas begin!"*

When difficulties arise, your intention of focusing on the interfaces (that is, the places where you connect with others) is a good one. If the reason you turn toward these boundaries is to prevent invasion from others, or to threaten invasion of them, however, your good intention may well have been wasted. You should approach the boundary to open the gates, smooth the path, and put up welcome signs, rather than to check defenses, post intimidating "no trespassing" signs, and scrutinize travelers' documentation. "Bring on the goodies," should be your attitude. "Let the superior ideas begin!" You invite others into your creative space simply to seek the best possible things for that space. Requiring others to actually add value as a condition of entry is also a good and legal practice.

---

1. Personal boundaries are really interpersonal interface proposals—one person's implicit offer to connect with others under certain conditions.

When you "own" a task or functional area, the product of your ownership is tightly bound to you. Sometimes your limits become its limits. A range of quality in your output is, of course, possible, from the minimum acceptable to the greatest possible. The minimum is determined by your own sense of the minimum acceptable quality or, if that is too low, the minimum acceptable to some other local authority. But you must not similarly limit the greatest output possible to your maximum capability. When role ownership is taken too seriously, this limit overlap between you and your product often occurs.

Some IQ aggregation may occur in teams where role ownership is a central organizing principle. In general, however, where roles rule, people will respect Turf at the expense of results. They are invited to cry Turf even when helpful invaders appear. You will hear them howling as solutions approach.

*In general . . . where roles rule, people will respect Turf at the expense of results.*

## SUPPOSED SOLUTION

*Create individual ownership.*
*Police boundaries around work responsibilities.*

## ACTUAL SOLUTION

*Share all the Turf with everybody who wants to help with it. Become attached to functions only according to how much you care about them.*

# GIVE EVERYONE SOME REAL TURF

As a way of removing the constraints of Turf, give everyone a piece of synthetic Turf at a team meeting and tell the team that it is their Turf, and their only Turf, forevermore. They can defend it, honor it, or do whatever they want with it. And they can tell all others they have no ownership associated with their little swaths of personal Turf.

*Give everyone a piece of synthetic Turf at a team meeting and tell the team that it is their Turf.*

*The intensity of your feelings will determine which activities you should pursue.*

The principle of IQ aggregation requires that passion be respected. On occasion, what looks like passion is really neurosis.[2] In most cases, your role should be to tend to those duties that you care about, even if they are tasks not in your official charter. Eliminating Turf and instituting shared accountability will increase the flow of creative input and the connections within the team. To benefit from the steady flow of ideas that will then arise, individual focus should be subject to dynamic reordering, initiated by individuals, driven by passion, and supported by the team. The optimal team structure exploits the ongoing shifting of focus that is possible with aligned people (see Chapter Eleven).

If no one cares about certain tasks, don't coerce someone to assume those duties, but rather eliminate them altogether. If a task is no one's opportunity, it probably shouldn't be done. Don't spread it around; eliminate it. Don't do things with many people (as a team) that aren't worthy of a single person's care.

When you see people caring about things, you have the surest sign possible that passion is in the neighborhood. As noted in Chapter Four, passion is a prerequisite for greatness. Your ability to care can serve as your focus guidance system. The intensity of your feelings will determine which activities you should pursue. Our observations strongly suggest that pursuing what you care about is the best way to satisfy your needs. We have also found that if you accept responsibility for what you care about most, your work will serve to fulfill the team's needs.

Of course, you can't care uniformly about everything. The very notion of caring presupposes you have different levels of interest allocated to different things. Your best chance of success is to deal with only those things that arouse your passion. Caring about everything is caring about nothing.

Caring is, by definition, selective. If a person truly cares about a particular aspect of the team's product, he is more likely to execute a

---

2. Discerning the difference between passion on the one hand, and neurotic, bubble-headed enthusiasm on the other is possible, though it can be a bit tricky at first.

clean finish on that aspect than someone who doesn't care, or someone who cares less. This outcome can be expected regardless of the "official" roles of the individuals.

## CARE MASQUERADING AS BLAME

Caring may appear in a whine: "We ought to do *X*, I'm telling you." When someone harps about something "the team" should do but insists that the task is not his personal job, that individual is often the ideal person to work on the problem.

Complaining about a given team behavior is equivalent to negatively projecting a passion. When you care about a particular topic and whine about it in the face of others' inaction, this care can often find its most productive expression by your "owning" the item in question. It could become your central concern, in fact, and you could resolve your issues with it by putting leadership into the system instead of complaint.

*It could become your central concern, in fact, and you could resolve your issues with it by putting leadership into the system instead of complaint.*

The thing you care about most is almost always the thing that you should do now. When team members focus on what they feel most passionately about in a project, chances are good that the product will be great.

"Task by passion" is the ideal role allocation strategy for the fully mature team. Of course, for most teams, attaining "full maturity" is more a moment to come than one to remember. Consequently, any role allocation strategy that moves a given team closer to the "task by passion" ideal constitutes progress. In general, developing loosely structured roles or lists of functional responsibilities by person, the contents of which change over time, will be an effective way to construct a framework for creating passion-based roles.

Regardless of how you arrive at your expressed/acknowledged role, your particular list of responsibilities, your role, or hierarchical position should never prevent you from adopting a superior idea or practice. If you truly care about a role or a function, "lack of resources" is not an acceptable excuse for not pursuing an idea that ought to be executed.

We have found the following team roles serve well in IP-heavy projects like software and high-tech development generally:

- Program manager
- Quality assurance specialist
- Developer
- Technical communicator
- Product manager
- Technical support person

These roles provide a structure around which to improvise. The roles themselves are analogous to the strings of a guitar; they mustn't be confused with the music itself. Don't be afraid to tune the guitar based on the song you need to play right now.

*The roles themselves are analogous to the strings of a guitar; they mustn't be confused with the music itself.*

# ANTIPATTERN: BOSS WON'T GIVE POWER

## PROBLEM

*You're a boss who is afraid that a team will go the wrong way if team members make more decisions.*

## SUPPOSED SOLUTION

*You're in control of teams reporting to you. Don't support ideas or practices that may interrupt your control. Your business is not a democracy.*

## ACTUAL SOLUTION

*Insist that team members grow up. Your true role is to encourage them to reach their fullest possible potential. Parents are not required at the mature workplace.*

*Late product delivery
is probably the most
vivid power
expression among
high-tech teams.*

If you're a boss, don't worry that you're "giving away" your power by supporting or participating in **Decider**. Using **Decider**, team members explicitly exploit only the power that has been heretofore subterranean, perplexing them and preventing them from operating at maximum capacity. Whether or not the enormous power of a team is wisely channeled, or even recognized ex officio, it is always present. Late product delivery is probably the most vivid power expression among high-tech teams. Lateness usually results from a failure to apply the power of team members who are late. Suppressed ambivalence, a lack of belief in the goodness of the cause, and other ambiguities consume the calendar. Problems related to the team members' connections with one another, with the erstwhile goal they share, and with their employer will all ultimately find (negative) expression.

As a team matures, it may indeed head in the wrong direction. As a boss, however, you can be a member of the team if you accept all the other rights and responsibilities of being a member. Simply vote "no" when you believe an idea is wrong. If you insist that all team members only and always implement the best ideas, and you give them a better idea, their integrity will ensure that they adopt it. This is all the power you ever had, anyway.

As the boss, you have the following responsibilities:

1. Reach your own potential.

2. Be on your team.

3. Be on a second team with other team bosses.

4. Be on a third team with your boss.

5. Maintain alignment and vision across your teams.

6. Make sure that your teams step forward to achieve their self-determined results.

7. Insist that your teams assume complete accountability for their own decisions.

8. Provide your teams with whatever time, skills, and technologies are needed to achieve shared vision, ongoing group cognition, and constant delivery of results.

9. Model what you desire from others on your teams.

10. Practice the virtues most important to your teams' success.

11. Contribute the true authority that your virtuous behavior confers on you.

12. Insist that your teams' members attain more of their potential as quickly as possible.

If your boss doesn't assume these responsibilities, vis-à-vis you or other teams in his sphere of influence, it is your job to proceed anyway. You must above all reach your full potential and optimize the potential of your immediate team.

# ANTIPATTERN: TEAM QUACKERY

## PROBLEM

*Team performance is deteriorating. There are always remedies at hand, like the nostrums of the past.*

An infestation of **TeamQuackery** behaviors will grow and subside according to the relevant available food supply: the aggregate tendency toward disbelief, despair, or cynicism. Once the host organization has been infected, the behaviors are nourished by the organization's advancing cognitive and ethical decay. What was everyday cowardice begins to show as spite. What was seen as a team's slow pace of learning is transformed into the team's inexplicable Oblivion about things of major importance. Large chunks of institutional memory disappear without warning.

Unfortunately, these experiences of decreasing team and corporate lucidity are legitimized to the maximum extent possible by reference to various local team mythologies and superstitions. Suspect team-related practices mushroom where ineffective beliefs about leadership and insufficient understanding of the dynamics of personal

*Any place where acts of personal bravery are not routinely witnessed . . . will most likely play host to bravery's evil twin, bravado.*

motivation are the norm. They proliferate alongside people who are enduring the quiet suffering of chronic mediocrity: these practices are especially vulnerable to questionable remedies.

Environments that lack a virtue often attract the missing virtue's travesty version. For example, any place where acts of personal bravery are not routinely witnessed (and celebrated) will most likely play host to bravery's evil twin, bravado. An environment that rejects critical thinking accepts instead the cynicism and idealistic fantasy that can jointly fulfill the available niche. An environment incapable of generating hope natively gives credulity all the opening it needs.

## SUPPOSED SOLUTION

*Improve "teamwork" or add "process."*

To remedy this situation, myriad "quack" solutions are proposed:

- Add more things to an old process or change to "a new process."
- Take personality tests and take a course in the categorization of people by their personality traits. Make everybody do the same.
- Retreat often, preferably with team-oriented physical activity focused on ropes and falling into one another's arms.
- Reorganize again.
- Separate people who "don't get along."
- Send out e-mails that feign optimism and "motivate" the team.
- Create in-house organizations charged with improving morale and proposing ideas like those in this list.

TeamQuackery results in an environment characterized by a lot of teamlike activity, but few desirable team results. It increases cynicism, especially on the topics of "teamwork," "retreats," and "management/teamwork training." Often, huge amounts of time and energy are wasted. "Good corporate citizenship" is required to be on constant display, even while products grow increasingly mediocre and ship at ever later dates.

Conversely, excellent ideas that could foster improved collaboration are discounted because work is already going on to "deal with those issues." This atmosphere leads to lack of accountability and tolerates immaturity. Adults should be responsible for the environment they create; instead, in an environment permeated with TeamQuackery, teamwork problems become "management's problems." Somebody "higher up" should fix the problem, goes the thinking—you just do what you're told.

Because certain activities have been deemed appropriate for solving teamwork problems in the past, they are automatically given credence today. As a result, superstition trumps rational thought. True solutions require a depth of thought and discourse that is—if not avoided—very difficult to pursue in many corporate cultures. The false solutions proposed are shallow, but they continue to win favor. This antipattern produces greater cynicism, which spreads indiscriminately to all programs, including the good ones. The actual prospect of creating an atmosphere truly supportive of great teamwork is reduced to another hokey management game.

The making of IP-heavy products requires that teams of people aggregate their relevant intelligence and other creative capabilities and apply those abilities. The teams encode what they gather, communicate its availability, and make their product accessible to those who might want it. This process relies fundamentally on team behavior. Collaboration is the heart of all IP product development.

Unfortunately, many people seem to experience problems in creating, maintaining, and optimizing the interpersonal connection on which maximally efficient collaboration depends. The generally unsatisfactory state of collaborative skills is the limiting factor in our overall progress. Indeed, efficient "multipersonal" creative effort is difficult to attain. Our collaborative inelegance, therefore, constrains our IP-generation potential, standing between us and our objectives.

The concept of high-performance teamwork has credibility with most people. The joys of a team that is really cooking are a pleasure that many have experienced. It seems that almost everyone has at least one triumphant group effort lingering as a memory.

*Somebody "higher up" should fix the problem, goes the thinking—you just do what you're told.*

*The generally unsatisfactory state of collaborative skills is the limiting factor in our overall progress.*

These pinnacles of teamwork notwithstanding, the everyday experience of your present team circumstances may be overwhelming. The day-in, day-out difficulties you face on a struggling team can soon erase any positive memory of your past experience on great teams.

Even in the midst of the daily quagmire, however, you may convince yourself that team functionality at a high level *is* possible. Sometimes, you may even think that *major* team achievements are within your reach—achievements that could make a difference. If you just knew *where* to reach and *what* to grab, you could do it. After all, the "great team" thing happened before. Unfortunately, you cannot muster the effort and resource to bring it off again. It can't be done now. Most of the time, you just accept your fate.

This context gives rise to TeamQuackery. Two conditions must be satisfied for a team to be considered enmeshed in this antipattern:

1. *The team is down on itself as a team*. The team sees itself as troubled, but doesn't know what to do, and isn't effective enough to care for itself. Members seem resigned to continuing the team's daily struggles, while thinking wistfully of better teams, better lives, better days.

2. *Team members hold false beliefs about the team*. On the one hand, the general discomfort caused by the team's perception of itself as subpar provides a psychological-emotional brew that nourishes wishes and fantasies (that is, hopes for simple solutions, silver bullets, and so on). On the other hand, a false sense of well-being may lead a team to minimize or ignore the need for team development. Thus, team members hold distorted beliefs at both extremes.

## TEAM QUACKERY FORCES: DISBELIEF, DESPAIR, AND CYNICISM

The state of high teamwork or flow is characterized by efficient, very-low-friction collaboration. When your team is in a state of flow, your ability to produce alongside your teammates expands dramatically. Your willingness to ride with their momentum and to abide by the rhythm of the work itself is greatly enlarged. You have great awareness of all the sensations, powers, and topography of your connection with the team.

Unfortunately, when the team is not in this state, the possibility that you could ever achieve such heights seems hopelessly remote. The effort would be costly and would fail. Perhaps you believe that you must simply wait for the magic. When you're not in the state of flow, its very existence seems dubious to you.

*When you're not in the state of flow, its very existence seems dubious to you.*

Things become even grimmer later, when your encounter with team flow seems more a myth than a possibility, and you face the stark reality of corporate life. Given the personalities of the current people ("especially Cindy"), you don't believe strongly enough to work toward a radically better team. "No matter what I do," you tell yourself "no one will support any change. Not here. Not now. Not these people. Not this company."

When potential solutions do appear, flickering for a moment in the darkness of this environment, you perk up a little. You look around and check out the new idea. If useful information is available that might enhance your life, you might even feel hope. Ultimately, however, you revert, regress, go back, and retreat. You pull yourself away from hope. Your system retaliates against the intrusion of new information, and you withdraw into the haze of more familiar practices. After this single flicker of light sputters out, the graying uncertainties return to enshroud you once again.

At this point you can initiate your own variety of TeamQuackery:

*"No!" You blurt out your customary negation, despite your better judgment.*

*"New information or not," you think, feeling the strength of your resistance mounting, "it sure doesn't apply to our situation! Nor to us!"*

*Murmuring to your coworkers, you toss doubts at one other. "This stuff doesn't represent real solutions at all! Let's snuff it out right now."*

Because most members typically don't understand the underlying team problems that dominate their world, many real solutions

*Chronic disbelief takes the micro-step to cynicism, rather than the leap to clarity sought by the skeptic.*

will seem off the mark. "What's that have to do with us?" says one. "Yeah!" comes the chorus. "Irrelevant! Rejected!"

By following this path, you can end up as the ur Quack. A lack of rigor in your thought regarding these problems will lead to pervasive doubt—not mere skepticism or doubt exercised appropriately case by case, but rather an endemic disbelief, unconstrained, touching everything, arising everywhere, with a special appetite for all new things. Chronic disbelief takes the micro-step to cynicism, rather than the leap to clarity sought by the skeptic. From there, the practice of **TeamQuackery** works its most pernicious effects.

## FORGETTING AND IGNORANCE

High-order teamwork often appears a capricious thing. Who can tell how, why, and when the magic of teamwork occurs? Did it really once happen to you? Perhaps it is only mythical, the stuff of wishes and dreams.

Occasionally, the overwhelming force of high-energy teamwork does materialize, within some randomly anointed team. Although the effects of the collaborative burst are obvious and singularly positive, the origins of the phenomenon remain obscure. For many, the actual nuts and bolts of the experience in this "time of grace" slip into fugitive memory. The sensation of well-being you experienced as part of a great team, and the way you actually achieved so much—these things become like a dream that dissolves, even as you attempt to fix it in conscious memory on first awakening.

You proceed warily then, left only with the belief that something, somehow, really worked once. Unfortunately, you are no longer in that rarefied state. You don't feel it happening. When you talk about it, your descriptions seem clichéd, even corny.

*You are not in the enlightened state of multipersonal flow that would be required to describe that state convincingly.*

*You never used the power of the energized state to reproduce it.*

How did you get there? You either never knew or you forgot. While you were there, you didn't stop to analyze how you reached that point or to try to understand how to make the state repeatable. You never used the power of the energized state to reproduce it.

# MYTHOLOGY AND SUPERSTITION

When the transcendent moment of teamwork ends, you may think that it has disappeared forever. Even if you do take the time to analyze the experience, you cannot explain it. If pressed, the explanations you produce for this most valuable team event will probably reveal little more than superstitions:

- The *chemistry* was right.
- It was *safe* to take risks.
- You had a *shared vision*.
- Things felt *right*.
- The environment was *supportive*.
- You had a *sense of common destiny*.
- You had *no choice* but to succeed.

The highlighted phrases in this list generally are not defined precisely. Definitions are necessary, however, if you expect such terms to be really useful. What's more, *you want them defined in a way that the team accepts unanimously.* This broad support would indicate that the definitions had some genuine value and were worth examining further.

Teams that permit such undefined terms to slip into their lexicon give teamwork a bad name. Using such vaguely defined terms is a loss twice over: No real exchange of information takes place, and the impression that teamwork is being discussed takes the place of real discussion. The words provide no conceptual foundation for building successful teams and improving team life. Even so, many teams use these terms as if they brought something to the game. When looking back at great team experiences, if you use such vague terminology to explain them, you would do as well—and perhaps even better—to attribute your bigger-than-life team success to wishing on a star or tossing coins in a fountain.

Teamwork consultants and educators often contribute to the general softness of discipline and may arouse legitimate suspicion regarding "teamwork" stuff. Unfortunately, many courses and "coaching" programs yield no lasting, favorable results.

*You would do as well—and perhaps even better—to attribute your bigger-than-life team success to wishing on a star or tossing coins in a fountain.*

*Many consultants
have never been
members of a team
that practices the
methods that they
preach—or members
of any team at all.*

The adoption of different terms and unfamiliar concepts may disguise the emptiness, to some extent. When choosing your own coaches, it is worth considering the fate of sports coaches who persistently fail to win. Teamwork coaches are seldom asked whether they have tested and succeeded with their methods with other teams. Many consultants have never been members of a team that practices the methods that they preach—or members of any team at all. Almost all work alone, not dealing with the day-to-day teamwork pressures faced by their students. Either they don't know their subject, or their information is only as good as their last team experience.

Many spout quackery. For example, they may attribute teamwork to something that occurred simultaneously during the emergence of the teamwork, without giving the matter any real thought and without testing the hypothesis. "When I was on a great team, it really worked for us to have pizza together every Friday."

## BELIEF IN CHARISMA

Many people tend to personalize the genesis and quality of historic team events. They attribute what is clearly a remarkable phenomenon—group coalescence toward a single purpose—to the achievements of some extraordinary leader. Usually, these leaders are no longer on the scene when team success is finally ascribed to them. Unfortunately, having minimized the leader's role earlier, it becomes overstated in later versions of the team's history.

You imagine:

*[Some person] of destiny somehow conjured up the genie of group achievement. If only that leader were here now. He is a wizard of connection. He can make great teams at will.*

You rationalize:

*This (absent) leader was a true visionary. In his wake, everyone cooperates. At his behest, everybody (even Joe) freely offers his richest gifts to the cause. This genius leader can do it because he has Charisma. Charisma is a substance that we, alas, all lack now.[3] The leaders we have now, well, they're good people. But they suck. And that's why we suck.*

Wistful fantasies of the achievements of different times and different teams, pining away for charismatic leaders, attendance at puny teamwork courses—all lead nowhere. It is easy to surrender to daily mediocrity and team death by a charisma vacuum.

## TEAM QUACKERY SYMPTOMS

TeamQuackery is characterized by a number of symptoms that include apathy, lack of energy, and/or misguided efforts at team-building.

- Good results are scarce.

A lack of improvement in a team despite concerted effort to create change is the surest indicator that something untoward is afoot. Attention and energy, when correctly applied, will invariably yield improved team circumstances. When they don't, their failure is an excellent indicator of pathological TeamQuackery.

- Your team has no shared vision and low energy.

You can assess this quality by evaluating how much you look forward to being with team members, or how tired (not stressed) you are at the end of a day's work. Alternatively, you can diagnose the team state by asking individuals on the team separately what "we" are doing. If the answers aren't the same or some teammates don't know how to answer, there is clearly a lack of shared vision.

*If the answers aren't the same or some teammates don't know how to answer, there is clearly a lack of shared vision.*

- People criticize other people who are not present.

No good result can come of even the best criticism without its object receiving it. Consequently, this behavior is folly, and folly is equivalent to waste.

- People state "what is needed" but take no effective steps to achieve it.

---

3. It is rumored that the Pond of Charisma is located near the Fountain of Youth.

- Some team members declaim a boss or bosses as "the problem."

If bosses actually *were* the problem (which they seldom are), no effective action is forthcoming from those who blame them.

- Your team goes to retreats.

Team members may experience substantial discomfiture,[4] consisting mostly of embarrassment at doing stupid things and achieving no tangible result. Perhaps your team attends retreats where members are rewarded by substantial enthusiasm and pleasure, or a team achievement (albeit orthogonal to the team's purpose). Unfortunately, there is no tangible result, even though the sojourn was pleasant. Perhaps your team retreats are simply boring, tackling inconsequential issues with no tangible result—even though it certainly felt like work.

The expected "tangible result" of team training (or any focused teamwork in which you participate) is a body of practices, useful in teams, that has been newly transmitted to you. You don't have a tangible result if

1. There's nothing new you as an individual can do when you return to work that will reliably produce improvement in the team situation that is commensurate with your effort.

2. There's nothing new that the team as a whole can do when members return to work that will reliably produce improvement in the team situation that is commensurate with the team's effort.

*Your desires for improved team life are laudable, but it appears that you are not serious about achieving them.*

If these symptoms characterize your attempts to improve team life, then you and your team are tolerating life in the TeamQuackery antipattern. Your desires for improved team life are laudable, but it appears that you are not serious about achieving them. If you were serious, your behavior would be substantially different. For example,

---

4. Alas, good teamwork often causes or heightens momentary discomfort; however, it also increases joy.

your participation in lame retreat preparation and execution work would be unacceptable.

TeamQuackery is tolerated because of the belief that teamwork is part of the emotional realm. Good teamwork will explicitly account for emotion. This statement doesn't mean that teamwork doesn't require constant thought. It also doesn't mean that teamwork that includes emotion explicitly is good teamwork.

It's time to get over emotional bigotry. All human processes involve emotions. You don't stop thinking when you start feeling, nor do you stop feeling in the presence of thought. Instead, you should be aware of what you are thinking and feeling at the same time. TeamQuackery thrives in an environment that ignores or prohibits emotional information. If you abolish your own bigotry toward emotional information, you will take a major step toward eliminating your tendency to embrace mediocre teams and their associated TeamQuackery remedies. Simply treat emotional information as a rich source of data about the people and events of your team life— typically the opposite approach preferred under TeamQuackery. As with other forms of bigotry, exaggerated responses of any type serve to hold the prejudice in place.

If you aim to eradicate TeamQuackery from your team, you face a real danger that your aggressive stance against faux solutions will be misinterpreted. Because the definitions are so tangled, your colleagues might assume that you are opposing teamwork instead of insisting upon it. You'll survive their doubts, because you will be more likely to create a great team. That achievement will surely vindicate you.

*If you abolish your own bigotry toward emotional information, you will take a major step toward eliminating your tendency to embrace mediocre teams and their associated TeamQuackery remedies.*

## SOLUTION

*Lead and participate in team solutions
that focus solely on results.*

To form a great team, you must give more of yourself and consistently express your common sense. Most important, you must

*Many people don't understand that one person at any level can create a great team, beginning at any time, by properly establishing and consistently applying his boundaries.*

demand more quality (more results) from the expense of your time. Many people don't understand that one person at any level can create a great team, beginning at any time, by properly establishing and consistently applying his boundaries.

Following are some boundary-related practices you might consider.

- Don't limit your right to develop your own understanding.

Whenever someone states an idea in your presence that seems wrong to you, assume that either the idea is wrong or that you are wrong about it. You have every right to insist on getting to the bottom of your discomfort by asking questions until either you are educated out of your discomfort, or the idea is set aside.

- Question every neurotic act.

Neurotic acts work against the stated objectives of the person acting neurotically. When you see a team member doing something that works against his goals (or the goals of the team), assume that (a) the person's goals have changed, or (b) he is neurotically interfering with the individual's or team's success, or (c) you are perceiving neurotically. In all cases, analysis and solicitation of more information will yield a better team.

- Energetically study and practice teamwork—and study your practice.
- Don't accept TeamQuackery in your teamwork study and practice.

*You should not accept TeamQuackery because you think the topic of teams is unfamiliar territory or is for sophisticates of human emotion.*

In particular, you should not accept TeamQuackery just because you think the topic of teams is unfamiliar territory or is for sophisticates of human emotion. You have probably been participating in teams for most of your life. You have feelings all day long, and you have experienced emotions over your entire life. You know how people react in team situations, especially your team. Use this knowledge to achieve results efficiently.

- If anyone has a new idea for your team practices or a proposal to teach the team a new idea, do not accept the idea if the proponent can't explain it in a way that makes sense to you.

- Establish minimal anti-TeamQuackery standards:
    - Define terms used to describe all key concepts.
    - Document all new team practices so that others can repeat your results.
    - Assess the probable results of adopting new team practices before adopting them. Adopt the view that teamwork can radically improve and that ways to do so can be understood and taught.
    - Expect training to produce a lasting and significant difference in your team life. When it doesn't, assume that the TeamQuackery antipattern is afoot.

## TYPECASTING

Many people have an unwarranted belief in the existence of simplistic and rigid personality types, especially those of the introvert and extrovert. Whatever Myers and Briggs had in mind, and Jung before them, and Freud before him, it is highly unlikely that they believed people were fixed for life into invariant roles that are so utterly and conveniently supportive of malfeasance. Some courses incidentally promote superficial speciation of team members into personality categories. Stereotyping and foolishness often result. Mythology is promoted. Extroverts don't know how to listen, and introverts don't know how to talk. "Oh, well, that's too bad," you say. "But it's just the way we are, and we're stuck with it. I just need to accept that either (extrovert) everybody wants to listen to me or (introvert) I have nothing worth saying."

It's difficult to listen when you want all of the attention and equally difficult to speak when you want none of it. Each person adopting The Core protocols is obligated to say whatever he or she genuinely believes will move things along most efficiently. That is the office and the responsibility of every team member. Being an "extro" or an "intro" does not absolve anyone from being an accountable "vert."

The superstitious exaggerations of personality types are merely the two most common neurotic adaptations to the question of positive

*Being an "extro" or an "intro" does not absolve anyone from being an accountable "vert."*

*Although personality clash plagues corporate life, the diagnostic literature makes no reference to it.*

or negative external attention: hope that you get some favorable attention versus fear that you get some negative attention. Both arise from feelings of favorable attention deficit. Mumbo-jumbo, pseudoscience prattle about personality types has little to add to this discussion.

## PERSONALITY CLASH

Some people believe in a disorder called "personality clash." Although personality clash plagues corporate life, the diagnostic literature makes no reference to it. The only known cure—which is little more than a folk remedy—is to create physiological distance between the "clashing" personalities. Apparently, the clash of personalities is like the clash of articles of clothing: Just don't wear them together. Both work well in their separate places. It's not necessary to judge either person. The separation strategy prevails, although distancing the combatants is rumored to promulgate new clashes in parts unknown.

The state of the practice is, to say the least, limited. You do not need any theoretical sophistication, however, if you simply and exclusively focus on results. Robust protocols will generate results.

*Ask for what you want.*

*Seek and offer help.*

# III

# Aligning

TRANSCENDENT MOTIVE

AND THE

EFFICACY OF HELP

---

*"I want."*

*Man. This whole thing is a little odd, you think. What next? You are on break at a hastily thrown-together off-site event. Growing out of that equally hastily thrown-together re-kick-off meeting. And the protocols, too. You are the one (nonvoting) guest of this team. Once team members figured out that they needed to really engage here (an idea you planted), that if they wanted to make a great product, be on time with it, and have a good time making it— or at least a better time than usual—well, then, they would need to engage more, and to actually live out their values a bit more vividly. So, after a few preliminary rounds of the usual blaming and complaining and challenging, the whole team began arguing boisterously, and eventually started making proposals according to this* Decider, *and making decisions, too, or at least trying to.*

*Even their trivial decisions—and, geez, you think back, when they first got going, they voted on every damn thing, when to take a lunch break, and then when to return, and so on—and what's more, even these things inspired controversy, noise, and (eventually) thought before some proposal finally commanded unanimous support. You were so annoyed when one person voted "no" to a regular kind of lunch plan. He held up the whole show. But it was amazing what happened after he vetoed things: a (surprisingly!) clear talk from the "no" voter (about how this was the first time they had ever really connected, finally, he said, and so they should use the time wisely while it lasted). Because who knows. Hell, he said, they had lunch every day, no big deal, and then he counter-proposed a working lunch. And it was the damndest thing: The whole team, everyone on the team (except the outlier who just counter-proposed), had just voted the complete opposite way not five minutes before. Well, now they turned right around and voted "yes" to the working lunch proposal.*

*And, even though you think the whole ruckus was annoying, it really did work out better than if the team had disbanded for lunch. It was shortly after this surprising reversal of opinion that the reality of the team's general situation showed up here. Things just started pouring out in the less formal environment created by eating a meal together, things about what each person thought he was trying to achieve with this product. It was obvious to everyone that there was no common point of view whatsoever about this product they were supposed to be building. All agreed (eventually) that it might not be so smart to build something together until they agreed just what it was supposed to be. Geez, how much do you have to think and talk about that one?*

*But, you have to admit, the team's vitality is way up. CheckIn gives team members an ongoing structure for saying what they feel. And that releases energy that is usually wasted in emotional detours and bullshit runarounds. Noise in the circuit is reduced. Rapid, reliable, interpersonal connections are hooked up. Quickly.*

*You wonder about the broader applicability. Even if a team agrees that the exchange of emotional information is important, it is just so weird to be real about stuff like this, and so much initial discomfort occurs that special tools to support real engagement—things like CheckIn, you guess, are really needed. Say CheckIn is a part of the everyday team deal. Then individual people don't have to muster up all that hellfire anti-inertial courage required to initiate connection at an emotional level. There's just a sort of default, regular place and words ready to use when you really need them. Creating high-grade communication pathways for the team each time they're needed is, well, it might just be impossible without the permission implicit in the protocols. Impossibly inefficient, that's for sure. But CheckIn institutionalizes emotional expression. So emotional disclosure becomes a normal part of the team deal.*

*Now Decider. Decider gives real-time access to communal decision making; but it also preserves, hell, underlines as never before individual power and individual freedom, especially from the tyranny of the majority.*

*It supplies the team a real executive capability, the ability to take action, a kind of team head. And unanimity! Who'd have thought that unanimity was the easiest thing to get? That it was even possible? That it clears up big messes instead of causing 'em? With the capability to choose as one, the team has its own kind of mental processes, like how they choose and deal with outliers. Which is really just like personal ambivalence. But there's no denying that issues are resolved with* Decider.

*Decider also evenly parcels out accountability. With this pattern, all team members are fully responsible for each group decision. Because any one of them can stop the show if he believes that an idea is dumb, just because he can stop the show, the team doesn't ever do anything that goes against its beliefs. That seems big.*

*Decider allows only actionable proposals. It lights a fire under the group's collective butt, gets people moving toward action, and keeps them going. Always. And yet, it seems like* Decider *provides good ongoing control and guidance mechanisms for effective team behavior. After initial actions are launched. It's efficient. Elegant. And you like the fact that a* Decider *proposal trumps any other activity taking place in the team.* Decider *is truly an effective means to get a team to act. And, once the team takes an action, it won't be able to complain about its lack of power or its lack of personal accountability; those options are eliminated. You love that.*

*So we have an accountable team. The emotional integrity of team members seems to be coming along fine, and they've got a reliable group decision-making capability. So good that you're all on this* Alignment/SharedVision *retreat thingy. Supposedly,* Alignment *draws team members closer together, helps the team shape up its purpose. Supposedly, it helps create an environment for a team to achieve its biggest, its noblest dreams. Maybe* Alignment *will sort of bring it all to life. Animate this emergent collaborative. Yeah, it's almost like its own entity. Or maybe it'll take a good* SharedVision. *But if these folks can build even more on their capabilities for clear communication and decisive action, well, wow.*

# The Elements of Alignment

## PERSONAL AND TEAM ALIGNMENT

In Parts I and II, we explored two of the three interdependent stages in the intentional team formation processes:

- Optimizing presence via increased disclosure and true engagement

- Aggregating value and managing accountability via unanimity

We now turn to the fullness of team formation: the establishment of personal and team alignment. This process is captured in the Alignment pattern and its related protocols. Part III also introduces the patterns required by Alignment: Investigate, Receptivity, AskforHelp, and WebofCommitment. Investigate and Receptivity help the team define individual goals. WebofCommitment is basically the group instance of the individual AskforHelp and focuses on the mechanics of how the team achieves its goals. Part III also describes AlignMe, an antipattern that commonly impedes the success of a team, and discusses unhealthy types of Alignment avoidance.

Alignment is the bringing together of diverse elements into a desirable orientation with one another. TeamAlignment occurs when each team member knows what he wants for himself and what he wants from the team, and what others want for themselves and from him (the terms **wants** and **goals** are used interchangeably in this book).

Obviously, your personal goals matter more to you than do corporate goals. Personal goals explain why you are involved. If a team knows what each of its members wants, then each person can get support from his teammates to achieve it. When others know your goal and have explicitly committed to supporting you in attaining it, then your responsibilities are altered: You can be held accountable for behaving in a way that will yield what you say you want. If you persist in sabotaging your own goals, moreover, then you can be expected to change either your goals or your behavior. When the facts of what you actually want are acknowledged, then you can radically increase your results-to-effort ratio by applying AskforHelp.

Personal goals motivate people; team goals motivate teams. Team goals are derived from product visions, and product visions derive from personal goals. The fundamental motivational unit is the personal goal. The integration of personal goals with product visions, product visions with team and company goals, and all goals with their ultimate achievement, is central to establishing and maintaining the flow of motivation, accountability, and behavior that leads to excellence. The integrity of this system of achievement is supported most explicitly by two Core protocols, WebofCommitment and PersonalAlignment.

It's difficult to integrate the interests, dreams, and visions of every member of a team, and those of every team on the team of teams that constitutes a contemporary company. Apparently, it is considered too difficult, because usually the effort is simply never made. Perhaps it seems impractical or without value. People who do attempt to achieve this integration will attain their objectives more easily than those who don't. This difference arises because of the genuine accountability found in a system where people state explicitly what they want and have aligned the team's and the company's

*If you persist in sabotaging your own goals, then you can be expected to change either your goals or your behavior.*

*The tolerance of mediocrity becomes the default practice for everyday life.*

interests with their own. The greater alignment provides for greater commitment than does a system in which the relations among these critical elements is summarily dispensed from on high or, more likely, not at all.

The problem is not just the general state of ignorance about alignment; it is compounded by the lack of standard means of achieving it, knowing that it has been achieved, and monitoring the state of alignment over time. The absence of interpersonal communications standards of this type restricts access to the aggregate vitality. This failure results in inefficiency and promotes chaotic lifestyles. The tolerance of mediocrity becomes the default practice for everyday life.

Even though **Alignment** is a single Core pattern, it has broad implications in the context of a Core team. It has extensive associations with a number of subsidiary patterns and protocols, and it touches on every aspect of **SharedVision** (see Chapter Twelve) and product delivery.

# NINE

# Alignment Pattern and Protocol

---

## PATTERN: ALIGNMENT

### PROBLEM

---

*You think there are not enough people or other resources*
*to get your job done well.*

*"I'd like to do that feature for this release, but there's not enough time."*

*"Sorry, not enough resources for that date. Gotta give up something."*

*"What feature do you want me not to do?"*

*" . . but not enough (headcount/time) . . . whaddya gonna do?"*

*"Given our constrained resources, it was a good effort."*

People often see a shortage of resources[1] where no such shortage really exists. Problems are then misdiagnosed as being caused by too

---

1. Usually you can't say that you need more "people," but you can need more "resources." You can ask for "headcount," but, linguistically, wanting more people is somehow anathema.

---

*Because workers have
an acceptable
explanation for the
problems at hand,
they're not concerned
with finding real
solutions.*

little time or too few people, or both, and wrong strategies are subsequently employed. This misperception is continually reinforced.

*High-tech workers fervently believe in time and people shortages.* Most don't give the issues much genuine thought and discussion. Instead, they respond to these perceived shortages by applying ostensibly higher-resolution planning techniques, hiring more people, and cutting anticipated features. Unfortunately, these responses compound, rather than alleviate, the underlying problems.

Because workers have an acceptable explanation for the problems at hand, they're not concerned with finding real solutions to the problems. If a team tends to see "shortages" where none have been demonstrated to exist, or sees others accepting possibly chimerical shortages as authentic, then developing and understanding the dynamics of particular cases would seem to be a helpful indicated practice for that team. Alas, it is more common to accept and promulgate the conventional explanation of too few resources.

The cycle begins with a good idea,[2] but it may be scuttled because, say, it's the "wrong time" for such an idea. If it is the right time, then the idea may be positioned as "too big" an effort.

"Not enough (people/time)," you protest.

You hear the latest shortage story—or you offer it—accompanied by the fatalistic shrugs of developers' shoulders all around. Once again, your disappointing, limited world, with its aggravating imperfections, wrecks your quality, constrains your potential, and generally hampers your enjoyment of life.

"It is disappointing that we can't do the thing," you admit, "but, after all, we are dealing with limited resources."

---

2. In an environment that is susceptible to imaginary shortages, any idea that actually manages to surface in a serious context is probably a pretty good one. Most lesser ideas are eliminated at earlier stages with a variety of techniques: persistent nay-saying, loose-cannon accusations, unrelenting argumentation, or simply ignoring the idea until its sponsor loses heart. This hazing of ideas happens long before an idea becomes a real question of allocating resources. Typically, any idea that is still standing after the preliminary rounds of negation will necessarily have some vitality and some credible champions. It may, however, be ditched because of the imagined lack of resources.

Much of the time, you have no idea whether a shortage really exists. You assume that the shortage is real, instead of carefully examining the situation. Many explanations based on insufficiencies arise from unexamined assumptions. Because unreasoned things are more likely to contribute to errors of behavior than are reasoned things, simply believing in the unexamined shortages will produce more problems in your life.

No matter. High-tech teams believe in the myth: A lack of resources, not a lack of resourcefulness, retards progress.

## SOLUTION

*Align your team around what each member wants.*

On a properly aligned team, most talent and time shortages are resolved by uncovering the untapped talent of the people already in place. Most of the remaining talent and time shortages can be eliminated by applying team genius to create radically better ideas and more efficiency.

Regardless of any mythical shortages or other obstacles encountered by the team, two things must happen after CheckIn and Decider are adopted: personal and team Alignment. Without them, the team may abort its mission or fail to become a truly high-performance team. These Alignments should be seen as significant team milestones. By substantially increasing productivity and integrity, Alignment will protect the team from the worst of the faux shortages. The team will improve its ability to deal directly, honestly, and effectively with resource allocation. It will increase its aggregate, available creativity, which could make it more productive by orders of magnitude. Although not a panacea, Alignment will mark a turning point in the solution of the team's resource problems and the beginning of the team's SharedVision.

Of the two types of Alignment, PersonalAlignment gets most of the attention, because it directly touches every person on the team.

*Because unreasoned things are more likely to contribute to errors of behavior than are reasoned things, simply believing in the unexamined shortages will produce more problems in your life.*

*Most . . . talent and time shortages can be eliminated by applying team genius to create radically better ideas and more efficiency.*

Team alignment really rides along for free when every individual on the team is aligned. Alignment provides a stable platform for each team member to do the following:

- Identify a personal goal
- Discuss it with the team
- State or restate the goal:
  - In as few words as possible
  - With clarity
  - With underlying commitment
- Create a practical plan for achieving the goal:
  - Using the team's help
  - Performing visible, intentional actions that will give evidence of progress
  - Executing practical assignments and providing status information

The PersonalAlignment pattern may appear conceptually simple, but it is difficult to implement. The team will find it challenging to overcome the obstacles that arise during the Alignment effort. The surprising result is the tremendous power released in the Alignment process, and the ways in which it touches the lives of the team and the individuals.

The Alignment pattern is intended to support the personal integration work of individual team members.[3] While this work is occurring, additional Alignment operations on the team are under way. The team effects will occur on their own, provided that several conditions are met:

- Each team member conducts his own PersonalAlignment.
- All members carry out their PersonalAlignments in the team's presence.[4]

---

3. Integration entails the manufacture of integrity; the creation of harmony among one's thoughts, words, and acts; and the establishment of mutually supportive relations between one's goals and one's behavior.

4. Or a representative subgroup of the team, provided that the entire team comes together and specifically integrates the individual Integrations.

- The Alignment takes place in a single meeting. If the process takes long enough, the meeting would adjourn for sleep and other necessities, but would reconvene without any other work coming between sessions.

Extraordinary salutary effects will reverberate throughout the team, offering clear evidence of team alignment. With both team and PersonalAlignment achieved, all major parts of the team have become functional. The team is prepared to create things. The first thing it will create is a SharedVision (see Chapter Twelve).

## THE ALIGNMENT PROTOCOL

The Alignment protocol governs behavior during alignment. It has five major steps and calls upon the PersonalAlignment, Perfection Game, and Investigate patterns.

1.  Team members begin to align themselves by applying the PersonalAlignment pattern.

All alignees start out with the same, default PersonalAlignment statement: *"I want self-awareness."* All further Alignment work necessarily stems from the application of self-awareness. If you haven't passed and don't mean to pass shortly, and if you are not aware of more pressing wants, then obviously, you want self-awareness.

Carefully review PersonalAlignment (see Chapter Eleven).

Spend sufficient private time in introspection and in receiving help, so you will be able to form and express your PersonalAlignment to the team.

Small groups of people can gather to listen to and investigate (see Chapter Eleven) one another, but only after all of the individuals have spent time alone and in receiving help.

Next, prepare clear, direct answers to the following questions. These answers must be captured in writing for each team member, and will be brought into the WebofCommitment (see Chapter Eleven).

- What do I personally want?
- What will it look like to the team when I am working on and/or achieving what I want? What external, observable alignment evidence will appear?
- What kind of support do I need from which members of the team to work on and/or achieve what I want?
- Can I accept particular assignments that will demonstrate the status of my Alignment-related work to the team?

When all members are ready, the group will meet to hear each set of answers to the questions. The group consists of subgroups of the team or the entire team, as determined by the team.

When each Alignment concludes, the alignee fulfills the alignee role (detailed in WebofCommitment) and asks the team for help:

*"Will you, <helper>, <my positive step>, <kind of help>, <details>?"*

For example,

*"Will you, all of you, help me practice my speech Thursdays at lunch from now until January 28?"*

or

*"Will you, Bill, as I work on my Alignment, coach me on that topic, two hours per week for three weeks?"*

Possible helper responses include the following:

- Yes
- No
- Request clarification or information
- Pass (see Chapter Two).

More details on the alignee's behavior during the help, evidence, and assignment parts of the discussion are found in "Personal Alignment Commitments."

2.   Team members use Investigate to help one another complete their PersonalAlignments.

Investigate is used by team members who are not currently working on their own Alignment, when they make themselves available to an alignee during the public portion of his PersonalAlignment. Investigate encourages the successful and efficient completion of PersonalAlignment. When well executed, it will also enhance the depth of Alignment. Investigate has broader applicability as well, supporting general-purpose personal investigation. This pattern generates investigators, where the subject of the investigation is the alignee.

3.   Alignees iterate as necessary.

Your first pass at PersonalAlignment, with the support of the team in Investigate mode, will generally produce a completed PersonalAlignment, but it may yield an inconclusive result or provoke a change of heart. It may lead to a deepening of the Alignment, or just confusion. It is acceptable to redo the public portion of a PersonalAlignment. Even if everything about your Alignment seemed clear, if you desire to change some or all of it, you may do so—provided that you share the changes with the team in full meeting.

*The key to a successful PersonalAlignment . . . is that you must want what you say you want.*

The key to a successful PersonalAlignment (and the team alignment that flows from it) is that you must want what you say you want. The degree to which this correspondence is true establishes the measure of your integrity. Your success with this endeavor will correlate with your overall success on this team. The team's aggregated Alignment integrity will likewise correlate with the team's overall success.

4.   The team improves the collected PersonalAlignment statements.

5.   The team completes a WebofCommitment and integrates it into the group.

For each person the team records the answers to each of the four questions in PersonalAlignment in a permanent document, which is accessible to all team members. This step documents the team's WebofCommitment.

## *Other Conditions*

Additional factors contribute to the quality and ease of Alignment, including these physical issues:

- Alignment is best achieved in a quiet, comfortable place, away from usual workplaces and workplace stresses.

- The team will maximize its effectiveness if it performs all PersonalAlignments as a team during a single, off-site session, taking as much time as necessary (usually several days) to do the work to everyone's satisfaction.

- If one or more persons on the team can't attend the off-site meeting, the team must proceed without them.

# TEN

# Alignment Antipatterns

---

## ANTIPATTERN:
## NOT ENOUGH PEOPLE

Instead of focusing on the qualities of individuals needed to achieve results, you merely focus on the number of individuals.

### PROBLEM

---

*You blame a headcount shortage for your lack of results.*

*The available qualities[1] on a team matter more than the number of people on that team.* If a given team task requires three distinct skills and your teammate Joe happens to have those three qualities, the following should hold true:

> *If Joe's needed qualities are available to him on demand,*
>
> *And Joe's workload is wide open,*
>
> *Then you can simply ask Joe to do the task. If he accepts, other things being equal, all will be well.*

---

1. *Qualities*, in the context of The Core, are positive, nonquantifiable properties of people, such as skills, virtues, and other winning personal attributes.

---

*Focusing on the number of people is a distressingly primitive way to measure anything relevant to development purposes.*

In that simple case, more people aren't needed. It is as if the whole team is on call inside Joe, like the cache on a processor. Thus, if·Joe knows himself well, he can volunteer for the task and then handle the job relatively quickly.

On a team with a more complex assignment, the qualities required usually mandate using the expertise of more than one person. However, focusing on the number of people is a distressingly primitive way to measure anything relevant to development purposes. When you estimate the needs of a collaborative effort to create intellectual property, the primary issues will not revolve around the headcount.

To collaborate effectively, then, you need certain *qualities* of people, with each quality having some degree of availability. Ideally, those needed qualities will also have some degree of transmissibility (that is, teachability or copyability), so that, over time, tasks may be more flexibly apportioned among team members without adding more than the optimal number of people. To paraphrase Einstein, you could say that the ideal number of people to provide the required qualities is as few as possible, but no fewer.

As of this writing, IP teams typically set schedules and hiring requirements by tasks, projects, and resources. They organize people by function. Some do a good job of estimating and budgeting their time and hiring and assigning people this way. Most, however, fail miserably.

*You cannot truly know how long it will take a person to create ideas and implement them.*

Of course, such a scheduling effort will seldom produce a literal budget or a literal schedule. You cannot truly know how long it will take a person to create ideas and implement them. If you wanted extremely accurate schedules, you would head in another direction. Schedules with more predictive value would be based on such elements as the specific qualities needed, their availability, and their transmissibility.[2] You would then lay out a spreadsheet with the following information:

---

2. Plus many more, lesser variables, such as environment, mood, and so forth.

- Specific qualities

- Amount needed

- Amount of quality available

- Some factor incorporating the effects of each quality's intrateam transmissibility

Suppose this information was all you needed to create a schedule.[3] The mathematics required to quantify the resources would be abstruse. To determine the required amounts of the required qualities, you could take the intersection of quality availability and quality needs of the team, and the effects of intrateam transmissibility over time. You could then measure the calendar time required for that population to achieve the goal. The population would need to be accurately inventoried for the needed qualities. Likewise, the amount of each quality required would have to be accurately predicted, the degrees of quality availability correctly factored, and the effects of intrateam quality transmission modeled without fault. Even if all these requirements were met, the results would so seldom match the actual person-time required, and spread across the actual calendar time expended, that it is ridiculous to continue in this direction.[4]

While it is foolish to consider using such a scheduling system, it would, if feasible, yield a much more accurate schedule than the techniques currently used, which call for dividing up the work and the budget according to the nonstandard unit of "person." This choice of using person-units is magnified by another patently incorrect idea: that each minute is essentially the same as every other minute. The final touch of folly is the assumed belief that all people will predictably consume some fixed amount of calendar time—at a rate and with a

*Using person-units is magnified by another patently incorrect idea: that each minute is essentially the same as every other minute.*

---

3. Which it is; the numbers are just a bit difficult to come by.

4. But consider the following questions: Are these not among the key issues in product development? Do you incorporate them in your planning? Or even try to do so? Who is using these vital elements in their scheduling and project planning? Where do you find a system that is realistic? It is difficult to take any project management system seriously unless it accounts for the key variables.

yield they themselves set—in the generation and encoding of ideas.[5] This system is a ludicrous, ineffective, and distracting proposition.

Budgets, estimates, and schedules have value because they describe how you feel and think today. They reveal very little about how you'll work tomorrow.

This misguided thinking shows up in lots of ongoing bluster, angst, and failure in everyday development life about scheduling and shortages. Therefore, it naturally seems that everything is so difficult because you are suffering from insufficient "resources"— that is, people.

*You* are experiencing a real shortage—but not the shortage you perceive. In spite of all the attention paid to these faux shortages, the problem is not an insufficient number of people or a lack of time. Your intuition that more people might solve your problems is basically a good one; but it's way too crude. You do need more of something that people provide, and more people might provide more of that something. What you need, however, is that missing element, not more people, per se.

*You are experiencing a real shortage—but not the shortage you perceive.*

## SUPPOSED SOLUTION

———————

*Add more people, strip down features,
or push out time in schedules.*

*Adding people because your team has too few of them is a solution to a problem that you don't have.*

Adding people because your team has too few of them is a solution to a problem that you don't have, even though (as suggested above) on some occasions it provides a real solution. It is, at least theoretically, true that adding people will eventually solve the real problem.

Your real problem is probably that you are working in a psychologically and creatively malnourished environment that is partly of your own making. However, no single person or institution

———————

5. How long does it take to have the right idea—say, an idea that eliminates 40 percent of the work while increasing results? What conditions might lead to such creativity?

should be blamed for such environmental shortcomings, not because no one involved is accountable for the ugliness, but because blame is such a self-defeating practice. Such environmental sterility, it must also be pointed out, also afflicts most non-business endeavors. The qualities you need from people, yourself included, are typically not as available in such an environment.

You don't need more people; you need more *from* people (yourself included) already on the scene. What you need is not just sheer, by-the-numbers volume of production. The problem of acquiring more human qualities for a project can be solved in several ways. Increasing headcount is the brute-force approach: If you hire enough people, odds are you'll get what you need. Eventually. Of course, there is an excellent chance that you already have what you need—you just don't have access to it. You can exploit these hidden resources by increasing your personal productivity and helping the people around you do the same.

## REAL SOLUTION

*Instead of adding headcount,
make the heads you have count.*

Try boosting your interpersonal and intrapersonal bandwidth. Generally, human connection runs at a fraction of the available interpersonal bandwidth. To use a further analogy from the computer world, the current situation is as if you have your 300-baud modem attached to a T1 line. You voluntarily, but needlessly, subsist at an impoverished level of human connection.

Often your connections at work have become suffused with negativity, and you have become inured to this situation. You can't be as creatively productive as you would be in a more positive environment. You can't relax into your creative work as things are, and you don't choose to change them. There is too much you don't say that would be helpful, and too much you don't do that would be successful. Despite the joy to be found in creating together, and

*You don't need more people, you need more from people (yourself included) already on the scene.*

*There is too much you don't say that would be helpful, and too much you don't do that would be successful.*

*In that moment, when trust unceremoniously displaces suspicious defensive effort, you feel truly weightless and extraordinarily lucid.*

despite your ability to make *work* any way you want it to be—work is often the parent of your regrets.

The picture is not completely bleak, however. You observe, and even help with, the many grand things that are created, despite the negativity. Exciting technologies continue to find their way into people's lives. Nevertheless, much withholding of self and distortion of personalities continue to plague society, leaving a vast overlooked potential.

What can you do? First, pin down the etiology of the problem in yourself. The chronic negative charge at work is created in part by ignorance—your colleagues' ignorance of you, and your ignorance of them. It is also partly created by your tendency to confuse the unknown with the dangerous. The typical reaction to strangers, even those with whom you work over a long period of time, is chronic, albeit low-level, fear or suspicion of the unknown. Much of the fear derives from your uncertainty about your colleagues' motives and goals, as well as their fundamental unpredictability. Even though you may intermittently sense goodwill emanating from them, often feel camaraderie with them, and even believe in their consistent good intentions, your fear lives on. You become used to it, and scarcely notice the weight. But when it's gone—when the suspicion lifts even for a moment—how good it feels to trust instead. In that moment, when trust unceremoniously displaces suspicious defensive effort, you feel truly weightless and extraordinarily lucid. Then you will see how badly you felt. That bad feeling, which you thought was the normal way to feel about going to work, derived from a lack of trust. It is common, but it is not normal.

Often you don't know the people with whom you work on a personal level. You do come to know their habits, but the features that you see are either those that they want you to see, or those that you furtively observe. It's not only that you are guarding yourself; your colleagues also guard themselves. You do get to know them—in a way. That is, you know something that is like them: the intersection of what they want you to know, and what you perceive of them without their active involvement. In any event, you do develop a picture of each of your colleagues. Almost all of these pictures, however, represent a well-defended, unrelaxed persona, which is how people appear when they believe they are not among intimates. When they are not feeling safe.

*You usually live with your coworkers in a bizarre state: familiarity deprived of intimacy.*

Oddly, you may not grow closer to many of your colleagues over time. You usually live with your coworkers in a bizarre state: familiarity deprived of intimacy. When you think about it, this situation is the worst of all worlds: Not only are you not close, but you are always together. The chronic, unappeased suspicion, combined with the twitchy, hair-trigger self-protective impulses, is—physically, psychologically, and creatively—very costly to maintain.

Casting off this burden—shedding the maintenance costs of many suspicions and some of the related stresses—will be the happy result of increasing trust. Trust of others comes from knowledge of them. For trust to be a wise strategy, you will especially need to understand others' intentions:

*"What does this person say he's going to do? Does he then do it?"*

True safety is what you feel when you trust. Dispensing with the horrendous cost of maintaining protectiveness, and ceasing to project the carefully wrought image of yourself to others with whom you work, you will be able to risk new, bigger things. Your sense of safety helps you decide whether a show of vulnerability or a personal revelation leads to punishment of any type. You ask yourself:

"Do I feel safe here? Safe enough to take creative or critical risks? Safe enough to grow? To be wrong?"

"Is he safe to talk to? Does he understand what I say? How does he feed it back? Is he receptive?"

"What makes her tick? How do I know what she will do next? How is she motivated? With what or with whom does she align herself?"

You constantly look for the answers to these questions and more like them, for each person. The more quickly you obtain your answers, the better for all, at least insofar as reducing the burden of interpersonal connectedness.

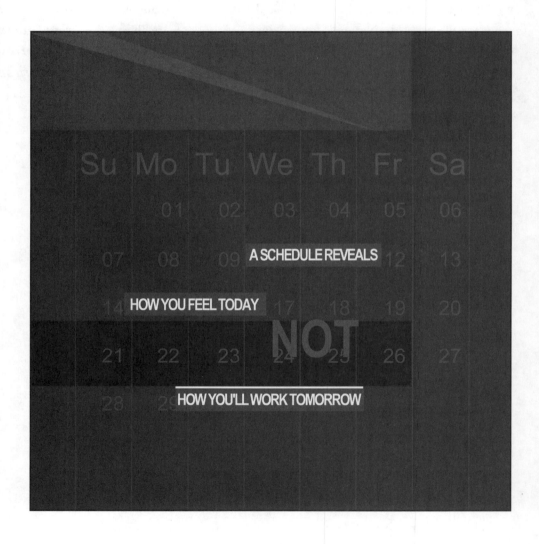

In working to intentionally increase trust and safety, you will require more personal information from your teammates and they will, in turn, need information from you. Your motives and goals are among the most powerful secrets you can reveal. They are also the most relevant personal information elements for all members of the team. You will be able to use or learn from this information why each of your teammates is where he is now. This information is highly germane.

The assumption that almost everyone has goals is the obvious starting place for bringing a team together. Nevertheless, workplace culture[6] typically doesn't acknowledge personal goals, doesn't especially encourage working to understand one another's goals, and certainly doesn't mobilize much direct support for the attainment of individual goals. Even so, awareness of goals is one key to understanding behavior.

Even if the corporate culture doesn't support this type of learning, you can't stand still and be a further victim of a culture in which you choose to live. After all, you help to create and maintain the culture. In fact, you have absolute power over the culture that lives within your personal sphere of influence. How you permit others to interact with you is a very powerful way of creating new culture.

Because nearly everyone has goals, nothing prevents you from sharing your goals with your teammates right now. You need only do so, and then invite others to share with you. Alignment is nearly a fail-safe way to join together with your team in discovering and stating goals. Once goals are disclosed, you can start planning to attain what you want and to secure from your teammates enough help to turn your dreams into reality. This Alignment of personal interests is sorely missing in most teams. Moreover, the intentional group disclosure and group reception of motives creates a team that is aware

*Your motives and goals are among the most powerful secrets you can reveal.*

*You have absolute power over the culture that lives within your personal sphere of influence.*

---

6. What is workplace culture, anyway, if not simply how you behave at work? How do you decide how to behave? By copying others usually; mostly, copying those people who are long gone. Is that how you want to behave? Is it the most effective way to behave? You follow this route by choice. Your fear of doing otherwise is typically profoundly exaggerated. How you choose to behave is the aspect of culture for which you are accountable.

*Alignment takes place on many levels. When you are aligned on one level, most often the other levels come along for free.*

of the Alignment of personal interests, is aware of the specific personal interests involved now, and is aware of how to attain the goal of Alignment itself.

Alignment takes place on many levels. When you are aligned on one level, most often the other levels come along for free. The Alignment pattern represents a major step on the road to being on a genuine team, where separate individuals become as one, yet suffer no loss of individuality while experiencing a massive boost in power to generate desirable results. People need only join together in stating their goals, visualizing them, planning for them, and securing help from one another to achieve them. This is the heart and soul of teamwork.

## ANTIPATTERN: ALIGN ME

An especially pernicious antipattern, AlignMe, may make an appearance during Alignment. Applying the nostrums described in Chapter Nine will usually control or eliminate AlignMe, but identifying it in real time can prove tricky. Even when you think you have identified it, you may not feel certain.[7]

AlignMe occurs when a team member, consciously or not, avoids concluding a PersonalAlignment. A number of avoidance strategies are possible but we will describe only two: the classic AlignMe and its subtype, **blatherer**.

The blatherer delays goal-setting in the following ways:

- Not passing, even though that's what he wants to do
- Not asking for time to prepare
- Not using preparation time effectively

---

7. We've observed this antipattern to some degree on every team alignment with which we've been involved. Unfortunately, the evidence of AlignMe generally becomes available to those involved only when the greater portion of time has been misspent already. The whole thing appears much clearer in retrospect

- Consuming inordinate amounts of team time while verbally wandering through his life, his problems, his work, and his family issues

- Suggesting counterproductive or ill-fitting goals

In short, the blatherer will talk about anything except what will move him toward attaining what he truly wants. In so doing, the blatherer abuses the team's willingness to pay its undivided attention to each member. The attention of team members is so rewarding that the person is reluctant to give it up. A person having difficulty discovering and stating what he wants will often blather on. Anyone who slows the team down and attracts attention at a cost to the greater work is not benignly drifting along. This kind of hey-stop-look-at-me behavior is one of the most damaging neuroses faced by teams.

In some instances, the sabotage is intentional. Intentional sabotage is actually preferable to oblivious sabotage (see Oblivion). But whether the damage is "inadvertent" or malintended, in all cases, stopping the team and not producing the best possible result is a great misstep.

The classic AlignMe actor is reluctant to conclude the Personal Alignment and will use blather techniques to retain the spotlight. Rather than merely glorying in and demanding more of the team's attentiveness (like the blatherer), however, the classic AlignMe person parasitically exploits the team's proffered support by shifting the responsibility for his Alignment from his shoulders to those of the team. The team's position of supporter morphs into the starring role when a classic AlignMe is at work.

While the team may accept this misappropriated responsibility for many reasons, and for quite a while, vanity is the most common explanation. Product developers revel in the triumph of solving a difficult puzzle. A troublesome, unending Alignment is nothing if not a puzzle. Those who are always ready to propose a theory or battle for intellectual supremacy in a group will abandon the simple purity of Investigate to chomp on the AlignMe bit. AlignMe merely masquerades as a puzzle, however. It is actually a frustrating conundrum—a problem with no solution.

*This kind of hey-stop-look-at-me behavior is one of the most damaging neuroses faced by teams.*

*Your vanity can be
seen—especially
later—in the
enjoyment you
experience from feeling
smarter than your
neighbor.*

When suffering from AlignMe in another, you devolve. Your vanity can be seen—especially later—in the enjoyment you experience from feeling smarter than your neighbor. You love to rescue anyone who will let you. You like to see yourself as The Big Helper. When vanity takes over your role—and that of others—in an Alignment, a lot of verbal and emotional noise hides what is actually happening. In AlignMe, bogus "answers" are provided to the alignee. The individual becomes inundated with psychobabbling advisors and will politely listen to as much "counsel" as desired. Identifying "what the alignee wants" can also become an intellectual competition, and solutions are dogmatically pronounced ad nauseam. The AlignMe alignee may approach others one at a time, taking hours to really "open up," seeking round after round of "advice" and "support." All the while, your vanity grows and flourishes because of your immense capacity as a helper and confidante.

## PROBLEM

*In an investigative session around your
PersonalAlignment, you can't or won't come to the point;
instead, you specify bogus wants or are passive.*

Some people seem to always prefer talk to action. All people sometimes do. When you are in this state and are talking, you also will prefer to talk about nothing rather than talk about something. The more significant the topic, the more you'll want to talk about nothing. Because your own Alignment is very significant, it exacerbates your preference for talk over action. It can become extremely difficult to focus on your behavior.

Every alignee will experience some difficulty in not wandering off topic in Alignment. The Investigate protocol will handle all but the most willful, or willfully oblivious, cases.

When you discuss an important personal issue, especially for the first time, you typically become distracted, forgetful, or confused. This involuntary leave-taking surfaces especially when you are

*When you discuss an
important personal
issue, especially for the
first time, you
typically become
distracted, forgetful,
or confused.*

receiving maximal benign attention and disclosing any weakness. And what you want must always be something you are missing. A weakness, in some sense.

Try this experiment. Pay special attention during a particular Alignment. An hour after it is completed, ask the alignee to restate his Alignment. You will know the exact wording of it (having prepared the experiment), but if the alignee didn't write down the Alignment statement or doesn't have it handy, he may not remember it. The effort of recalling this statement may cause an uncharacteristic stutter and, invariably, a word or two will be slightly off. Often, the whole thing will be wrong or forgotten.

This avoidance tendency causes individuals to blather when discussing PersonalAlignment. Instead of working to finish the process and get down to business, it is common to talk in circles or tell stories. This tendency is exacerbated in a group setting.

AlignMe is inaugurated when someone tries to have the team perform his PersonalAlignment. Usually, he wants the others to carry the burden of thought, effort, and intention that go into a Personal Alignment. The others, of course, want to be helpful and show themselves to be good citizens, and together they generate another instance of the AlignMe antipattern. AlignMe is a very expensive time-sink at a very important time for the team.

## ALIGN ME SYMPTOMS

Watch for the following signs of the AlignMe antipattern:

- Alignment blather occurs.
- The alignee does not get help offline.
- The alignee does no thinking offline about the Personal Alignment.
- You, as investigator, feel obligated to "do an Alignment" for the alignee or "to align" him.
- You imagine that you will hurt the alignee's feelings by asking that person to work on the Alignment offline.
- Your team takes no offline time during the Alignment process.

# ALIGNMENT BLATHER SYMPTOMS

The following symptoms are typical of **Alignment** blather:

- Talking in circles
- Telling stories
- "I don't know"
- "I'm confused"
- Long pauses with no result
- Anger at the investigator
- Victim affect
- You, as investigator, feel sorry for the alignee and patient with him
- You try to convince the alignee to continue
- You pull information out of the alignee

## SUPPOSED SOLUTION

*Be patient. Play along. Offer lots of help.*
*Don't offend the alignee.*
*Propose several **Alignment** statements.*

If you are the alignee, you get free attention. You have the focused attention of everyone in the group, and it costs nothing. You need not reveal anything. You can tell stories and talk about whatever you want. Your teammates seem endlessly interested in you, and you don't have to answer questions honestly or at all.

If you are the investigator, it may seem appropriate to let the blather continue. You can tell yourself, "This is helping," or "We'll get somewhere when he finishes this story." Most of all, you can tell yourself that you are helping this person by just listening.

Do not tolerate blather or other **AlignMe** behaviors. They are signs of laziness of thought and action, and they indicate a lack of intention on everyone's part. AlignMe is an outrageous waste of time; it shows a lack of commitment to CheckIn and PersonalAlignment.

You must speak up during blather. Say, "I don't think we're getting anywhere. Could you think about your Alignment offline and we'll work on it later?"

Demonstrate your commitment to the alignee. Don't let that person break his PersonalAlignment commitments to the team.

## ACTUAL SOLUTION

*Be intolerant of blather, obfuscation, confusion, and passivity.*

The real solution to the AlignMe problem is to ask the alignee to think about the Alignment out of the presence of the team. Any team discussion of AlignMe symptoms will conclude that break time is needed during the Alignment process to allow individuals to do their Alignment work. Inevitably, the group will reach a consensus: Each individual should align himself. The group is there to provide support and help, not to do the Alignment work.

*AlignMe is an outrageous waste of time; it shows a lack of commitment to CheckIn and PersonalAlignment.*

*Inevitably, the group will reach a consensus: Each individual should align himself.*

# ELEVEN

# Alignment Patterns

---

## PATTERN:
## PERSONAL ALIGNMENT

---

Understanding and attaining what you want.

### PROBLEM

---

*You don't know what you want.*

Most of the time, you are unaware of what you want.[1] Your lack of awareness does not eliminate your wants; it prevents you from placing your intentions where they can do you the most good. You will still generally decide in ways that move you somewhat closer to what you want. But when you're not conscious of all the reasons behind your choices, you reduce by some amount your chances of satisfaction. With respect to your team, the extent to which you lapse into "want oblivion" is your contribution to the aggregate team oblivion; your puzzle piece is randomly tossed with all the others to

---

1. If, in your case, most of the time you are aware of what you want, then at least some of the time you are not aware of what you want. Some of the time is sufficient to create the opportunity discussed here.

---

create the grand jigsaw that would, if assembled, solve the mysteries of your team's results.

## WHAT I WANT

You can use PersonalAlignment to help you understand what you want. You must answer two questions, as truly and as deeply as you can:

- What do I want?
- What's blocking me from having it?

It is probably safe to say that many people work without truly thinking about why they are working. Certainly, many do not contemplate it on a daily basis. What is your purpose in working? If you are oblivious of purpose when you go to work, you likely do so because of some kind of unthinking inertial impulse, or, perhaps, because of a general sense of financial need or desire. Maybe you work just to avoid the untidiness and discomfort of quitting or changing jobs. In effect, sometimes at least, you work without deciding to decide to work.

Why do you spend most of your waking hours on your job? Why are you giving this work effort the largest part of your productive daily energy? What are you doing that will make any difference in the long term, anyway? And, for that matter, who are these people with whom you work, and what are you doing, working alongside them each day, all day?

*Much can be gained by looking at the difference—if any—between how you spend your life and how you say you want to spend it.*

Much can be gained by looking at the difference—if any—between how you spend your life and how you say you want to spend it. Many people allow their jobs to take precedence over other important parts of their lives. On the teams we've worked with, for example, many people believe their jobs impinge overmuch on their personal health and/or that their jobs excessively diminish the amount or quality of time they spend with loved ones.

If you believe that your work takes a certain toll on your life, then certain inferences can be drawn. Very good reasons actually do exist for maintaining health and/or family relations, for example, while simultaneously achieving at work. You must have a very compelling reason for choosing work over health or family. "Well," you might say, "Well, I just have to, because . . . ," and then you list the common things listed at this juncture (deadlines, competitive situations, pressures of one sort or another). You've been routinely giving yourself, your spouse, or your children this or a similar stock response, but it cannot substitute for the more lucid thinking of which you are capable.

That you choose to do what you do is an important fact. You choose to do things that you *say* you don't want to do at the cost of your integrity. Worse, this obviously self-contradictory stance then serves as a placeholder for thinking things through. Any reluctant expenditure of vast chunks of your life shows a lack of appreciation for the importance of what you want.

You will find little social support behind your attempt to discover what you want. There is no real established body of wisdom regarding it, and no set of everyday guidelines to help you accurately determine what you want. Moreover, no common educational process imparts either the wisdom or the practicalities of this higher order of self-care. Nor are you likely to find any classroom teaching on the art of organizing your life around actually achieving what you want.

For some, the very idea of focusing on what you want, or even just encountering the phrase "organizing your life around actually achieving what you want," will have connotations of extreme selfishness. The whole idea may exude a kind of "badness." ("Is that all he thinks of? Himself? What a selfish pig.") Obviously, our aim is not to promote selfishness or untrammeled acquisitiveness as substitutes for virtue. To the contrary: In our experience, it has been nearly universal that when people work to clearly articulate what it is they want, they invariably want for themselves purely good things. They seem to really crave things that would improve not merely their own lives, but also the lives of all the people around them.

Seeking things that enrich all at no one's expense is not selfish. So, by being aware of what you want, you have what you need to organize your life around achieving it. This situation stands in stark contrast to the alternatives. How else *would* you organize your life,

*Nor are you likely to find any classroom teaching on the art of organizing your life around actually achieving what you want.*

*When people work to clearly articulate what it is they want, they invariably want for themselves purely good things.*

anyway, if not around achieving what you want? You could theoretically organize your life around these other kinds of achievements:

- Achieving nothing

- Achieving whatever you happen to achieve but without prior cognition or admission (because those would be tantamount to wanting)

- Achieving what others want

- Achieving what you don't want

No doubt, there are other permutations; but, when you think about it, once your basic survival is somewhat assured, if you proceed to organize your life at all, the only real choice is to do so around attaining what you want. Regardless of your religious outlook, cultural background, nationality, ethical beliefs, or any other traditional factors that may influence your values and thinking, you probably would rather achieve what you intend to achieve.

Of course, achieving the intended does require forming an intention in the first place. That intention would be "what you want."

In spite of popular prejudice, good teams are not really about teammates who take care of one another; instead, they are about the mature self-care of team members, of their self-sufficiency. Only the sufficiently supplied can afford to give help; seeking and providing help is something good teams are about. Any isolation, any deprivation of support, or any personal solitude of a team member occurs by his choice. Help from others is readily available on a team where, by default, everybody cares for himself. Mature self-care is simply the most efficient way to distribute the burden of the care of the people on the team among the team members: Expect that each person will take care of himself. The elegant solution of self-care resolves the problem such that

*Mature self-care is simply the most efficient way to distribute the burden of the care of the people on the team among the team members.*

- All teammates are cared for.

- Each team member is in the charge of the person to whom he is closest.

- No one carries extra responsibility.

Unfortunately, when you do decide to think about what you want, still more demons will arise. For example, your tendency to depreciate yourself is likely to emerge. Self-sacrifice may seduce you with the losses of the Mutually Exclusive. Or it may bewitch you with the zeros of the zero-sum game. You may feel encouraged to think of things in black-or-white terms: "If I get what I want, then [whoever] wouldn't get what he/she/it wants." Thinking of good things for yourself is often accompanied by a nearly involuntary assertion of belief in the mutual exclusivity of two good things.

This kind of thinking follows a template: "If I were to [*acquire a positive element that I've been denying myself*], then I would [*suffer a negative element that has been the story for denying myself so far*]." Some examples will illustrate this line of thought:

- "I can't do what I want because I have a mortgage."
- "I can't say what I think because they would fire me."[2]
- "I can't make a great product because I have small children."

All too often, people suffer self-denial and then attribute this suffering to some ersatz sense of responsibility or some immutable law of nature. *The motive power behind such thinking is almost always a long-standing and juvenile belief in the inevitability of bad flowing from involvement with good things.*

Sometimes, though it is rare, undesirable results may come from involvement with good things. So there is always *some* chance that the worst possible consequence will result if you treat yourself a little more kindly. For example, your boss just *might* fire you if you voice your carefully considered opinions; but it's quite unlikely. If your boss is more likely than average to do that, you don't really want to be there anyway. The common fear of bad consequences stemming from good things causes many people to squelch their impulses to discover their truest desires. They repress their healthy, mature, and natural tendencies to care for themselves, and embrace the bogus "greater good." They forgo a good thing for "the good of

*Thinking of good things for yourself is often accompanied by a nearly involuntary assertion of belief in the mutual exclusivity of two good things.*

2. Getting fired can be a good thing, especially if you get fired for telling the truth. Why would you want to work in that situation anyway?

*Another common
behavior used to
avoid discovering and
attaining what you
want is to pretend . . .
that you are shallower
than you really are.*

X," where X represents "the team," "the kids," or "the company" or something, anything, as long as the martyring person forgoing the goodies actually believes in X more than he believes in himself.

Another common behavior used to avoid discovering and attaining what you want is to pretend—even if just to yourself—that you are shallower than you really are, and that you have shallower wants than you really do. You might say, "What I really want is to be independently wealthy, but . . ." A minimal amount of investigator questioning will reveal that "independently wealthy" is not the end of the matter, but just the beginning. Wealth, in this case, is almost always a metaphoric thing, and it expands to reveal a more basic human desire—perhaps for something like freedom or power. Shallowness is a difficult posture to maintain in the face of fearless investigation.

If you don't know what you want, you simply can't make great products. If you are unaware of your desires and motivations, they will inevitably taint your art and artifacts. They will also appear as frustration, manipulation, and misunderstanding directed at the team and its products.

To really achieve what you are capable of, you must first learn to get to the heart of what you want. You must learn to do this in a renewable and repeatable way. That is the most helpful act for you individually, and it will prove to be the most productive for your team, as well. Otherwise, your vision, your team, and your product will all be determined by your listless toss of the dice.

## SOLUTION

*Discover what you want. Tell your teammates what it is.
Ask for their help. Expect them to do likewise, or to pass.*

## THE PERSONAL ALIGNMENT PROTOCOL

Complete the following **PersonalAlignment** exercise. You are encouraged to ask others for help early and often. Expect your helpers to use the Investigate pattern, and when you help others with their PersonalAlignment, you must use the Investigate pattern.

1. Ask yourself, "What do I want? What—specifically—do I, personally, want?"

2. When you think you know what you want, write it down.

3. Now ask yourself: "Why don't I have what I say I want already?" Assume that you could have had it by now. Almost always, there is some internal blocking element preventing you from getting it, or you already would have it. Write down your answer.

If your answer to the question in step 3 blames or defers accountability to uncontrollable circumstances or other people, pretend your last answer to step 3 is just a story, a myth that somehow deprives you of your full power to achieve for yourself. Before proceeding further with this protocol, you must make an imaginative leap to a more personally powerful stance. You likely will have to increase your self-awareness. Increase your perception and your receptivity. In any case, change *something* now about the way you have executed this protocol so far, because it hasn't worked. Then go back to step 3.

4. If your answer to the question in step 3 is more than a few words, reply to the question again, simplifying your answer.

5. If your answer to step 3 doesn't refer to a personal issue:
   - Increase your commitment to yourself in this process.
   - Consider whether you are afraid, and, if so, what you fear.
   - Consider whether your answer to step 3 shows integrity.
   - Change *something* now about the way you have executed this protocol so far, because it hasn't worked. Then go back to step 3.

6. If you have gone back to step 3 several times:
   - Employ AskforHelp (again, if necessary)
   - And/or take a break and go back to step 1.

7. If your answer to step 3 points to a problem or constraint that, if solved, would radically increase your effectiveness in life—work and play—you have identified a *block*.

8. Until you are certain that what you say you want is what you really want, remain at this point. If you have remained here for a while, you are still uncertain, and your team is moving on, adopt the default alignment: That is, you want more self-awareness and you don't know what's blocking you. Go to step 13.

9. If you are not certain that eliminating the block identified by your answer to step 3 will be worth a great deal of effort, go back to step 8.

10. Check out the block with people who know you and with people who know about blocks, if possible. If you are unwilling to utilize AskforHelp with your team, go back to step 8.

11. Determine what virtue would be powerful enough to shatter the block.

12. Decide whether this virtue is what you really want: the power that would yield what you *thought* you wanted (in step 1). If it is, write it down. Go to step 3.

13. Create a very concise sentence that begins with the words: "I want . . ."

14. If your sentence has unneeded words, go back to step 13.

15. This sentence is your PersonalAlignment statement. Check it out with all of your team members.

16. Ask them if they can think of a shorter, more direct way to say the same thing.

17. Promise them to take specific, visible actions that will show your commitment to obtaining what you want. Tell them what they can expect to see you doing, commencing now.

18. Ask your team for help. Will they do *X*, when you signal them by doing *Y*? In your request for help, there should be specific actions you are asking them to do that will help you obtain what you want. It is very important that *you* initiate this action-reaction sequence by signaling to them that you are working on

your PersonalAlignment. It is not up to your teammates to initiate status checks or to police your PersonalAlignment. Ask for your teammates' help using very specific language, such as: "Bill, when I [*do something positive that demonstrates my commitment to attaining what I say I want*], will you [*show a sign of support, encouragement, and/or proffer any requested substantive help*]?"

19. Write or rewrite the following:

    - Your PersonalAlignment statement

    - Alignment evidence[3]

    - The support you ask for from your team[4,5]

Examples of support include the following:

"When I say, 'This takes courage for me,' will you applaud?"

"When I say, 'This takes courage for me,' will you then sit down alone with me, listen to what I say, repeating back to me each idea I say?"

"When I give a daily report on how I took care of myself, will you do the wave?"

"When I say, 'I'm going to add some hope,' will you give me a high five?"

---

3. *Evidence* consists of the *short-term evidence*, behaviors you will demonstrate beginning now and that show you are practicing your Alignment. It also consists of *long-term evidence*. What will your life look like in five years if you perfectly achieve your Alignment? It is important that evidence be positive and measurable. For instance, "I'll stop being negative" is not positive. What will you do instead of being negative? "I'll be happier" isn't evidence because the rest of the team can't tell whether you are happier. "I will say 'no' at least once per day" is evidence for someone working on self-care who has a problem saying "no" to people. It is a positive step and it is measurable.

4. Support must be positive and consist of one thing. For instance, "Will you catch me when I am quiet and not saying my ideas?" is not support. It focuses on a negative behavior and is vague. The positive version is "When I say, 'I have an idea,' will you say, 'Let's hear it!'" Support must consist of a specific positive signal that is given by the alignee and a specific positive response given by the team.

5. Sometimes an alignee finds himself in a dilemma. The individual wants support for his ideas and wants the team to support them by saying "Good idea!" This issue is problematical because the team might not like the idea. The way to solve this dilemma is to have the team support the action of stating the idea, rather than the idea itself. The team can always say, "Good job stating your ideas, Kate," even if they don't like the particular idea.

## Personal Alignment Commitments

This protocol requires the following commitments from the alignee:

- Pass early if you are going to pass. Pass later only if you fail to pass early.

- Move to the deepest desirable point in the shortest possible time.

- Be truthful.

- Be receptive to the effective assistance of others.

- Reject assistance that impedes your progress.

- Don't just "go along," or merely humor the **Alignment** process. If you are inclined to do that, pass. This choice preserves the integrity of the experience for others.[6]

- "Pretend" as needed. That is, try out new ideas about yourself before discarding them.

- Be accountable.

- Avoid storytelling.

- Insist that when you give your support signal, the team members follow through with their support.[7]

## The Personal Alignment Statement

A **PersonalAlignment** statement begins with the words, "I want." The most common and successful **Alignment** statements have the form

*"I want* X,*" or "I want to* X.*"*

where *X* is the virtue or power that you have decided will break through your biggest block.

---

6. If you have the urge to "fit" or "combine" the Alignment process into some other process you have already experienced or change it in some way that makes you more comfortable, then pass. Alignment requires that you pretend that it works as designed.

7. It is common to have to remind a team several times of what they agreed to do to support you. This omission does not indicate a lack of support for you personally, but rather a general lack of accountability in your team culture.

## Align Yourself

The benefits of the **Alignment** pattern begin to flow when you commit to identifying a significant personal goal. The experience of finding out what you want focuses you on finding and removing personal blocks[8] and securing the help of the team.

You must answer the following questions to align yourself:

- What do I want?

- What problems or blocks do I have that prevent me from getting what I want?

- What virtue or power would enable me to remove the blocks?

- Is it possible that the block remover is what I really want? (Without it, I will never get what I want.) If necessary, reconfigure the block remover to become a personal want.

- If you translate a block remover into a want, start over with the first question.

*Personal Blocks.* Personal blocks prevent you from attaining what you want to attain. For example, you might want to be a leader but have a terrible fear of public speaking. This fear of speaking is a first-level block. When applied iteratively, **PersonalAlignment** leads to wants, which lead to blocks, which translate into other wants, which point to other blocks, and so on. Your fear of public speaking, for example, might be uncovered as a fear of rejection, and you might want courage to overcome that fear.

*Finishing Your Personal Alignment.* What removes a block can become translated into a want. The steps in the **PersonalAlignment** protocol outline a way to identify blocks and make block-to-want conversions. Until the lowest-level personal block[9] is reached, **PersonalAlignment** is not finished.

---

8. A *personal block* is typically an inhibitory behavior you practice or a deficiency you suffer. In any case, it is "blocking," standing in your way if you are going to attain your **Alignment**. If no blocks were present, you would have your **Alignment**.

9. At least the lowest-level block that is psychologically available to the alignee during this time. There doesn't seem to be any real end to blocks.

*Alignment depth for a team correlates closely with the quality of the team's products.*

Eventually, no more blocks can be found, and the last block is identified. *The virtue that would eliminate that block is the thing to want. Attaining it becomes the* PersonalAlignment.

# ALIGNMENT DEPTH

**Alignment depth** encompasses the level of blocks and the extent of the blocks themselves. **Alignment** depth for a team correlates closely with the quality of the team's products. This relationship makes sense; any challenge that fully engages you or stresses your character will reveal the same virtues and weaknesses as the most recent challenge of its kind or the next challenge. This relationship holds, whether the challenge is to deliver a great Web site or to do a PersonalAlignment.

## Common Alignments

The following are the most common **Alignments**. This is a partial list, and is not meant to serve as a constraint or a boundary.

*I want:*
Faith
Hope
Passion
Self-awareness
Self-care
Courage
Wisdom
Peace
Maturity
Presence
Joy
To love myself
To value myself
To feel my feelings
To believe in myself
Integrity

Fun

Ease

To accept myself

To be honest with myself

To be patient with myself

## *Faux Alignments*

Although it is difficult to condemn a whole word or phrase to the trash
heap as a faux Alignment, we have found that certain "alignments"
are always indicators of something amiss in the person's understanding either of PersonalAlignment or of the phrase in question. A few of
these could conceivably be reasonable PersonalAlignments under
certain circumstances; even then, a different phrase will do the job
better. The following often masquerade as Alignments:

*I want:*

Confidence

Self-confidence

Self-control

Strength

To solve problems

To listen

To be understood

To understand

Fame

To be rich

To retire

To be the best _____

To not _____

Sanity

Knowledge

Focus

Balance

Patience

Security

All of these faux **Alignments** suffer from at least one of five problems:

- The word/phrase carries meaning that isn't about getting what you want. The meaning may instead be about pleasing others. For example, someone might tell you to "be strong" when you are faced with a loss. You might then tell yourself that you need strength. More likely, you need to focus on your feelings about the loss.

- The word/phrase is ambiguous. Many people think that they want confidence. What precisely is that? It isn't clear, and it is difficult to make clear. Figuring out exactly what you want when you say the word "confidence" will lead to a more specific virtue, such as "courage."

- The word/phrase deals mostly with other people. For example, if you want to understand, or to be patient, you are probably referring to yourself in relation to other people. **Alignment** is limited to what you do for yourself, not for others. You cannot do something for other people that you don't do for yourself. Perhaps if you have trouble understanding others, you really want to understand yourself, which is self-awareness.

- The word/phrase masks some deeper desire or fear. People who state that they want to be rich or famous may really seek something that they fantasize comes from being rich and famous, such as love, wisdom, or courage.

- The word/phrase focuses on a negative quality. **PersonalAlignment** must target a positive quality that is desired.

## ANALYSIS OF PERSONAL ALIGNMENT

*Shallow Alignment poses a challenge for a team if the team ignores its own experience with . . . the depth and sincerity of a given Personal Alignment.*

Shallow **Alignment** poses a challenge for a team if the team ignores its own experience with—and intuition about—the depth and sincerity of a given **PersonalAlignment**. The utility of any given alignee's work is at stake.

You could be stuck[10] on an abstract, impersonal **Alignment** when, for example, as an experienced team member you claim, "I want to improve my effectiveness," or " I want to be a better coder." These goals are not unworthy **Alignments** for someone for whom the achievements would represent breakthrough thinking and doing. For someone who is beyond the fundamentals, however, the challenges they bring are not as richly rewarding. Often, you are unable to perceive the wants that drive you. Even so, if you do not proceed to greater depths, seek more challenging personal ambitions, and fulfill more personal desires, team trust will be eroded and the team's belief in itself can be greatly reduced.[11]

The problem is not that you are a shallow person. With a little help and applied **Receptivity** (discussed later in this chapter), you will doubtless create an admirable **PersonalAlignment**. The problem generally lies with the rest of the team:

- When the team behaves as if it is hearing a deep **Alignment** when it knows it is not
- When it hears things that don't make sense but is incurious
- When it doesn't respond to a shallow **Alignment**
- When it tolerates blather

Team members must be clear with the alignee and with themselves about any discrepancies or dissonance during an **Alignment**.

The **Investigate** pattern will reveal most inconsistencies or circular thinking in any lightweight or confused **Alignment**. The team can point out these problems to the alignee. This type of quality enhancement activity consolidates the team's learning, exercises its ability to offer support, and promotes courage. The discovery of the team's courage and integrity as part of an overall movement toward team alignment begins here. Expect to encounter a wide range of quality with **Alignments**, as with product development efforts or any

*The discovery of the team's courage and integrity as part of an overall movement toward team alignment begins here.*

---

10. *Stuck* describes a pathological, possibly obsessive, attachment to an object or an idea.
11. When someone is (to use the BootCamper's typical phrasing) "way in," and others aren't, the "in" person seems more vulnerable and alone.

other undertaking. It is essential that the team learn how to address these issues. You might perceive a note of dissonance in a low-quality Alignment but not mention it to your teammates. To support the developing trust within the team, be honest about what you hear. Nonjudgmental yet direct and honest expressions will provide motivational power to the alignee. If anything will inspire the individual to seek a greater depth of Alignment that will bring good results, his peers' depth and their candid support will.

When individuals align themselves, the team helps investigate goals and the plans for achieving them. Few are able to articulate what they want without the assistance of the team. The Investigate pattern is the most efficient way to provide genuine help.

Investigate describes the first of two helper roles played by the team. In its second role, the team builds and maintains the Webof Commitment. The alignee receives ongoing support as the team follows the Investigate and WebofCommitment patterns.

Investigate promotes the safety and security of the alignee, maximizes team learning, maintains the flow of relevant information, and helps the alignee finish composing his Alignment in the shortest time possible. As the team works its way through the Personal Alignments, it builds a WebofCommitment, based on the "help contracts" accumulated during its completion of the Alignment protocol. These contracts state that teammates will help one another in specific ways and provide periodic Alignment evidence to one another.[12] Keeping the promises made during Alignment and faithfully supplying public evidence of progress will support the team's new, more interpersonally committed culture.

The WebofCommitment pattern is the resulting context of Alignment. When all team members are aligned, the team is automatically aligned, but it is essential that the Alignments be integrated. Webof Commitment describes effective practices for this integration. The aggregate of the personal goals will be expressed in the team vision.

*Keeping the promises made during Alignment and faithfully supplying public evidence of progress will support the team's new, more interpersonally committed culture.*

---

12. Alignment *evidence* is visible proof that you are getting, or working on getting, what you said you wanted in your PersonalAlignment.

Initially, the team focuses on the PersonalAlignments. As a result of its participation in the Alignments, the group becomes increasingly more connected. This escalation of connection serves as the foundation for team alignment. Whereas PersonalAlignments provide specific assignments that the team can intentionally execute, team alignment is more involuntary, unconscious work.[13] There is little explicit activity associated with it, but this work is absolutely critical.

## HOW AND WHY
## ALIGNMENT WORKS

The revelation and acceptance of all team members' personal motives catalyze the release of boundless team energy into their milieu. This energy enables the team to produce more and makes it much more of a joy to do the work together. Energy flows from person to person, and from person to product. This energy leads the team to the experience described earlier (see Chapter Seven)—
*a team in flow.*

When you reveal what you truly want to your teammates, you always increase your accessibility. You become more admirable in the eyes of your teammates, and the team intensifies its identification with you. Your environment is thereby greatly enriched. Something shifts for you. The effects of PersonalAlignments on the team are felt incrementally, but, about halfway through the Personal Alignments, the bulk of the available human energy typically makes a wholesale shift from potential to kinetic. This shift is fueled by a profound increase in members' accessibility to one another, and in the wholesale increase in intrapersonal identification within the team. The result is dramatic, like a dam bursting. Virtues once contained are now released. They surge through the team, engag-

*The result is dramatic, like a dam bursting. Virtues once contained are now released.*

13. In general, when we use the word "Alignment," we are referring to the more visible piece of this pattern, PersonalAlignment.

ing the members' highest instincts and calling forth their most profound capabilities.

Several forces cooperate to unleash this energy, most notably the solidarity and identity of the team. The team now knows itself and is empowered by the feelings of individual members, which include great relief, increased attraction to one another, and a deepened empathy with one another.

The members of the team both feel these things and think about them. For the first time, the team members are aware of one another's feelings, feel these feelings in unison, and think about them together. The forces are fueled by feedback loops. That is, increased feelings of attraction increase empathy, and vice versa.

## RELIEF

Saying what it is you want—with candor and credibility—creates substantial relief for others. Now your colleagues have a mental road map for you and for how you function. Their awareness of where you would like to go and what you would like to do has given them new capabilities. Now your teammates can explain your actions to themselves. They may also be able to predict your responses. When they observe you behaving inconsistently, they know that they need to investigate you further.

*Saying what it is you want—with candor and credibility—creates substantial relief for others.*

## ATTRACTION

In Alignment, you find out that others want things just as you do. Others are vulnerable in ways that are familiar to you. When you admit that you want something, you are admitting imperfection. The reality of others' inner motivations is more attractive than the superficial personae and misguided "privacies" you had been perpetuating in silent conspiracy with them. In fact, you may have the feelings and thoughts you experience when you have a "crush" on someone. Primarily, however, you feel relief to be with people you find attractive. You enjoy a palpable relaxation and offer a new, more compassionate level of engagement with your colleagues. At last, you have feelings of being among your own kind at work and of "being home."

*The reality of others' inner motivations is more attractive than the superficial personae and misguided "privacies" you had been perpetuating in silent conspiracy with them.*

*Each individual
commits to being that
person who can make
a difference.*

# INSPIRATION

There is more behind the Alignment experience than the whole-some effects of vulnerability. You discover during Alignment, and then disclose to your team, that what you really want is something internal to you. This realization is important for each person on the team. Each team member seems to crave higher quality of character, and is willing to work toward observable improvement in behavior. Each person is, at heart, seeking some virtue that would enrich his life and world.

Central to the Alignment experience is your recognition that the rest of the team wants good things, which will make a positive difference for you, as well as for them. Everyone wants to make a difference. Moreover, each individual commits to being that person who can make a difference. With these realizations and the multiple new points of connection you begin to experience innocence, hope, commitment, and—something everyone hopes and believes will be the foundation of working life—inspiration.

# EMPATHY

As you actively listen and support the continued development of these revelations, your relaxation and comfort intensify. In fact, the predominant feeling among the team members is increasing trust, the source of all relaxation. You start to enjoy the experience. You can finally relate to these people, identify with what they want, and observe them become what they want to be. You feel as they do.

Everyone on the team has lofty goals and nobler concerns. When the fear of colleagues' unspoken agendas diminishes, you empathize with and embrace one another's excellent wants.

*When the fear of
colleagues' unspoken
agendas diminishes,
you empathize with
and embrace one
another's excellent
wants.*

# RESULTS

Sarcasm, irony, and cynicism subside to a more natural, less strident, and more productive level. You'll experience the joy of genuine humor. In fact, humor and laughter will gain a greater share of the team's emotional space. Laughter becomes much more frequent, and it sounds more heartfelt and genuinely joyful. Postures change; shoes come off; people recline. Comfort expands its turf.

Looking for greater relaxation and comfort, team members may notice that their environment is a bit stuffy or otherwise unbeautiful. They spontaneously begin to improve it. They shift furniture and rearrange the décor, buying little things and making bigger ones— all activities devoted to creating greater physical comfort and more beauty for themselves. The effort costs little or nothing. Transcendence over shortage is beginning. "Having fun" emerges as an explicit value. Fun tends to show up where it is valued.

On team after team, the results have been remarkably invariant. Within a matter of hours, the team moves from one level of effectiveness to a much higher one. This shift is obvious and profound. During PersonalAlignment, the team accomplishes in a day or two what years of quality improvement efforts or other team exercises fail to produce.

Team members in this setting become caught up in mutual fascination. They may not take breaks. At BootCamp, they struggle to pay adequate attention to the pressures of the simulated product development they are conducting. They may not take good care of themselves physically. They may not break into subgroups to complete the Alignments more quickly—they don't want to miss a word from anyone. Suddenly the team is the most fascinating thing on earth to its members, and the connections with teammates truly are compelling.

If you are aligned, you experience the comfort of being on a genuinely connected team. You begin to sense the unlimited power of the team, although your full awareness of your power will not reach its zenith until the act of creation—when you make a product together.

You are encouraged—not only by the structured process of PersonalAlignment, but also by the increasing openness of team members to one another. As you show more of your humanity, you find that others are receptive to "the real you." You reduce your defensiveness, freeing additional creative energy. Healthy positive feedback emerges at this point, and members feel increasingly able to reveal additional vital and intimate motivational information.

*On team after team, the results have been remarkably invariant. Within a matter of hours, the team moves from one level of effectiveness to a much higher one.*

*Suddenly the team is the most fascinating thing on earth to its members, and the connections with teammates truly are compelling.*

The most important thing about the initial and ongoing disclosure is not that it is intimate (which it is), but that the information is vital to efficient operation of the team. Usually, information discussed during Alignment happens to be somewhat personal as well as extremely useful. Typically, people keep these things private. This denial strategy is futile, however; it mystifies others without protecting you.

A PersonalAlignment statement is a simple declarative sentence briefly expressing what you want. After Alignment, team members might ask one another, for example, "What was your Alignment?" The phrases "PersonalAlignment," "goal," and "what you want" all map to the objective in a PersonalAlignment statement.

*Alignment may be discussed in many contexts, but it always means the same thing: that everything relevant is "lined up."*

Alignment may be discussed in many contexts, but it always means the same thing: that everything relevant is "lined up." If you are aligned, your thoughts, words, and deeds are congruent, both in your individual context and in the larger team context. They are *aligned*, as in a straight line, the shortest distance between two points. When aligned, you always seek the most efficient attainment of your goals. What you say you want is consistent with how you act. Saying that you want something implies that you are willing to change to get it. Otherwise, you really don't want the thing, and you are not aligned.

## PATTERN: INVESTIGATE

### PROBLEM

*You see others better than you see yourself;*
*but the difficulty of communicating what you see prevents*
*you from exploiting this ability.*

When someone tells you what he sees in you, it is sometimes difficult to hear the scrutiny. If it is something good, you probably laugh it off, interrupt the speaker, or change the subject. If it is a weakness, some way in which you continue to hurt yourself, you may become defensive or angry. Typically, the information is not given to you in a fully supportive way. Sometimes it is called "feedback" and is really unsympathetic criticism. Such criticism is usually poorly intended and thus off the mark.

It is unfortunate that we do not have highly effective, institutionalized methods for teaching and learning how to give and receive information about each other. There is no better source of information about you than people who know you, including individuals who work with you. By using nonspecified, idiosyncratic feedback and other more or less unsupportive techniques for critiquing group members, teams miss out on the extraordinary benefits of sharing critical information about one another.

The ability to see others better than you see yourself has enormous potential for a team. If you could exchange personal information with less turbulence, each team member could exploit the others' superior capacity to see him, and then learn what they see. Each team member could offer this service to the others.

By sharing personal information, teams can see and achieve much more. They can be more lucid. They can create better things, more quickly. Unfortunately, team members generally avoid confronting one another with their differing perceptions.

*It is unfortunate that we do not have highly effective, institutionalized methods for teaching and learning how to give and receive information about each other.*

## SOLUTION

*Inquire into one another as a naïvely curious and nonjudgmental investigator.*

Teams fail to share information effectively—instead, there is too much accusing, teaching, and telling, and very little listening. It is helpful to your teammates if you inquire deeply into their inner workings. Your inquiries are what they need. The answers to these questions lie within the heads and hearts of your teammates. They simply need your support in revealing and clarifying these answers.

*There is too much accusing, teaching, and telling, and very little listening.*

Even when you think you know "what is wrong" with one of your teammates, you really don't. Telling that person or others "what is wrong" with him will only result in cynicism and hurt feelings. If you really want your teammate to grow, support that person. Investigating his motivations and thoughts is one of the most beneficial acts of comradeship possible.

## THE INVESTIGATE PROTOCOL

1. Become a detached but fascinated inquirer.

Imagine that you have just started a compelling inquiry into the motivational structure of an alignee. You are calm and completely detached from the outcome of the investigation. Find out as much as possible about the person's experience in developing a goal without disturbing his progress. You don't need to participate a great deal. You are filled with unfamiliar thoughts triggered by your intense perceptivity. You are happy when your teammate's thoughts, feelings, and ways differ from yours—that is how you learn.

2. Ask only questions that will increase your understanding.

Ask questions to acquire information. Maintain the posture of an interested person, handicapped by ignorance. (See "Intention Check" in Chapter Six.)

3. Don't ask inappropriate questions.

For example, avoid the following types of inquiries:

- Questions that attempt to lead the alignee or that reflect your agenda. This problem can arise when you have strong feelings about the subject.

- Questions that attempt to hide an answer you believe is true.

- Poorly thought-out questions. If you are not aware of your own intention before you ask the question, don't ask it. (See Intention Check.)

- Questions that invite the alignee to wander off into too much analysis or irrelevant material. Questions that begin with "Why" can spur this problem.

4. Use a few formulations for your questions.

Consider using the following forms:

- "What about *X* makes *Y Z*?" For example, "What about your coding makes the experience frustrating?"

- "How does it go when that happens?" "Will you slow down the process and describe it to me?" "Take a specific example and slow it down."

5. Ask questions only if the alignee is engaged and appears ready to learn more.

If your teammate seems to be bored, stubborn, resistant, or going in circles, then stop investigating. The alignee must adhere to the commitments in PersonalAlignment if you are to continue to any good effect. To break up this block, say, "I have a sense that I am pulling information out of you against your will. Let's take some time to think about this issue and talk about it later." You can also just be quiet. (See "Align Me" in Chapter Ten.)

6. Give opinions rarely and only after receiving the alignee's permission.

Stick to your intention of gathering more information. If you have an interesting thought, a good idea, or theory, say, "I have an [ . . . ]. Would you like to hear it?" The alignee can then answer "yes" or "no," or state conditions under which your input would be welcome.

If you feel that you will explode if you can't say what's on your mind, that's a good indication that you shouldn't speak.

7. Never argue during PersonalAlignment.

Arguing distracts you from the task at hand. If you feel yourself becoming combative, check out.

8.   Don't talk to anyone other than the alignee.

Focus your attention on the alignee using the protocol for questions in numbers 1 through 7.

### *When to Use Investigate*

The Investigate protocol is helpful in the following circumstances:

- When an alignee asks for your help with a PersonalAlignment.
- In an Alignment situation, when an alignee has explicitly stated that Investigate questions are welcome.
- In general, when you are learning about a phenomenon, with an eye toward exploiting it.
- When you are working on your own PersonalAlignment.

### *Investigate Commitments*

The following commitments are required of an investigator:

- Intensify your curiosity.
- Widen your Receptivity.
- Ask well-formed questions.
- Set aside your biases toward and prior experiences with the alignee. Observe the alignee with innocence and a fresh perception.
- Accept what the alignee says while at the same time perceiving more than usual.
- Do not tolerate theorizing about the alignee.
- Do not tolerate diagnosis of the alignee.
- Do not tolerate therapy during Alignment.
- Do not tolerate any distraction away from the alignee.
- Use Investigate or CheckOut.
- Do not tolerate AlignMe.

*Examples of Investigative Questions*

What is the one thing you want most from this project?

What blocks you from getting what you want?

If that block were removed, would you get what you want?

Is there some virtue that would enable you to eliminate the block?

What is the biggest problem you see?

What is the most important thing you could do right now?

If you could have anything in the world right now, what would it be?

If you could do anything in the world right now, what would it be?

How does it go when that happens?

Would you explain a specific example?

Would you slow it down into steps?

# PATTERN: RECEPTIVITY

## PROBLEM

———————

*When you feel stress, you assume that something is missing.*

## SOLUTION

———————

*When you feel stress,*
*you are not receiving what's available to you.*

*Adding resources to overcome a perceived shortage is analogous to throwing logs on a fire to smother it.*

*The mother of all shortages (in or out of the high-tech business) is a shortage of Receptivity.*

*In fact, a smart person is not the person who knows the most.*

Engagement increases the value of time in general by increasing the value of each moment. Receptivity is a virtue that evolves and is energized by engagement—a requirement for success. It is the only reliable technique with which to overcome perceived shortages. Adding resources to overcome a perceived shortage is analogous to throwing logs on a fire to smother it. Until you have exhausted your receptive capacity and fully deployed your ability to receive, no real benefit accrues from asking for more resources, because they can't be fully received.

Most resource shortages on a team are genuine shortages; they are just not the shortages you imagine. Usually, the actual shortage isn't people, money, or time. The mother of all shortages (in or out of the high-tech business) is a shortage of Receptivity.[14]

When mediocrity is tolerated because there "aren't enough people" or there "isn't enough time," you can be sure that the qualities of the people on hand are not fully engaged. You can also bet that truly efficient means to apply those qualities have not been brought to bear on the problem.

It is extremely useful for a team to become proficient in Receptivity. To do so requires practice, however. A team's high performance and joy or its waste and misery correlate directly with its degree of Receptivity to the myriad incoming data.

Any investment you make in analyzing what is happening on your team typically brings a manifold return. Many people think being *smart* is the same as *knowing*, as if smartness were something you acquire. Others think that mastering technicalities[15] indicates intelligence. In fact, a smart person is not the person who knows the most. Likewise, a smart person is not someone who retreats into technical gobbledygook (highlighting a deficiency of integrated reasoning and self-expression skills). The smart one is not the authority, someone who did something notable yesterday. Smartness is what you do now.

---

14. The notion of a Receptivity shortage gives us a bootstrapping problem to contemplate: How can you receive the capability to receive?

15. "Technicalities" does not describe technical knowledge that is valued. A technicality is usually a diminution.

The smartest person in any environment is the person who is learning the most from it. If you are paying attention to your immediate environment (the basis of Receptivity), you will find more than enough information, creativity, and energy to achieve the necessary tasks. A receptive person is smart simply because he treats each encounter as if it were infinitely rich and behaves as if the many dimensions of any encounter can supply all of the information he requires.

The smart person is proactively receptive. He adopts an investigative posture with respect to the information-saturated environment. This individual's work is really a quest for more information. You might hear a smart person ask questions of the following forms:

> "Tell me more about . . . ?"
> "What else do you know about that?"
> "What do you think of . . . ?"
> "Will you show me . . . ?"

These questions and others of their ilk are the basic tools employed by any effective product developer. Taking the investigative approach to all phenomena yields enormous supplies of information, generally provided freely by others. The occasional summaries of the smart person's investigations are orderly, simple, and lucid. If an explanation is too complex or, worse yet, too technical for a rational, intelligent person to understand, then the subject of the explanation has not been thoroughly investigated. The investigator is in the beginning stages. Of course, if the person doesn't recognize this fact, he has not gotten very far into the inquiry.

The information is there if you want it. It's just a matter of your willingness to receive it. Transmission, though fun, halts learning to a large degree. When you preach what you already know, you're usually not learning. Consequently, you don't want to enter into a "teaching" or "preaching" position very often. It is most profitable to teach only when someone asks you to do so, which indicates that the listener is in a receptive frame of mind. Occasionally, it is useful to experiment with small teachings to

*The smart person is proactively receptive.*

*Transmission, though fun, halts learning to a large degree.*

*"Why would an otherwise normal human being, a creature who can think, present me with this lame idea?"*

determine a person's Receptivity to you. Only rarely will you teach people who realize that they don't know something important and want to learn. Even if you succeed here, the experience is hardly ever as rewarding for the teacher as it is for the recalcitrant students.

What if someone expresses a lame idea? If you tell yourself, "This guy's a fool," or "That's a stupid idea," what have you received? Nothing. A small pain, a wince, and a living confirmation of the world's uselessness and the tribulations of your job. If you simply tell yourself that you are the smarter person, you might stoke up your ego by a smidgen and feel a bit of pleasure. You gain nothing of value, however. You also incur the cost of adding a new little lump of fat on your already-plump ego. That's not smart.

Alternatively, you could be receptive to the idea. You could investigate this puzzle further. You could ask yourself, "Why would an otherwise normal human being, a creature who can think, present me with this lame idea?"

Now you have posed an interesting question. Through your Receptivity, you have created an opportunity to grow smarter. You have identified something worth pondering. What could this person possibly have been thinking? You can start an investigation into what's going on with that person, the meaning of the idea proposed, and the significance of when the idea was brought to you. Assuming (utilizing Pretend) for a moment that the entire sideshow was for your benefit, why at this moment in your life is the person offering you a lame idea?

What you learn will depend on your Receptivity to information that might ultimately be useful to you, even if it initially causes discomfort. In this case, if you initially rejected the idea, you might consider *that you miss the point much of the time.*

You observe that the lamer (the person with the lame idea) is considered smart and functional enough to work with you, however suspect that distinction. You assume you have judged the idea correctly, at least at the surface level: It was lame.

Because you are smart enough to perceive the lameness of ideas generated by people judged smart enough to work with you, you can also see that your colleague could have recognized, if he so desired, that you would probably reject the idea. As people rarely offer ideas simply for the purpose of having them be rejected, something else is afoot. Either you must be wrong about the quality of the idea or something less obvious must have been behind the lamer's expression of the idea. Perhaps you might look at the situation this way: Your coworker was not really offering a lame idea, but instead expressing something (indirectly or incoherently,[16] though he may or may not be aware of it). In this light, you rethink the idea, just to double-check. No, the idea was, in fact, lame. You realize now that you wish it weren't a lame idea. You conclude:

> *At least one person believes that low-quality thinking and wasting your bandwidth with lame ideas is acceptable.*

Of course, the lamer could be a sage in disguise, analogous to the court fools of olden days. If so, perhaps he is trying to draw your attention to this time-wasting situation. Probably not, however. You decide to veto the sage theory, but file the idea away.

Late on a sleepless night, you might consider a new question: What if the lamer and others were trying to teach you? Perhaps they had to be inexplicit because of your defensive posture. As a result of this experience, you must ask yourself, "If the people around me believe that there is no cost to me or anyone else if they cause me to spend my time with no gain, how did they reach this conclusion?" Could they see that you don't have much faith in yourself?

It must be true. You tell others that your time doesn't matter when you don't create restrictions about how you let others spend it. If your time doesn't matter, then your life doesn't matter. If your life doesn't matter enough to you, it surely won't matter to others. After all, you are the closest to the situation, and best able to judge it. You know that you have wonderful ideas and a variety of accomplishments, but you begin to see that you aren't doing very much now with who you are or creating who you want to be. This situation

*You tell others that your time doesn't matter when you don't create restrictions about how you let others spend it.*

---

16. This incoherence may be overstated. The lamer's words and intention are incoherent, but there is little doubt that the context of this lame idea contains a message to you, whether you receive it or not.

*With minimal investigation into any problem, you will find—if not all of the answers—more or creatively richer approaches.*

could arise only if you had given up on yourself and stopped believing in the truth of what you see and feel. You no longer are in awe of the limitlessness of your own mental ability and the richness of your world, teeming with ideas and imaginative events, both large and small. It appears that you have stopped believing in that promise.

You begin to wonder if you are even awake.

Perhaps depression has been creeping up on you.

This scenario depicts one path that you might follow. In this example, you were unaware of your problem until you began thinking about what was otherwise a trivial, or at least commonplace, event. When a problem must be solved, assume that the answers are present in the information at hand.

With minimal investigation into any problem, you will find—if not all of the answers—more or creatively richer approaches. Those solutions should be the only ones that you can reach in the moment. If you are present enough, engaged enough, and of a sufficiently receptive frame of mind, just check in with yourself and expect the moment to hold something for you. You will soon discover why you haven't been shipping on time or why the product isn't as good as you know you can make it.

**Receptivity** counts. The breadth, depth, and height of the world's availability are not distractions. They are your resources. Applying these resources effectively is your goal.

Another kind of **Receptivity** occurs in programming, or other computer-mediated creative tasks. During arduous and prolonged debugging, when the bug is finally found and squashed, you suddenly realize: "Gosh, that's why that was there!" An artifact that had been present all along held the information that would have led you to the bug. For some reason, however, you had dismissed this artifact as not useful to your debugging.

This type of omission is common in problem solving. When the solution materializes, you see all of the clues that you had previously missed or misread, but that are now painfully obvious. These items are usually things perceived but paid little attention to when you first noticed them—you didn't think they were relevant. Small things—like a person giving you a lame idea. When it makes no difference, when you have exhausted yourself and arrived by brute force at your demon bug, all at once you see the meaning of those annoying little symptoms you had dismissed as unrelated to the "real" problem. They were unworthy of investigative effort because you already "understood" them and had accounted for them in a theory of things that hadn't really been thought through anew. More Receptivity could have revealed the one missing idea. Before the solution was found, you kept looking at it and ignoring it, while it was screaming, "Hey you! Look at me! I'm the bug!"

Receptivity. Data are coming at you—all that you need. Just reach out. Put out your sensors and fill 'em up.

*Before the solution was found, you kept looking at it and ignoring it, while it was screaming, "Hey you! Look at me! I'm the bug!"*

# PATTERN: WEB OF COMMITMENT

## PROBLEM

*It's difficult to know what you want and even more problematic to ask others for help.*

When you *do* know what you want, getting it becomes easier. Unfortunately, many people are likely to backslide in their persistence or the quality of their attempts. This problem occurs because they still must deal with the issue that has blocked them from getting what they want. They need help from others.

The most valuable asset for a team that wants to create great intellectual property is integrity. This is particularly true when meeting deadlines. Being late is always the result of disintegration. You say you'll be done at a certain time but you fail to meet your schedule. When teams are late, the problem doesn't just happen in one moment. Lateness is the product of months, maybe years, of broken commitments and acts of disintegration.

*Lateness is the product of months, maybe years, of broken commitments and acts of disintegration.*

Disintegration touches every part of the team and has a negative effect on everything, not just timeliness. Lack of integrity results in lack of passion, lack of effectiveness, and lack of quality. Lack of integrity represents a system crisis for a team.

Teamwork consists of nothing more than a set of handshakes or commitments and a few predefined interfaces. A commitment is a type of integrity interface. Teamwork happens when you connect with your teammates. The quality of your teamwork will, therefore, reflect the quality of the handshakes. Do the handshakes have integrity? Are the deals kept? Are deeds and words aligned? If a team doesn't honor its commitments, it won't create great software.

## SOLUTION

---

*Create a structure within your team that will help you get*
*what you want.*

Many processes such as Alignment evolved at BootCamp. WebofCommitment evolved over many BootCamps and is built from AskforHelp and PersonalAlignment. After escorting several teams through the PersonalAlignment process, we realized that Alignment was exponentially more effective when the team supported each PersonalAlignment, which most members spontaneously did, anyway. An alignee must commit to his own PersonalAlignment, but the team should commit its support as well. That way, everyone is much more likely to get what he wants.

An obvious avenue for creating this team involvement is to have each alignee ask the team for help. Once the team agrees to provide that assistance, commitment to a PersonalAlignment statement is multilateral. Each person's Alignment is supported by the entire team, first by the observable and self-predicted behavior of the alignee, and then by the rest of the team's fulfillment of its promises of support.

The disclosure of individual wants, their virtually universal attractiveness, and the determination and commitment among all team members to help each other attain what they most want creates a beautiful conceptual structure. One BootCamp team, for example, dramatized its Alignments and mutual exchange of commitments to help one another by memorializing this conceptual structure physically. What emerged through this ritual were the incredible synergistic powers of uniform PersonalAlignments. The team members dramatized the dynamics of what happens to the team when the promise of Alignment is fulfilled.

They demonstrated the relations of their Alignments to one another by sitting in a circle and throwing a ball of string to their teammates in turns, stating their PersonalAlignment, then throwing the ball of string to someone to whom they were especially connected, while simultaneously holding on to the string. For example:

> *"I want courage," starts Joe (his Alignment). "When I try to be courageous, I will signal you by first saying, "This is scary for me, but . . ."* Joe *then wraps the string around himself and throws it to Mary.*
>
> *Mary catches the string and says, "I will help you have courage, Joe, by applauding the courage (her commitment) you show after you say, "This is scary for me, but . . ."*
>
> *Mary then continues, "When Joe has courage, I find it easier to be passionate (her Alignment). I will show my passion by shouting, 'Woo-hoo!' when I think something is really cool." She throws the string to Bill.*
>
> *Bill says, "When you shout 'Woo-hoo,' Mary, I'll do it, too. When Mary has passion, I am willing to lead."*
>
> *And so on.*

The string was wrapped around each person before being tossed to the next. At the end, you could see the physical web—the WebofCommitment was born. The WebofCommitment consists of the actions a team takes to complete its team alignment. This interweaving of the products of PersonalAlignment signals completion and connection.

A team that has established its web is more efficient. If a team member is struggling, the problem is almost certainly related to his Alignment. Other team members need only gently ask, "What's

*Anyone could
approach any other
person who is
demonstrating strange
behavior and ask,
"What are you
working on?"*

your Alignment again?" to reset the PersonalAlignment work. This process has a healing, safe, and supportive effect. The alignee will say, "Oh, right!" and proceed to demonstrate more aligned behavior.

Imagine a world where everyone understood this language. Anyone could approach any other person who is demonstrating strange behavior and ask, "What are you working on?" to invoke memories of safety and connectedness in that person. We take this step on our team and with BootCamp alumni all the time.

The WebofCommitment is constructed by the team. Each person contributes to this web:

- When the individual contributes a PersonalAlignment statement, he adds one goal to the body of team goals.

- When the individual asks for specific help and receives commitments to provide that help, he contributes multiple Alignment contracts.

- When the individual commits to specific behaviors that will alert the team that he is working on, has obtained, or is closer to obtaining the PersonalAlignment goal, he contributes written contracts to act with integrity regarding what he claims to want.

- When the individual commits to providing others with the help they request to achieve the goals of their Alignments, he contributes written responsibilities to others' Alignment contracts.

The resulting WebofCommitment should be tangible, of artistic integrity, and on continuous display—perhaps in a large team-created painting. A team ceremony should be held to celebrate the importance of each individual PersonalAlignment, to recognize the WebofCommitment, and to highlight the completion of this work and the achievement of team alignment.

The work of SharedVision immediately follows the completion of Alignment. If the SharedVision work is complete, it can be included in the art and ceremony associated with the completion of WebofCommitment.

# THE WEB OF COMMITMENT PROTOCOL

The WebofCommitment protocol has four steps:

1. Each alignee should create a list that includes the following:

   - A PersonalAlignment statement

   - Positive, measurable evidence—both short-term and long-term—that will show he is getting what he wants

   - Support commitments from his team in the form of (1) a specific positive signal he gives to his team and (2) a specific positive show of support his teammates give to him

2. Post the list in a public place—on a bulletin board, as a poster, or in an e-mail.

3. Conduct a ceremony for the entire team to do the following:

   - Highlight each PersonalAlignment

   - Bring the PersonalAlignment process to a close (optional)

   - Celebrate the team alignment

4. Keep your commitments to one another, and track whether commitments are kept. Renew all elements as needed.

It is difficult to identify the help you need from the team. Start by asking your teammates if they support you in making the proposed change. Suppose you want to care for yourself. You usually spend your energy caring for others, which is causing problems. You might decide that the action the team will see that shows change is that you will say "no" when appropriate. The help you could ask for is, "Will you support me in saying 'no'?"

To make this change more specific, you could ask that each time you say "no" to a team member, he will say, "Good job saying 'no.'"

To make this change exclusive to the team, you could request a simple physical gesture as a way for teammates to acknowledge that they see that you are working on your goals. Often, this show of understanding and support is sufficient for the alignee.

*It is not the job of team members to correct you constantly so as to keep you behaving with integrity.*

The most common mistake made in asking for help with PersonalAlignment is to ask others to support something negative about your behavior. For example, you might ask, "Will you tell me to shut up when I am not listening?" or "Will you ask me how I feel when I am zoning out?" In other words, "If I am doing the old behavior that I don't want to do anymore, will you tell me to stop?" These requests leave the responsibility for correcting behavior up to the team members.

Such choices miss the point of PersonalAlignment and WebofCommitment. It is up to you to act with integrity with respect to your PersonalAlignment. It is not the job of team members to correct you constantly so as to keep you behaving with integrity. The purpose of the WebofCommitment is to create a supportive structure for the new behaviors, not to fight the onset of old behaviors.

We must remind nearly all of our clients and students to ask for positive help during PersonalAlignments. Focusing on old behaviors and giving responsibility to others can prove very seductive.

When you are unsure about what to request, simply ask for support. "Do you support me doing $X$ when $Y$ and $Z$?" It's more creative, fun, and supportive to think of something others can do for you that feels rewarding and positive—like a present to you for behaving with courage. In fact, it is best to do something that feels like "going overboard." It may feel like "too much" to ask others to cheer you on or compliment you, even though the request seems perfectly acceptable to them. You have simply been depriving yourself of good things to this point. Push the limits. Let others show their support of your goodness.

Signal others, "Now is the time to do $X$." If you ask teammates to compliment you on showing your passion three times a day, you're handing over a lot of responsibility for your Alignment to them. You must take responsibility for your Alignment by initiating the response. You could ask, "When I say, 'I'm going to show passion now,' will you applaud?"

Finally, it is important that you make sure that others give you what they promised. Too often, alignees obtain their team's agreement to show support, but when the time comes and the rest of the team forgets or becomes distracted, the alignees accept that situation. Tolerating it, they insist on it. Alignees behave as if they are looking for evidence that they didn't deserve the support. This behavior is unacceptable on a team that wants to be great. If your team members agree to support you in some fashion based on a signal that you give, *make sure they follow through*. If you don't, you support mediocrity and broken commitments. In every case we have seen, the team is just distracted, not averse to the agreement. The team members simply need you to care enough to remind them to keep their promises. Being great means not accepting the old way of doing things. Being great requires that you act intentionally, changing your behavior after thinking about the ideal ways to behave, and then following through with courage.

Remember that "the old way" was not about being on a team, but rather focused on being a lonely individual among other lonely individuals just trying to survive. To change the way you personally work, you must decide to behave differently from day to day, and from moment to moment. This effort may seem silly when you describe it aloud, but it takes a lot of work and intention to take advantage of all a team has to offer. It takes work to let yourself get and feel support, and to behave as if you and the work you do matter.

*Being great means not accepting the old way of doing things.*

*"The old way" was not about being on a team, but rather focused on being a lonely individual among other lonely individuals just trying to survive.*

## PATTERN: ASK FOR HELP

### PROBLEM

*You act as if help wouldn't help.*

Three behaviors characterize the best teams:

- They routinely ask for help.
- They establish and maintain high levels of interpersonal connection among their members.
- They live in a state of SharedVision.

The most critical of these behaviors is *asking for help*. Indeed, this act catalyzes connection and SharedVision. Failing to ask for help— failing to *continuously* ask for help—is at least a waste of potential. While seeking help always leads to more efficiency and greater freedom, failing to ask for help always leads to inefficiency and constriction. After all, the biggest resource available to all team members (and the resource most underutilized by them) is the capability of other team members and of other people who would be willing to help, if asked.

When you don't want to learn something, you usually don't. This case holds

- No matter how many teachers or other authorities insist that you ought to learn, and

- No matter to what lengths others go to offer you help.

*As the help being offered becomes more valuable to the putative recipient, that individual's lack of genuine acceptance becomes more vivid.*

As a helper, you can be assured that, if someone doesn't ask for help, that person won't truly accept the help that is offered.[17] This phenomena gains visibility in proportion to the criticality of the issue at hand. In other words, as the help being offered becomes more valuable to the putative recipient, that individual's lack of genuine acceptance becomes more vivid.[18]

In the very first hour of our BootCamp course, we give a little speech. We say the following to the attendees:

> *Ask us for help. After all, we do know how to do BootCamp. We've done it, and watched it be done, over and over and over again. Moreover, we generally won't interject what we know because that won't work. If you want to know what we know or get our help in some other way, you must ask.*

---

17. In the case that a person wants to be rescued, an offer of the help for which the person was secretly "wishing" will probably be accepted. The important aspect of this transaction is that the "victim" who needs help and doesn't ask isn't necessarily getting help by being rescued. He is probably receiving some affirmation that "wishing" for help is more effective than asking for it.

18. Consider, for example, telling a friend that he should stop smoking because of the long-term deleterious effects on his health. This effort is hopeless, even if withering argumentation and irrefutable evidence are cogently presented.

BootCampers generally ignore this statement. They start holding frustratingly circular meetings and building schedules and plans that are empty of content.

It takes at least one meeting with the manager characters[19] we play before students begin asking for help. Why do the campers ask then? Because the managers ask them, "Have you gotten enough help from those consultants (that is, us in a different role) we hired?" The answer is always "no" or an easily uncovered lie. So the managers usually leave the meeting with an agreement from the Boot-Camp team that they will ask for help and send a memo to the managers once they have done so.

Students then utilize the AskforHelp pattern and begin moving along quickly to a SharedVision. Every time they get help, they realize great results. But it always takes repeated nudging from the managers before the BootCamp team will request help on significant team difficulties. It takes a lot of pressure to persuade the team members to do something so obvious, something that works really well, time after time, and something with virtually no downside risk.

Modern culture emphasizes the need to go it alone, to be strong, not to need anyone. This tendency may result from bad decisions people make as they go along in life. Perhaps when you have made yourself vulnerable by asking for help, you were hurt in the process. A common conclusion from this experience is, "I won't get help from anyone in the future." It sounds like a kid holding his breath—like hurt feelings without a mature outlet.

## SOLUTION

*Use each other as a resource.*

Materially, the cost of seeking help is small, even negligible. Given the nearly universal neglect of the limitless help-seeking

---

19. These manager characters are called Black Hats. See Appendix A, which provides the BootCamp materials.

*"Have you gotten enough help from those consultants . . . we hired?" The answer is always "no" or an easily uncovered lie.*

*Asking for help—and then securing it—is also one of the most rewarding efforts any person can make on a project.*

opportunities that are always available, however, it must be admitted that the psychological cost of this endeavor is high. Nevertheless, our experience and observations suggest that the act of asking for help is one of the safest investments of effort possible. Asking for help—and then securing it—is also one of the most rewarding efforts any person can make on a project.

The effectiveness of asking for help is contingent on your use of a simple, direct, and highly specific protocol called AskforHelp.

## THE ASK FOR HELP PROTOCOL

The AskforHelp protocol involves two roles: an asker and a helper.

### Asker Role

When you are the asker, you must inaugurate the help transaction, as follows:

1. State some form of the following question to your intended helpers: "[Name of the person you are soliciting],[20] will you help me [verb] [object being created, goal being reached, and so on] . . . ?"

2. If you have a specific activity or activities you desire from the helper, and especially if these are the only activities you are willing to accept, express these specifics before encouraging the would-be helper to answer your request.

3. You must always shape your help request (as in steps 1 and 2) so that you ask a question that begins "Will you . . . ?"

4. After asking for help with a Core-legal question, say nothing until your question is answered.[21]

---

20. If any possible ambiguity exists regarding the identity of your intended helper.

21. Unless the helper begins blathering, changing the subject, or otherwise avoiding a simple "yes" or "no." In such a case, interrupt and implement AskforHelp again (return to step 1).

*Helper Role*

When addressed directly and properly with a request for help, focus your full attention on the asker. There are only four legal responses to a valid **AskforHelp** request:

1. If you are unable to fully engage with the asker on the request for help, immediately say, "[Name of asker], I can't discuss this request right now." Then, if possible, arrange a mutually convenient time to discuss the issue.

2. If, after focusing your attention on the asker and listening to the request, you don't want to carry out (or even further discuss) the request, tell the asker, "No, I won't do that," or simply "No." Then say nothing else.[22]

3. If you are willing to help with or willing to discuss the request, but need more information about the request, its purpose, or any specifics, ask, "Will you tell me more about the specifics of what you require?" You can then ask questions about the request to get the information you need. Once you understand the specifics, then answer "yes" or "no," which ends the protocol. Otherwise, go to step 4.

4. If you want to offer help, but believe that you cannot or should not give the help requested, decline the request explicitly before proceeding further. Answer something like "No, I won't. But I will [state the thing you think would be more helpful]. Would that be helpful to you?"[23]

---

22. When saying "no," the urge to explain yourself is a rescue. Typically the motivation to rescue is a mistaken belief that you are bad or deficient in some way if you don't do everything you are asked.

23. For instance, if a five-year-old asks you to tie his shoe for him, you might decide that it would be more helpful to support the child while he tries to do it himself. Frequently, the help offered is far more helpful than the help requested.

## Asker Commitments

The following commitments are required of the asker:

1. Have a clear intention. A person who is aware of his desire for help may often misstate this intention to secure help and somehow induce in the helper the urge to rescue the asker. (A rescue occurs when help is offered but not explicitly requested.) Examples include the following:

   > "I could use a little help."
   > "I need . . ."
   > "If I had some help . . ."
   > "I want help here."
   > "Help!"

2. Be utterly clear, in your own mind and in your request, that you are the asker—the supplicant in the help transaction. This recognition is important to the helper because your asking must be freely offered, the helper must perceive that you know that he can decline the request, and the transaction must carry no penalty to the helper if he does decline.[24]

3. State the specifics, if any, of your request.

4. Assume that the person from whom you're requesting help accepts the responsibility to say "no." That is, don't excuse your failure to ask for help by claiming responsibility for determining others' limits.

5. Don't apologize or otherwise obscure your intention.

6. Accept "no" without any additional internal or external emotional drama.[25, 26]

---

24. Otherwise, you aren't really *asking* for help. You are *demanding* help.

25. Strong feelings may arise when a well-formed request for help is declined. Remember, there is no a priori obligation to help you for anyone, except, perhaps, your parents.

26. Treat a "no" as if the person deserves your appreciation and respect. In this case, the helper had the courage to tell the truth. This response is much better than a helper who says "yes" but really wants to say "no."

7. Accept the help offered as completely as possible. If you don't understand the value of what is offered, feel that it wouldn't be useful, or believe that you have already considered and rejected the idea offered, assume a curious stance instead of executing a knee-jerk, "But . . ." rejection. (See this chapter's earlier discussion of Investigate.)

8. Ask for something positive.

9. Accept genuine help.[27]

## *Helper Commitments*

The helper must make the following commitments:

1. To say "no" when you don't want to help, or even when you aren't sure you want to help

2. To say you have changed your mind and don't want to help if you begin to help and decide that you really don't want to do so

3. To fulfill completely any of your commitments to help

4. To say "no" without drama or rancor or soliciting approval from the asker

5. To offer what you believe is truly helpful if you have something that you believe would be useful to the asker, even if it is not exactly what he originally requested.

## *Common Questions About Asking for Help*

There are five common questions about asking for help.

- What are the hours for help? What if I'm bothering somebody by asking for assistance?

---

27. In some cases you might implement AskforHelp and then reject what is offered because it isn't what you wanted to hear. To get results, it is important to take help if it is truly helpful, even if it wasn't your idea of what the help should look like. This response is the same as your CheckIn commitment to always support the best idea.

You should use AskforHelp in anticipation of needing it. That is, help is always good. Help in a time of trouble is, in part, a failure to ask for help. The helper can always say "no."

- What if I don't feel I need help?

Waiting on the feeling of "needing help" merely guarantees that you will wait too long. In general, everything you think you know about seeking help is wrong. Many times, you don't realize that you could benefit from help because you need it so much.

- What if I don't know where I need help?

Knowing that you desire help provides the grounds to seek it. Try saying, "I don't know exactly where I need help, but I am sure that you could help me with something," or "Would you investigate me?"[28]

- Who should I ask for help?

*Almost everyone has had the experience of talking to someone about a technical problem that the listener knew nothing about and having that connection be helpful.*

Help is not really about soliciting expertise, though it may include that task. Rather, it focuses on connecting with another person and articulating your hopes and fears. Almost everyone has had the experience of talking to someone about a technical problem that the listener knew nothing about and having that connection be helpful. It is helpful because you connect with the other person, not because the other person necessarily has "the answer."

In general, use your best thinking and intuition to determine who to ask. Ask yourself to whom you should turn if you want to get the most results in the long term.

---

28. In the case that the person you are asking knows the Investigate protocol.

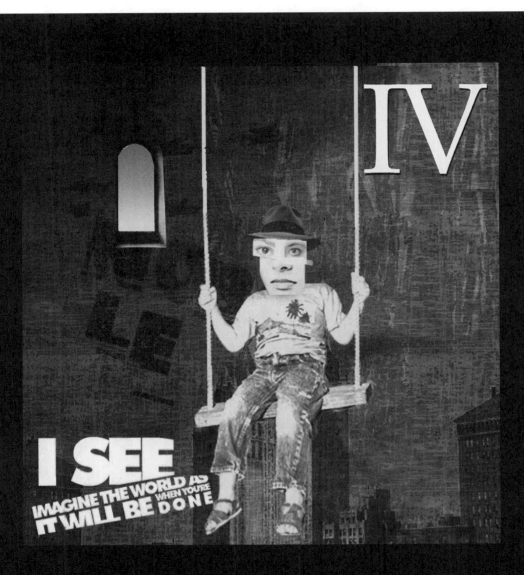

*Imagine the world as it will be*

*when you're done.*

# IV

# Shared
# Vision

NOBILITY OF PURPOSE,

THE PURPOSE OF WORK

*"I see."*

*Geez, you think. That* **Alignment** *stuff was hard. But when we got it done, it truly rocked this team. In a good way. The people are now living in a more or less continuously checked-in state. They are also just sucking up the feeling of emancipation that comes with their ability to act independently and efficiently (now with quick, incisive strokes, and unanimous to boot!). And they are clearly profiting from the power of their completed* **Alignments**. *If ever a team could prepare for one, this team is really ready for the creation of a* **SharedVision**.

*You wonder: Most of the work required to achieve a* **SharedVision** *has already been done. Although the original mission, the reason we went on this retreat, has not even been addressed yet! Still, the team has made progress. . . . Hell, maybe it indirectly contributes more toward fulfilling the product design and development responsibilities than anything else. And we've tried damn near everything else over the years.*

*The team's chaotic birthing stuff, for the most part, seems to have passed. Those pointless and lengthy arguments, the quiet ones hiding out with their unexpressed but pertinent perceptions, the leaky, repressed emotions, and the unending, wandering discussions—all seem to have shrunk from major hindrances to sporadic and minor annoyances. Team members' resistance to good new ideas is way low. Seems like maybe they're—we're, you think, having started to vote yourself—maybe we're experiencing our first real, hearty draught of life in an* **EcologyofIdeas**. *For once, everybody seems to get the value of listening fully to all ideas, whatever their source.*

*Until a team reaches this plateau—man, it does feel good—it's hard to see how truly effective development practices are possible. Without this con-*

*nection, this engagement, no team can show the kind of hyperefficiency that is possible. But how are we gonna take it back? you wonder. Those grossly inefficient team behaviors "in the real world," maybe they're just what happens when you rush an immature team to production. When a team attempts to leap straight from introductions to critical production, it's almost certainly going to yield crummy products, and they'll cost more, too. Now a team that invests a few days in its own development, you think, presuming it's real development, like this, that team can really cook.*

*Since* **Alignment** *and* **WebofCommitment***, a major, major improvement in team (what?)—team maturation—has happened. What caused that, you wonder. Several factors come to mind.*

- *The team has successfully conducted its own* **Alignment***.*

*Until a team has worked through its initial* **Alignment***, you can see that it is really more of a loosely structured, marginally cooperative federation of undefined interests. It's not a focused, product-generating machine like the team is going to be.[1] Hell, all those teams you've been on, the members were ready to bolt at the first hint of any seemingly better situation. Product design and implementation decisions somehow make their way through those old kinds of teams, but they lack unanimity of purpose, unity of means. After passing through* **Alignment***, however, this team "bonding" or whatever the feel-good word is, is way more solid, secure.*

- *This team wants to—can't wait to—express its newly explicit values.*

*And another thing: It seems like all the virtues the team requires for its creative work have been identified as de facto values. These values, in turn, showed up in the most common* **Alignment***s, and/or they were plenty referenced in various* **Alignment** *statements. More important, you suddenly realize, the team values—the things people want—have been explicitly, intentionally practiced during the process of* **Alignment***. Key definitions*

---

1. A team is not really civilized until it has finished an **Alignment** cycle. In BootCamp, teaching an unaligned team the finer points of collaborative intimacy, **SharedVision**, or an efficient development technique is almost impossible. The teaching difficulty reflects the typical high-tech team's barbarous "listening" style. This style is characterized by continuous argumentation, rejection as a condition of discourse, and judgment preceding acquisition of information. In short, the team members are uncivilized.

*have been put out there, and lots of experiments have been conducted. The goodness of early practice (although some of it was pretty extreme and amateurish), simply the idea of practicing what you need to get good at, and with plenty of individual actions behind it, has really been made vivid. There are a lot of people thinking about that, in fact, and it's kind of engaging the whole cognitive layer of the team.*

*It's like some of the team members become identified with, or maybe even "owners" of, specific team values. How'd that happen? Maybe, you think, maybe it's because you publicly commit to work on a given virtue as a part of your* **Alignment**. *Everybody knows you're working on it, and you're acutely aware of this desired quality, so you're going to be sensitive to its violation, and you're also going to be aware of actions that will highlight it. This is just the richest interpersonal infrastructure you could imagine. So rich that if anybody, the owner or whoever, really cares about a virtue, he feels perfectly free to challenge or reward—whichever seems right—those who connect with his pet virtue.*

*Here's another thing: This team has developed to a point very near (or even at) self-sufficiency.*

*Generally, you bet, even teams like this need to connect to one or more other like-minded teams—just to get enough outside stimulus. You still wanna import new energy and genes and things. It can just be encouragement, validation, or a challenge to the team regarding its values. Whatever. But you can't really go it alone, even as a team.*

*And another thing: This team is generating its own unique, high-bandwidth communications system. Really. New words, special myths, special signals and responses. A whole culture.*

*And the commitment structure. A richer, bidirectional, team/individual commitment structure has been developing. The central thing here is the high level of personal accountability. No stories. You know, it's amazing: Simply because each team member has revealed what he wants and has committed to achieving it (with the others' help), each and every one of us can be held accountable to behave as if we want what we say we want. Either that, or we have to change what we say we want, and then behave as if we truly wanted that new thing. But there's no real escape. Once it's what you really want, there ain't no more hiding.*

As a result of all this disclosure and commitment, life on this team is feeling much more comfortable. But also more serious. It is more comfortable because there is infinitely less pretense, posturing, and time wasting. It is more serious for each of us, because each is attempting to achieve exactly what he wants to achieve.

In the past, at some level, on those earlier teams, or even this one, all the team members were probably trying to get what they wanted. But now, no more privately trying: After each team member has publicly identified personal goals and acquired the true riches of the team's help, the likelihood that he will get what he wants has increased beaucoup. Big time.

There is also more than a little bit of new charge to things for now. In the past, we could postpone, whine, blame, wait, cry, or do whatever we needed to do to marginalize achieving our own goals. Now, you think, now, if someone doesn't get what he wants, that individual fails in front of the team.

Plus, you think, there's something to all this help stuff. In helping one another achieve **Alignment**, team members metamorphosed into a much more grown-up, much more mature kind of entity, where loyalties are much more pronounced and empathy toward one another is more genuine. There's a true feeling of concern—and its corresponding supportive behavior—that replaces the rescuing, and the stilted, fakey, empathy-show seen in the early dynamics.

This team, having come through the **Alignment** process, also becomes a much more attractive asset to its members. Individuals now see—hell, you think, I now see—the value of continuing this team experience, the rarity, the power. So what if some job offer comes along.

# TWELVE

# The Elements of Shared Vision

The three major team development phases are now complete: increased presence and connection (CheckIn), unanimity in action (Decider), and personal and team alignment (Alignment). The team is now formed. Most likely, the team members share the same view of the nature of the team and the nature of teamwork itself. This common point of view, which seems almost palpable to the team, has not yet been articulated, however.

What is a SharedVision if it doesn't result in—or come from—a common point of view? Note that SharedVision is not a statement or a goal, but rather an existential phenomenon—a state of being a mature team that is intentionally attained. The SharedVision pattern describes how to accomplish this "multipersonal" state.

In The Core, SharedVision is an overarching pattern that describes the application of the team's collective imagination to the problem of formulating a group intention. This intention provides an "architecture of purpose" that will support the realization of

*SharedVision is not a statement or a goal, but rather an existential phenomenon—a state of being a mature team that is intentionally attained.*

that intention over time. The SharedVision pattern has several effects:

- It provides the context for the ongoing application of the team's PersonalAlignments.
- It supports both long- and short-term team objectives.
- It defines a lexicon for the elements of contemporary team vision building.
- It describes protocols for efficient, high-quality vision building.
- It enables the creation of meaningful vision statements.

The SharedVision pattern integrates the essential components of vision. It represents the intersection of all vision-related elements in The Core. As a consequence, this pattern is tightly coupled with the following patterns:

- Metavision: the vision of visions
- FarVision: an imaginary picture of the world as it will be when the team finishes its work
- Version: a sequence of discrete product visions and product releases, each of which represents a step toward the realization of the FarVision

The SharedVision pattern also depends on the CheckIn, Decider, and Alignment patterns.

Experiencing SharedVision and articulating a vision statement always signal the start of a team's intentional creation of products. This result is the first fruit of a team—a promise of things to come.

*Recoil is liberally mixed up with the benefits of any new hope you may discover.*

If you are a member of a team in a state of SharedVision, you will also likely suffer from Recoil, a distressing syndrome that is felt most acutely immediately after you have experienced a genuine connection to your own and your team's true power and potential for greatness. Recoil is liberally mixed up with the benefits of any new hope you may discover.

You will also seek a means to rapidly improve all you touch and do on your team. Your vision, and the hope that comes with it, will fade if the team members tolerate mediocrity. The inadequacy of contemporary Feedback, one common set of undesirable practices in contemporary life, will become apparent. Fortunately, the pleasures and the deep efficacy of the PerfectionGame will offer a genuine solution to the devilish problems associated with aggregating the desirable and purging the mundane outputs of your team.

# ASPECTS OF SHARED VISION

*A development team driven by a SharedVision is rare.* Although many specific reasons can explain this rarity, the frequency of SharedVision on teams is generally governed by prevailing beliefs about proper modalities for team-based creative collaborations. Namely, it is typically deemed acceptable to proceed to collaborate without the collaborators sharing any vision. A person insisting that something called "shared vision" must first be in place would likely be viewed as iconoclastic.

*In most intellectual property creation efforts, a team has been directed to make a product together.* The members of an institutionally sponsored team, who must coexist with one another professionally, share accountability for creating a product to meet the needs of their sponsoring institution.

*The people on the team come from various backgrounds and will—by both disposition and job assignment—play various functional roles.* In the high-tech world, the team members will have different titles: engineers, programmers, and product developers; test developers and quality assurance engineers; webmasters and web developers; database programmers, database administrators, and database architects; and program, product, project, and process managers. There are also producers (at associate, executive, senior, and junior levels); sundry "creatives," such as artists, musicians, audio engineers, and animators; members of the technical staff, system architects, product designers, and technical writers; technical communicators; product, line, and family marketers; marketing communicators, public relations and advertising marketers; user interface designers and designers of every shade and hue; and system, application, and

*Most people tend to give too much credence to the purported differences among people and not to their similarities.*

maintenance engineers. Naturally, to top it all off, there are the leads, supervisors, managers, general managers, and executives.[1]

All of these classes of people (and, no doubt, uncounted other classes) are considered to be **developers**. That one developer actually writes some machine-oriented code or assembles some bits and snippets in a particular way, while another developer writes no code, and assembles nothing, is irrelevant for our purposes. That one developer crafts a message, while another creates the product that makes the message credible, and a third checks the integrity of both of the other developers, is really a minor difference. All of these team members are developers, because each is developing some element of the product.

Most people tend to give too much credence to the purported differences among people and not to their similarities. Each developer can have a tremendous influence on the product and on the rest of the team. Each can introduce critical defects, or set a team spinning fruitlessly. Each can increase the product quality immeasurably, or help bring a laserlike focus to the team's commonly chaotic energy.

In addition to the incredible range of designations and the wide variety of functional specialties, the members of development teams bring diverse educational backgrounds to the task at hand. There are computer scientists, electrical engineers, and graduates of other types of hard and soft science. There are liberal arts graduates from history, sociology, and psychology, as well as members of the fine arts cadre—practitioners and scholars from theater, media, and music. There are an increasing number of kids, who have bypassed higher (or lower) education in favor of the immediate application of their uncanny skills. High school dropouts work alongside Ph.D.'s. Often, these dropouts are more facile with their technical efforts than are their elders. Of course, the reverse is also often true.

On a good day, this polyglot horde is a team. If it is united at all, it is joined by a common impassioned relationship with the team's

---

1. Equally diverse but thoroughly different collections of individual titles will apply in other types of creative collaborations.

tools and machines, the products it produces, and the team's collective capacity and individual love for making its machines and tools actually *do* something. On the many "other-than-good" days, these people are only physically near one another—for the most part.

*Development includes many vital activities beyond writing code and testing code.*[2] In fact, writing code is not usually the critical task in the progress of development. The critical factor that actually governs the speed as well as the quality of development is the degree of team unity. A team characterized by one product vision per person[3] will suffer from unilateral, unrelated, and undirected actions. In the worst case, individuals who are in such a group will carry out mutually negating actions.

*Team unity is limited by the lack of a single, explicit, universally accepted focus that comes from a SharedVision.* Disunited teams are characterized by a complete absence of common intention, the result of the unaligned diversity normally encountered in immature teams.

*The team members' diversity, along with the usual load of entropy, requires that a compelling force be harnessed to propel the team forward with a single purpose.* A team derives its motivation from its vision. When a high-tech team actually delivers anything, not only is it a result of the team's technical capacity to do so, but the effort also reflects the productive channeling of the team's creative urge and the unifying force of its collective will to actualize a vision.

*In The Core, a vision is an imaginative construction of the state of the world when the team has finished its work.* A vision, especially the FarVision, depicts the world that will exist when the team has achieved its goals. The products a team makes are the means to realizing this world vision.

*A vision is an experience you have. It is not limited to what you can say, see, or imagine.* When a vision is explicitly depicted or stated, the expression of the vision is largely iconographic. Created while the

*A team characterized
by one product vision
per person will suffer
from unilateral,
unrelated, and
undirected actions.*

---

2. Or doing the corresponding tasks in other IP-based disciplines.

3. One vision per person is not the highest number of product visions possible. In particularly disunited groups, each individual has many visions of the product under way, depending on when you talk to him.

*A good vision
statement is a
placeholder or special
team totem.*

*Vision is about objects
and effects that exist
only in the
imagination.*

*Almost exclusively,
developers study
things orthogonal to
envisioning and the
development of team-
related skills.*

team is in a state of SharedVision, a vision statement is even more symbolic than is usual with such statements. A good vision statement is a placeholder or special team totem. It excites team members' memories so that they can resurrect the state of SharedVision that existed when the totem was created.

*The vision statement or other icon of the vision serves as a proxy for the vision-world that doesn't exist beyond the team's imagination.* Vision is about objects and effects that exist only in the imagination. This point explains why a vision is a vision and not a direct perception. An icon of the vision experience—typically a statement—is a necessary construction for the team. It will occupy a ritual space and support the envisioners over time, as they gradually realize the vision in the products they make, and in the world their products create.

*A simple but tenacious ignorance generally limits the team's visionary capacity.* Whatever the team members' educational backgrounds, most developers' institutional learning has focused on things other than the essentials of collaboration. Almost exclusively, developers study things orthogonal to envisioning and the development of team-related skills. In a classical education, the schooling is very technical. For software or Web developers, much time is spent learning to create optimal algorithms, understanding common data structures, appraising and creating system architectures, learning computer languages, and building compilers. Other software developers' education is equally technical but different, being spent mastering the technical guts of the currently prevailing commercial system software architecture and acquiring whatever skills its technologies require. Technical learning is necessary but insufficient when human interconnection is the blocking factor.

*Consistently placing technical things first leads to antipatterns of team behavior.* In particular, the vision-related antipatterns in The Core, Blinder and Technicality, can ensnare and defeat technically bigoted organizations. The former antipattern is spawned when a group seeks to maintain its unalloyed ignorance of visions. The latter antipattern is achieved by mixing into the ignorance far too large a dose of technical matters.

*Blinder produces the most extreme obtuseness regarding visions.* Even milder cases of Blinder nourish an unhealthy lack of understanding of the role and purpose of visions.

*Technicality results in a bloated valuation of mastery of technical details.* This concentration is a wasteful emphasis for the team. Technicality rewards the technical mastery associated with a given project or job (rather than results) and punishes its perceived absence.

*Both Blinder and Technicality will undermine a team's capacity for the deeper experiences of SharedVision.* Both antipatterns have effects that are as serious as they are common.

*A **Metavision** is a vision of visions.* Teams thrashing about, unwittingly hobbled by Blinder or infested with Technicality, necessarily suffer the inefficiencies and discomfort wrought by an incoherent Metavision. Conversely, a robust Metavision is the only effective remedy for Blinder and Technicality. A team's Metavision is its seed vision.

*The quality of an institution's Metavision will constrain the quality of all descendant visions, and will determine the quality of the products created and the life lived within that institution.* A Metavision provides a "vision gene pool" from which all other visions descend. From these visions come the products. If the team's or institution's Metavision is lucid, every other necessity of success is much more likely to follow as a result. Conversely, if the institutional Metavision is not crisp and is not readily expressible in both the words and the behaviors of everyone involved, unpredictable, selfish behaviors usually follow, along with the minimum of discrete (though inefficient and often contradictory) creative acts.

*A Metavision provides a "vision gene pool" from which all other visions descend.*

*Although team members hold diverse beliefs about development, virtually all developers share one intellectual characteristic: They lack expertise in creating a state of SharedVision for all teams, for all projects, at all times.* Team members typically join a team or a project with very different beliefs about what it means to develop something. Obviously, a paucity of Metavision will not help to resolve these differences. Most developers seem to persist in the belief that the primary work to be achieved is a technical task (as detailed in Technicality). They generally agree that

*Most developers seem to persist in the belief that the primary work to be achieved is a technical task.*

"good communication" is important, and they might even believe that "good teamwork" is desirable or necessary. Beyond those agreeable if ineffectual ideas, however, team members may maintain their divergent views of the nature of developing a product. For that matter, even a single person holds many contradictory beliefs.

*Adopting The Core requires that all participants accept as a paramount belief that effective product development is a vision-driven process.* In particular, the teams must subscribe to the idea that a SharedVision is a prerequisite for the most effective behavior possible—the true source and producer of successful product development teams and efficient efforts.

*The Core model of SharedVision consists of three essential elements, which must be created by the institution and the team in sequence:*

1.  The creation and application of a Metavision. Preferably, the Metavision should permeate the institution. Failing that, however, it is acceptable for the team (or some larger unit) to create its own Metavision.

2.  Following the promulgation of the Metavision are one or more subsidiary states of SharedVision. These states are inaugurated by the establishment of a FarVision by and for those who will implement it.

3.  All effects of SharedVision states are sustained, refreshed, and their objects further developed by the creation and delivery of multiple Versions. The defining characteristic of a product Version is that its release moves the team (and the world) one step closer to the world of the FarVision.

# PATTERNS INVOLVED IN THE SHARED VISION PROCESS

The SharedVision pattern describes the achievement of a pleasurable and efficient group state of being. The members of a team in this state have a unified mode of perception and a profound sense of connection with one another. The group sees and feels as one. All team members in a state of SharedVision see team-relevant things in essentially the same way. None of the team members sees things as he would see them alone. The experience is generally thought to be superior to a more isolated one.

The principal effects of SharedVision derive from the group's continuous validation that an object of compelling beauty and importance can be, and will be, achieved by its combined thinking and intense, concerted action. Attempting a goal like that typically found in a vision statement of this class of team requires substantial ambition.

The SharedVision object is something that each team member would most likely see as impossible to attain on an individual basis, were it not for the ongoing validation and sustained support of the other team members. The object itself is—or at least becomes—loaded with supreme meaning for the team. Nothing is more important.

The team's commitment to attaining the SharedVision object is a passionate one. So animated is the team's fervor that the only real difference between a shared delusion and a SharedVision is the rational, step-by-step behavior of those experiencing the vision, which contrasts with the irrational and often random behavior of those experiencing a delusion. When examining the team besotted with a SharedVision, a third-party observer might decide that, although the fulfillment of the team's ambition is unlikely, it is just possible that members of this group could achieve it. "If anybody can do it," the observer might well say, "this team can."

The members of a team in a state of SharedVision perceive most important things similarly, because they hold the same beliefs about their purpose as a team, the products they will make, and the process they will use to make them. Usually, they share a few key generative algorithms about what they are making and why.

## METAVISION

The Metavision pattern deals with the role of visions, their importance, their use, and their development. A credible Metavision

*When examining the team besotted with a SharedVision, a third-party observer might decide that, although the fulfillment of the team's ambition is unlikely, it is just possible that members of this group could achieve it.*

incorporates an understanding of the technologies for creating, maintaining, and ensuring the fulfillment of visions throughout an institution. It represents the ideal. Many times, however, a subgroup or even just a single small team may arrive at its own guiding Metavision, because the institution as a whole lacks a prevailing credible Metavision. The formulation of a Metavision is one appropriate response when Blinder is rampaging in the environment beyond the team boundaries. It is useless to await the formation of a Metavision by someone else.

## FAR VISION

The FarVision pattern describes a team's unanimously supported answer to the question "What will the world look like after the 20 (or another large number of) years we will be working together?"

## VERSION

The Version pattern presents the product vision, as well as the plan for and the process behind the current product release. The release always brings the world of the team's FarVision a step closer.

# Shared Vision Patterns and Protocols

## PATTERN: SHARED VISION

### PROBLEM

*You work without deciding together*
*what you are going to create.*

Teams face vision problems in three areas.

### PROBLEM 1: NO VISION

The lack of an active vision doesn't just inhibit success; it actively promotes evil. If your behavior has no cause, you promote meaninglessness with every act.

### PROBLEM 2: FALSE VISION

A false vision is worse than purposelessness. Hypocrisy compounds the basic evil of visionless acts by turning idealists into cynics.

CHAPTER
THIRTEEN
SHARED VISION
PATTERNS AND
PROTOCOLS

280

*Ultimately, a life lived
without the vitality of
vision can never point
beyond itself.*

Hopelessness results if your behavior has a different cause than the one announced.

## PROBLEM 3: VICTIMIZATION AND SCAPEGOATING

People who are involved with projects with no vision are not victims. Those whose work has little purpose and much commotion cannot legitimately cry out for relief. Those who suffer relationships that have no noble end in mind will find no one to blame. Ultimately, a life lived without the vitality of vision can never point beyond itself. This type of situation results exclusively from the choices of the individuals involved. Victims of visionless projects will find no refuge in The Core. Instead, those who accept emptiness as a normal condition of existence must simply endure that which they accept.

Many of the ruling visions in thousands of institutions—visions supposedly defining the purpose of myriad teams—are hollow, soulless visions. Consider, for example, the statement "We strive to be the world leader in information technology." The main reason that a company will embrace such an empty vision and persist with it is that each person in the company chooses to accept lameness in the communal statement of purpose.

Lifeless visions usually come from executives or official company "visionaries," but these folks have no exclusive rights on the emptiness franchise. Whether the antivision authors are the habitually dominant voices on a team or are special staff members or consultants assigned to the task, it is a virtual certainty, in the case of a lifeless vision statement, that the relevant staff was not included in the vision formation. Any group that is aligned is too smart to create a meaningless vision, provided, of course, that the team members' intelligence and wisdom are rendered accessible via something like Decider.

The inferior vision, which ostensibly embodies the true purpose of the company or team, will not be completely embraced by employees. In fact, it is usually not embraced at all. The widespread softness of support, outright rejection, or the hypocritical fealty to a lifeless vision is the root of much of the cynicism encountered in contemporary corporate life. If the stated purpose of corporate reality is wrong, then either the stated purpose is not the real purpose, or all employees are engaged in purposelessness. In either case, integrity is nipped in the bud.

Even a corporate vision that is only moderately impaired will not resonate with employees deeply enough to engage them at the highest levels. Worse, because the official vision unofficially languishes among employees, conditions favor the contamination of the local culture with habitual hypocrisy and a cynicism toward all things "official." Such a cultural infection, once it gains a toehold, is likely to overrun any virtues that the culture may actually have. The contamination will sap the institution's vitality and continually plague both the people and their products.

Employees who get their hands dirty—such as people in vital production or customer-related domains—will generally not be willing to make time to produce a functional vision. This reluctance probably reflects the reality that no one pays attention to visions in the culture. This response, in which people generally refuse to connect with random visions that are pronouncements from on high, is actually a healthy development. Corporate catchphrases, which tend to be trotted out occasionally, put on slides, and plugged into the spaces where official visions are supposed to go, do not attract support from the broader staff.

Moreover, any uninspiring promulgated vision—even though it may be meritorious in and of itself—will be counted as just so much management baloney. In many institutions, "the vision" is not even known to the employees who must fulfill it. In other organizations, no real purpose—other than today's daily bread—drives the effort.

For their part, employees must not be thought of—or see themselves—as victims of "a lack of management vision." Employees suffer needlessly and do little about it. They vainly hope that something better might materialize and continually gripe about poor leadership.[1] These employees must be content with their

*If the stated purpose of corporate reality is wrong, then either the stated purpose is not the real purpose, or all employees are engaged in purposelessness.*

*Employees suffer needlessly and do little about it. They vainly hope that something better might materialize and continually gripe about poor leadership.*

---

1. Waiting for others, for any reason, is always a bad idea.

CHAPTER
THIRTEEN
SHARED VISION
PATTERNS AND
PROTOCOLS

282

story: Things are awful because "management" or "the company" lacks vision.

Stable malcontents are oblivious to the role they play in being satisfied by a lifeless vision. Nonetheless, it can be inferred from the following argument:

- *Employees in a lame-vision situation don't usually quit their jobs (at least not directly, or with integrity) over the lame vision.* Lameness of vision is much too frequent to commonly inspire that response. If workers did quit their jobs over the matter, the situation would be corrected over time and would be much less common.

- *Employees so situated usually don't work effectively to change things.* If they did, the situation would not be so prevalent.

- *Because they don't leave and don't fix the situation, employees in an environment with a lame vision endorse it.* Although workers might howl at such a characterization, lameness of purpose or vision can be seen as something insisted on by any employee who tolerates it. For an individual to perceive himself as "stuck" in a situation where happiness and the production of great results are impossible, the environment must serve many personal purposes.

People do create more effectively, with more conviction and passion, when they are creating to further their own cause. Employees jointly pursuing a dream in their daily work, while enjoying the whole-hearted support of their employer, have a strong, natural alliance with their employer that inspires them to work together to bring about desired change. This alliance will persist as long as the employee and the employer hold the cause to be satisfactory. Because the identification is so strong and mutual, it will generate more loyalty from employee and employer than would otherwise be the case. In an era of short-tenure jobs, accompanied by enormous recruitment and training expenses, more loyalty to the team and its sponsoring institution is a much-needed virtue.

The central challenge in creating a team is learning how best to work with the right number of people on a team to accomplish the following goals:

- Provide for yourself
- Make a positive difference in the world
- Secure the loyalty of team members
- Promote the best results for everyone involved

The answer to this challenge lies in the vision and the steps that the team members must take together to create and fulfill that vision— to master the art of SharedVision.

Unfortunately, very little time is spent in most environments developing the capacity to understand vision and express it to others. In reality, having and sharing a vision has much more to do with high-quality interpersonal interactions than it does with the important, but ultimately secondary, technical aspects of a project. Developers are routinely charged with making products, building a Web site, or undertaking some other creative and collaborative production of intellectual property while they and their institutions are unknowingly deeply entangled in the Blinder antipattern.

The experience of SharedVision is intrinsic to a team's experience of the pleasurable and efficient group state of being. The existence of a state of SharedVision is a necessity for successful high-tech teams. Many have witnessed the miracles that can occur when a creative team "clicks"; others have also seen the travesties that result from a lack of SharedVision. As described in the antipattern TeamQuackery (discussed in Chapter Seven), experts are only now beginning to understand and explain what transpires on a team to cause the state of flow to suddenly materialize. Until recently, there hasn't been a body of practical knowledge with which to teach teams how to intentionally repeat this fruitful experience. Even though you may have experienced SharedVision, and perhaps you may have longed for a time when you could once again reach the levels of effectiveness you attained in your earlier experiences, there has been no clear procedure to follow.

*Teams that dwell continuously in the state of flow are rare.* Our understanding of the enhanced interpersonal connectivity experienced by a team in the state of flow, though by no means comprehensive, is sufficient to make it available to all teams, at all times.

*Many have witnessed the miracles that can occur when a creative team "clicks."*

CHAPTER
THIRTEEN
SHARED VISION
PATTERNS AND
PROTOCOLS

284

*The rarity of teams
experiencing
SharedVision is poised
to end.*

*Divergent visions will
exist on a team that
has not taken the
trouble to hear the
multiple singular
visions and converge
upon a single
SharedVision prior to
commencing its work.*

This ultrahigh-performance state can now serve as the minimum expectation of the team experience. Applying The Core patterns in the context of any team will invariably propel a team into the state of flow. Thus, it is no longer necessary to wait for the random "clicking" of creative teams. The rarity of teams experiencing SharedVision is poised to end.

Because much development deals with the creation of intellectual property, little can be completed without an articulated vision. At the very least, you will require a limited, next-version kind of vision—that is, a feature list. Additionally, you will need some sense of how this vision can be accomplished. The imaginary object of your efforts will guide your team while it is bringing the product to life. The vision's quality portends the product's quality. The absence of such an imagined object, or its inconsistency from team member to team member, will stall and misguide the team.

The extent to which your own imaginary object matches that envisioned by your teammates establishes the extent to which you will be truly working together. The extent to which your object differs from that of your teammates sets the extent to which you will work at cross-purposes. Everyone on the team has an individual vision of what is being created. Bringing these visions into Alignment is the work of SharedVision.

*Every person and every team has a vision, regardless of whether the effects of these visions are taken into account.* An untended team vision that goes unarticulated and undiscussed will have negative effects on the team's productivity, as will any vision that is mandated from outside the team. Divergent visions will exist on a team that has not taken the trouble to hear the multiple singular visions and converge upon a single SharedVision prior to commencing its work. You can count on that.

Typically, the unfiltered, unexpressed, and unaligned motivational forces of any collection of individuals are, prior to Alignment, hidden—secrets, private inspirations, compelling unmet needs, greed, generosity, manipulative impulses, a dollop of purity, a note of hope, and, if you're lucky, a few spontaneously aligned points of view.[2] Into this stew of unknown, complex, and partially destructive motives are tossed the usual broad-ranging technical and behavioral problems that accompany the acquiring of daily bread. Now stir in hundreds of disparate solutions to those and other problems envisioned by each of the mostly isolated team members. Sprinkle in the teammates' own emotions (especially their fears) and the incoherent fantasies that accompany them. This brew is the everyday fare of a team characterized by multiple singular visions.[3]

It's not that difficult to imagine the team behaviors that emerge while "realizing" multiple singular visions. In the beginning, team members try to negotiate a static, technical understanding of what they're creating. This attempt forestalls any effort to create a connection and forge a common understanding of how to relate. Instead of developing high-bandwidth interpersonal protocols and establishing broad **Alignment**, team members become absorbed by **Technicality**. The negotiations can go on for months. One team we know spent four months with 100 people creating "specs."[4]

Product development, when it is really cooking, is unlike the static spec you may eventually be able to negotiate. Product development is unbelievably dynamic. The environment changes; the market changes; the product development strategy changes; people change. The meticulously wrought static understanding is suddenly transformed into an incorrect description of the goals of the effort. At that point, the people following this increasingly irrelevant document[5] will revert to their private, unshared visions of what they're creating. One or two team members may attempt to change the spec

*Product development, when it is really cooking, is unlike the static spec you may eventually be able to negotiate.*

2. The spontaneously aligned minority generally accounts for whatever favorable results an otherwise unaligned team produces. These results, though admirable, are attained at a disproportionately high personal cost to those who are aligned enough to prevail.

3. This blend is just a way of lumping together all "nonshared" visions so that we can proceed. To be sure, a rich variety of things that are called team visions are not related to SharedVision. To the extent that they cause the quest for a SharedVision to be abandoned or minimized, they are wrong-headed, and often tragically so.

4. These specs, as we consistently find, were not results-oriented, but were vain attempts at control. In almost every case, action will produce many times more results than planning.

5. Which will turn out to be very few people.

CHAPTER
THIRTEEN
SHARED VISION
PATTERNS AND
PROTOCOLS

286

to accommodate what has already been achieved in the product. *Ex post specto—specifications after the fact.*

The chaos created by many active individual, unshared visions generally causes one of two things to happen. On a reasonably well-formed, somewhat healthy, though perhaps immature team, one where direct communication remains possible, a discussion about creating a SharedVision begins in earnest. The team members, groping in the dark, may try to establish a common set of core values and beliefs about the product they're creating. In that way, they sense, they can individually generate independent decisions in real time. These decisions, based on their common understanding, might align. Should that happen, the team and the product's prospects will be infinitely preferable to those created by real-time subordination to rapidly aging specs.

The second thing that happens has to do with less healthy teams. There, the project is launched without any Alignment. The situation deteriorates until someone or something arrives on the scene. If the new element is a person, it usually takes the form of a boss or another authority figure who will assert a quasi-dictatorial leadership. This person will "share" his vision with the team.

No matter how bright or creative this individual might be, or how valuable his ideas, a technical mandate dictated by one person naturally lacks the quality and the aggregate vitality that is possible when the vision is the product of many individuals. Nonetheless, the imposed structure "takes" for a short time, because in the face of sustained deterioration and diminishing hope, an imposed structure is urgently desired by most team members.

*A "share this" visionary imperative will diminish the emotional engagement of the players.*

Not only is the imposition of a single-minded vision less effective than other possible organizing structures, but it also reduces the team's ongoing vitality, diminishes its flow of creativity, and precludes members' commitment to any real vision. A "share this" visionary imperative will diminish the emotional engagement of the players. This dwindling support, in turn, reduces the value of the end result—assuming that the team persists and the product ships at all.

*First and always,*
*make sure that your team is aligned around its vision.*

## SHARED VISION PROTOCOL

Creating a SharedVision has three steps:

1.  Envision a vision-driven life. Turn that image into a metavision
    with and for your team and your institution.

2.  As a team, decide what kind of world you will create. Answer
    two questions together: (1) How will the world be different
    when you finish your work? and (2) What will life be like for
    you and your customers? From your answers, create a FarVision,
    and write a FarVision statement.

3.  Deliver one version of your product after another, and deliver
    each version on time. Each version must be designed to validate
    the single—the one and only—message you promulgate with it.
    The product must also palpably contribute to the increasing
    legitimacy of your FarVision. That is, each version must demon-
    strably bring you and your customers closer to the world of your
    FarVision.

# PATTERN: METAVISION

## PROBLEM

*There's no purposeful, institutionally supported approach*
*to the management of visions.*

When you lack a vision of visions, it is because you haven't thought
things through. If great products come from great teams, and great
teams depend on great visions, then the vision of visions—what they

CHAPTER
THIRTEEN
SHARED VISION
PATTERNS AND
PROTOCOLS

288

*Having a Metavision means (at least) that your teams will be creating visions intentionally.*

are, how to get them, how to make them real—is of the utmost importance. If you think things through, you will naturally want to define a vision before all else.

Metavision is a recursive idea. It requires that you first have a vision about visions in order to routinely and collaboratively make great products. Many people casually toss about the terms "vision," "mission," and "goal" without really thinking about those words and deciding what they mean. Such issues are fodder for Metavision.

Having a Metavision means (at least) that your teams will be creating visions intentionally. When you create and promulgate a Metavision, you are committing to a shared understanding of what a vision is, how you achieve visions, and how you know when you have one; you also agree that you won't proceed on a project until you have one. When you make and fulfill the commitments implicit in those kinds of decisions, you have an operative Metavision.

While you may have prior experience with visions on teams and recognize their power, achieving them was likely somewhat accidental. Now you must decide to work with visions on purpose. Decide to create and extend your Metavision by determining how to achieve a SharedVision in a repeatable fashion, with any team that wants to achieve it.

Most individuals, teams, and companies have no understanding of the role played by visions in their world. In Core terms, they lack Metavision. Developing the initial version of your Metavision will require several things:

- Learning what is believed to be true about SharedVisions

- Imagining what those beliefs mean to you

- Together with your team, thinking through the whole complex of SharedVision elements and dynamics

- Deciding that this experience is what you require for your participation on teams

- With your team, defining the vision experience you communally seek, what it will look like in practice, and what is required of the experience in practical terms

When you create a **Metavision**, you build a structure—an imaginary space wherein visions roost and breed. A successful **Metavision** sees its domain of interest as a *visionarium*. As with any other type of *-arium*, the environment must be carefully controlled to support the desired kind of life. What conditions prevail inside a visionarium? What vision species is supported in your visionarium? What ecological balance will enable vision to thrive? What is the ideal vision habitat?

These matters should inspire the deepest thought and discussion. If you do not collectively think about what visions are and what purposes they serve, you limit the numbers of visions and the quality of visions you can have.

*A successful Metavision sees its domain of interest as a visionarium.*

## SOLUTION

*Envision the practice of vision making*
*and then practice it continuously.*

Develop team awareness of the critical role played by visions and achieve consensus about that role. Never personally proceed with a team effort that lacks an explicit connection with a viable **Metavision**. Never move to the next phases of development until you are satisfied that the team has reached its desired vision state.

Establishing a **SharedVision** is not difficult or expensive if it is properly prioritized. The work consists of the following tasks:

- Establishing your inaugural **Metavision**
- Developing your inaugural **FarVision**
- Defining and making a **Version**

This effort should not consume much more than two to four percent of the team's time, or approximately one to two weeks per year. The return will be many times greater than the cost. The

CHAPTER
THIRTEEN
SHARED VISION
PATTERNS AND
PROTOCOLS

290

powerful leverage of ideas is dramatically illustrated in the experience of a SharedVision:

- Unity grows over time, rather than dissipating.
- Good information gains accuracy as it flows, rather than deteriorating.
- New ideas become aligned, rather than diverting and factionalizing.

In achieving a particular goal, what seems to count most is not the vision itself, but rather that everyone shares it.

# PATTERN: FAR VISION

## PROBLEM

*You work hard, burn out, and wonder why you bother.*

*Without purpose, you have a random effect on the future.*

You always play a role in creating the future, whether you choose to manage that role or not. Perhaps it is true of you that you can see no greater purpose to your work than supplying your own material needs and those of your company. Without purpose, you have a random effect on the future. That is, the world that results from your efforts is an accidental world.

Your team's FarVision must answer this question:

*What kind of world are you building?*

The initial answers to this question are not always satisfying, because you don't usually think of your daily activities as world building. When suddenly faced with such a question, you feel unprepared. You might avoid a direct answer. You might ask for clarification of the question. You might try to "talk away" the emptiness of your preliminary answer. Regardless of the response triggered by this query, there is real value in asking and answering the question, because it focuses the mind on the larger opportunities available.

CHAPTER
THIRTEEN
SHARED VISION
PATTERNS AND
PROTOCOLS

292

*If you really are
building a world, and
if you are doing so
unconsciously, you
literally don't know
what you are doing.*

*Like other team
qualities, team
integrity is the
aggregate of the
personal integrities of
each team member.*

If you are unable to directly and unself-consciously answer this question, you may want to examine why you don't see the significance of your daily grind. Of course, the question of *what kind* of world you are building makes no sense at all unless you accept the implication that you are, in fact, building a world. Most of the time, of course, you may not consciously engage in the task of world building.

Nevertheless, your engagement in world building is a simple truth. You have beliefs. Every day you act on those beliefs. Your actions have external effects, and ultimately they cause your beliefs to materialize in the world. In essence, you change the world to look more like your beliefs. You build a world.

If you really are building a world, and if you are doing so unconsciously, you literally don't know what you are doing. While you might not identify your purpose as "the creation of a world," having a larger motivating purpose gives you a frame of reference for choosing alternatives. It is difficult to see how you can truly meet your daily challenges unless you bring a sense of purpose to each moment.

Maintaining a broader purpose seems a necessary precondition of enjoying the highest levels of personal integrity. To have integrity, your intention, your words, and your actions must be aligned. If you know what kind of world someone is building, and you are building the same kind of world, then you can work together on this goal, with much less noise and wasted effort cluttering the environment between you.

Like other team qualities, team integrity is the aggregate of the personal integrities of each team member, enhanced or diminished however much by the effects of the interpersonal synergy. The aggregate level of integrity has a positive correlation with desirable results.

Without a central purpose, an individual or team finds it impossible to make enlightened choices. Each day you make many choices. Before doing so, you check the alternatives against your larger purpose and envision how the alternatives might play out in the world you want to create. Wise choices, those that promote your world's completion at reduced cost or in nearer time frames, are maximally useful to your purpose.

Even without the context of a larger purpose, you still must select from alternatives. Without an organizing purpose, however, your choices will be made according to whim and spontaneous, sometimes bizarre, and usually inconsistent motives. Inefficiency, apathy, premature cynicism,[6] and failure result when individuals or teams make product design decisions in this way. The Core, on the other hand, provides you with a purpose template: to build a world. Individuals, teams, and institutions have found that the most challenging, useful, and satisfying task is world building.

Many worlds and many kinds of worlds are possible. There are vertical worlds: the academic world, the business world, and the government world. There are planetary worlds: Earth and Venus. There are imaginary worlds: the computer-based, literary, and artistic worlds. There are cultural worlds. To avoid complexity, we will divide the worlds and world types into **your world** and the **real world**.

Your world is a uniquely personal environment that you have built over the course of your life. It incorporates a complex blend of many elements. Among these elements are the main structures through which you filter all your experience:

- Your cognitive inheritance[7]
- The memories of your experiences and the "knowledge" you extract from them
- Your contemporary perceptions—what you choose to notice, absorb, and ingest
- Your current beliefs

For ecumenical purposes, we'll give the name "I-World" to the world that emerges from this vast individual filtering and retention system. I-World defines what you expect from life, especially from life in the real world. I-World is the world as you see it.

---

6. The cynic mistrusts all motives but the selfish. Would it be too hopeful to wonder if any other kind of cynicism exists except premature cynicism?

7. This inheritance includes your own "DNA-inherited" cognitive capacity and the somewhat suspect collection of certitudes passed on from your parents, their parents, and the pool of ancestors before them. They contribute to your personal survival, as well as cause personal difficulties.

CHAPTER
THIRTEEN
SHARED VISION
PATTERNS AND
PROTOCOLS

294

*The terms "real
world" and "reality"
are extremely value
charged and are
commonly used in
ways that imply
judgments.*

*You can't escape
noticing that O-World,
or reality, is most
often viewed and
discussed as if it were
a malignant,
withholding, and
fundamentally cruel
place.*

We will term what is called "the real world" as "O-World," the other world. O-World represents the intersection of all the I-Worlds capable of informing you.[8] It is where you coexist with others. It is also known as reality. The terms "real world" and "reality" are extremely value charged and are commonly used in ways that imply judgments. The presumptions behind these judgments are usually unelucidated and unsupported.

It is surprising that O-World's reality seems generally held. In fact, this supremacy of O-World to I-World is usually accepted without question. The references to "reality" and the broad acceptance of the term imply acceptance of the ideas that "reality" is understood and that all possible worlds have been fully explored, all issues resolved, and all solutions to thorny questions effectively transmitted. That concept enables people to say with such certainty, "But in reality . . ."

Conversely, I-World is often considered a fantasy world. It is disdained as subjective or personal if it is brought up seriously. Discussion of interiority is so unsettling as to be effectively taboo.

You can't escape noticing that O-World, or reality, is most often viewed and discussed as if it were a malignant, withholding, and fundamentally cruel place. It is a place of shortages, dashed hopes, and bitter expectations. The "real world" demolishes childish fantasies of abundance, peace, and productivity. This pervasive view of the "cold, cruel world" must arise from something unusual, powerful, and primitive within people.

I-World is regarded as fanciful, characterized by dreams, nightmares, and hallucinations (things typically considered unreal). O-World information, on the other hand, is serious and important. It counts in ways that your dreams don't. The distinction remains in your mind every step of the way. With the collusion of all others who share these worlds, you promulgate the myth and make sure that O-World trounces all I-Worlds. The idea that reality is brutal, unforgiving, and dangerous is expressed again and again.

Another reason that the question, "What kind of world are you building?" is a good one is because building a world is the only effort

---

8. It is useful but incorrect to view O-World as a strict intersection.

that almost universally seems worth the investment of a mature human's productive lifetime. Which world is worth building must be addressed in your answer to the question, "What kind of world are you building?"

The world as you leave it is what you collectively create by your embellishment or diminishment while you are here alive with one another.

*Building a world is the only effort that almost universally seems worth the investment of a mature human's productive lifetime.*

## IF YOU TOLERATE IT, YOU INSIST ON IT

Four laws define your level of vigilance in world building:

- If you tolerate it, you insist on it.
- If you insist on it, it will be supplied.
- If you see a problem, you own it.
- If you ignore a problem, you'll see more of it.

The tendencies to tolerate the intolerable and to perceive a problem and neglect to resolve it are very human. They are impulses that express your internal confusion, and especially your mistaking tolerance with peacekeeping. "It's okay," you might say politely to a colleague who dropped the ball. "Don't worry about it," you shout after him, as he leaves your office with relief. But then you think maliciously, "Just because your commitment is meaningless."

Deep in your brain, this failure hurts. Sometimes you may not feel the full extent of the hurt, but you know that you have just tolerated a broken commitment—like so many people do every day. "No big deal," you think.

Such lapses happen routinely, even on the best teams. Mistakes don't hurt. What hurts is the lack of explicit agreement about the meaning of commitments and the causes of the failures to meet them. What hurts is that you force yourself to believe you can forgo the need to uphold your own values. In response, your values fall. Eventually, you don't have them anymore.

All along, the situation has been hurting you. The discomforts, pains, and stresses that accumulate within you can be usefully

*What hurts is that you force yourself to believe you can forgo the need to uphold your own values.*

CHAPTER
THIRTEEN
SHARED VISION
PATTERNS AND
PROTOCOLS

296

viewed as a persistent invitation to exist more explicitly, to increase your presence. You might want to check in more deeply.

A person can only achieve his potential by being intolerant of the malignant and embracing the beneficent. The consistent practices required by such a personal policy inevitably lead to more rational and simpler ways—not only in you, but also in your environment.

The millions of product teams that make up the high-tech industry could become the central emerging community. They may well be the most critical cultural elements and, boom or bust, they constitute the most influential segment of civilization in this era. Unfortunately, many such teams are blocked from grander achievements by their failure to really think things through and walk through the design of the world they are creating together. They haven't dreamed it and visualized it all the way to the end, and the team members haven't connected around it. They have no common picture of how their vision will look in either the long or the short term. Generally, these teams lack a thoroughly imagined, well-scrubbed intention behind their work, which motivates and drives them onward, despite anything and everything. They do not share a common purpose that is powerful[9] enough to attract the required resources, and to transform team members' SharedVisions into accessible, real products.[10]

In some eras, a spectacular surge of vitality propagates throughout the cultures of the time. Often, it is a key idea that ushers in the vitality. A great idea-compressor/effects-intensifier incites tremendous change. Medieval monks, for example, committed to preserving sublime knowledge that they themselves could never know, and they devoted themselves to memorializing imaginative acts of which they would never dream. Immense cathedrals of stone, built by several generations of workers, defied all prior beliefs and constraints on building massive structures. The Pyramids, which remain standing after thousands of years, remind us of the possible—the appropriate—

*The pyramids, which remain standing after thousands of years, remind us of the possible . . . scale of transpersonal envisioning and implementation.*

---

9. Resources are magnetized by powerful visions.

10. Real products, of course, would include units of executable software or other similar conceptual objects. "Real" does not mean "physiologically palpable."

scale of transpersonal envisioning and implementation. These pyramids serve as the legacy of our ancient forbears. They continue to stand today, perhaps never to be surpassed, challenging modern teams to contribute at the highest possible level.

Perhaps the vitality of our era can be found in the idea of connectedness. Perhaps we are in the beginning of the Connected Era. People will increasingly function in a less time-bound/place-bound style. And yet their presence and levels of engagement may well be greater. The curious, easy intimacy of things like chat suggest this is so, as does the marked majority preference for ATMs over interaction with bank tellers. Regardless, the presence of our networked, connected colleagues will certainly be more virtual. The energy and focus of contemporary civilization (if not yet all—or even most—governments) have shifted tremendously away from isolated, time-delayed engagement with the greater world, and toward the more connected simultaneous I/O of the Connected Era. Much of this "connection energy" has been nurtured by and distributed through the successful cultures of many Information Era companies.

## SOLUTION

*Insist that work you do have a long-term, noble purpose.*

Detach yourself from present trends; assume abundant resources; decide what the world will be like when your work is done. What values will rule? What technologies will support the reign of values? Which of the technologies will you have created?

Achieving a useful FarVision requires an aligned team that meets the following criteria:

- It demands candor and insists on integrity.
- It is fueled by passion.
- It is focused on achieving positive effects.

Such a team is also devoted to eliminating any weaknesses that inhibit the full personal engagement of its members. Its members

CHAPTER
THIRTEEN
SHARED VISION
PATTERNS AND
PROTOCOLS

298

also remain committed to incessantly ask for help from one another and from external parties. They tolerate only the truth, and change their ways readily based on demonstrated results. The team has an explicitly formed intention to create things that make a positive difference. It plans to spend the time required over many years to make a difference of the scale appropriate for human life.

The factors previously inhibiting the team from creating a SharedVision are addressed by the virtues the team members began practicing after their PersonalAlignments. On an aligned team, the Alignments are honest and true. The virtues sought in these Alignments eliminate or diminish the personal blocks identified by the team members. The team members begin to practice (in full view of one another) the virtues they have each chosen to pursue immediately after their Alignments are established.

While people who experience it readily see the value of the Alignment process, at first many may wonder about its relevance to SharedVision or to product design and delivery. Because of Alignment's obvious interpersonal significance, even people who have reservations about its relevance are willing to pursue the process once it is launched, however.

Prior to undertaking an Alignment, you might wonder how everything ties together. You might ask, "How does my wanting to show more courage help with a SharedVision or in defining our product?" When the team has completed the Alignment, as satisfying as the experience may have been, it may still prove difficult to see the direct relationship of the Alignment process to achieving a Shared Vision. Alignment and SharedVision are related in ways that might best be shown in an example:

*You might ask, "How does my wanting to show more courage help with a SharedVision or in defining our product?"*

- Say your PersonalAlignment is that you "want to show more courage." Then, when you start a team task, you will see just how much your newfound commitment to showing courage is (and has been) needed.

- Assume that you then effectively show courage.

- Adding your courage to the team picture will cause a positive change.

- Multiply this positive change by the many times you will perform your PersonalAlignment.

- Now consider the positive changes coming from every team member. How much positive change is that? Enough to launch even the most pedestrian team into the state of SharedVision.

With this post-Alignment quality boost, a much more functional team rapidly emerges.

Remember that the qualities now available to the team include not only your courage, but also the entire collection of desirable elements that the various other team members are now pursuing. These goals typically include passion, connection, creativity, fun, self-care, and integrity.[11] Not only are these virtues theoretically more present, but they emerge in powerful, fresh modalities uniquely configured to your team.

Because of the nature of Alignment, the team also experiences near-constant cognition with regard to each of the virtues being pursued by anybody on the team. After all, the team members are obligated—usually by the explicit Alignment contracts—to externally demonstrate their support to a team member when that person exhibits a certain behavior. The teammates will enact—and carefully watch others enact—new strategies of personal power. There will be lessons aplenty. When this sudden influx of power is combined with the team's newfound competence at stimulating and maintaining such a flow of power,[12] there is little that cannot be achieved.

Teams are not finished with the vision-inculcation process until they have encapsulated their vision in a vision statement. The vision statement serves several purposes:

- A constant message to the team over time regarding the state of their team at the time the vision was made

- A map for guiding the team throughout its implementation of the Version

*When this sudden influx of power is combined with the team's newfound competence at stimulating and maintaining such a flow of power, there is little that cannot be achieved.*

---

11. These elements, along with courage, are always among the most popular Alignment wants.

12. The team's competence in this domain will be seen by its persistence in the proper use of The Core patterns (or their functional equivalents).

CHAPTER
THIRTEEN
SHARED VISION
PATTERNS AND
PROTOCOLS

300

- A message to the rest of the world regarding the intention of the team
- An image of how the world will look when the team's work is done

## THE FAR VISION PROTOCOL

After having completed Alignment, write a statement with your team that best expresses what the world will look like when your work together is done. Unless the statement leaps out at you, use the Passionometer protocol to align the team around its core values.

- *The FarVision must be imaginative.* Look as far into the future as possible. Twenty years is a good starting point, but the date chosen must always be beyond your ability to extrapolate current trends. That is, it must be the work of intention and imagination, not analysis.

- *The FarVision must be measurable.* Ideally, progress can be measured, as well. The desired result may be an observable, external thing or event, such as "put a man on the moon." Alternatively, it might be softer and more difficult to measure, such as "create infinite, free bandwidth." Your FarVision could also be values-driven, which is more difficult but still possible to measure, such as "eliminate poverty" or "create ubiquitous radical democracy."

- *The FarVision statement should be just a few words,* ideally no more than ten words. If it is more than six words, ask your team to reevaluate it.

- *Use the PerfectionGame to perfect your FarVision.*

- *The team should unanimously support the FarVision,* using Decider.

Next, form a product vision—a vision statement for the first Version. This statement should follow the same guidelines as the FarVision statement. It should describe the most important thing the team can do *now* to move toward the world depicted in its FarVision.

Examples of FarVision statements and Version statements follow:

**Put a man on the moon.**

Version 1: Orbit the earth.

**A computer on every desk.**

Version 1: Software that's easy to use.

**World peace.**

Version 1: Peace in our country.

## THE PASSIONOMETER PROTOCOL

The Passionometer protocol provides a straightforward technique for discovering what a team cares about and how much a team cares about it. Its most common application is the creation of the team's vision statement.

1. On index cards team members write down meaningful words or phrases that they associate with the world of the team's FarVision.

2. Toss the cards onto the floor faceup. If repeats are found, throw out the extras or keep them together as a set.

3. A facilitator holds up each card (or set), and team members show their passion for the word or phrase by making noise or vivid gestures, or by another means.[13]

4. The facilitator, with the advice and consent of the team, makes three piles of the cards based on the responses from the team as he flips through the cards one at a time:

   - Highly passionately supported

   - Somewhat passionately supported

   - No real passion

---

13. One person, vividly demonstrating his passion, can "peg" the Passionometer. What is being measured is the aggregate team passion, not the number of votes for a card.

CHAPTER
THIRTEEN
SHARED VISION
PATTERNS AND
PROTOCOLS

———————

502

5. Repeat steps 3 and 4, using only those cards that are highly passionately supported until the cards are narrowed down to a set of five or six.

6. If the team remains stuck, repeat Passionometer on the highly passionately supported cards.

———————————————————————

# PATTERN: VERSION

## PROBLEM

———————————

*You are engaged in a feature war with a competitor or have an unwieldy list of feature requests from customers.*

Short-term product needs work against longer-term well-being. How can you sustain your vision over the entire time it takes to realize your vision?

## SOLUTION

———————————

*Create a sequence of product Versions. Each Version must accomplish a discrete step toward the FarVision.*

*Always create a version that the team agrees is the most important step to take now toward achieving the FarVision.*

Always create a version that the team agrees is the most important step to take now toward achieving the FarVision. As you deliver each Version, you should become increasingly more explicit with your marketers about your FarVision. Tell them how each Version relates to the world you are building.

When creating each version of your product, add only those features that support the current Version message. Before it is time to ship the product, stop adding features, stabilize the product, and ship it on time. In this way, you will have a product that hangs together, is timely, aligns with a FarVision, and supports a message that your marketing people can advertise.

# FOURTEEN

# Shared Vision Antipatterns

## ANTIPATTERN: BLINDER

### PROBLEM

*Your team is hindered by its blindness to the need
to create SharedVisions.*

Many teams are oblivious to the state of their visions. Teams mired in Blinder are twice-blind: They can't see the need for vision, and they can't see that they can't see it. As a consequence, teams perform below par with less joy and less effectiveness than could otherwise be achieved with the same people and resources.

The opposite of vision is blindness. Blinder refers to many levels and types of blindness:

- You're blind if you agree to do something with a complete lack of preparation, as in *flying blind*.

- Blindness results when you have near total loss of vision and don't believe you do. That is, you are blind because you don't perceive on many levels.

*Teams mired in
Blinder are twice-
blind: They can't see
the need for vision,
and they can't see that
they can't see it.*

*A severe case of
Blinder requires that
all team members
continuously assert—
primarily in what they
create—their
commitment to
mediocrity.*

- You are blind when you make others blind.

- Blindness minimizes your field of vision, like the blinders worn by racehorses.

Many degrees of **Blinder** are possible. With a mild case of **Blinder**, a team might be extremely ignorant of the vision imperative. In a more severe case, the extreme ignorance is accompanied by a whole new level of voluntary blindness. That is, in a profound case of **Blinder**, a team is not only ignorant, but stubbornly ignorant. In the face of clear information or experience, the team explicitly prefers its ineffective ways.[1]

Although you might empathize somewhat with the vision blindness (that is, ignorance) of a team infected by **Blinder**,[2] a severe case of **Blinder** requires that all team members continuously assert—primarily in what they create—their commitment to mediocrity. It becomes difficult to empathize with **Blinder** at this juncture.

The following behavior patterns are often noted with **Blinder** teams and individuals:

- Extreme, in-the-moment, faux pragmatism

- Overreaction to competitors' moves

- Dictation of vision, or vision as an ex officio statement, "Share this"

- A commitment to **Oblivion**

- Reliance on authority or hierarchy for conflict resolution and decision making

- **Metavision** cut off before it has finished gestation

- Too many or meaningless goals, vision statements, and mission statements

- Bizarre **SharedVision** attitude—for example, "Of course, we've got a vision. Anybody here not understand that?"

---

1. Perhaps the only way to cling to ignorance is to glorify it.

2. To a certain extent, accidents of fate or the general poverty of a work culture could partially excuse extreme ignorance. No doubt, everyone on the team could sense the need for some centrally organizing team purpose. On a particularly weak team, no single person has the courage to insist on a better team experience.

- FarVision dismissed out of hand as too impractical

- Odd emotional affect, often macho, with crude self-aggrandizing expressions regarding visions

- Labeling the vision as an alternative technique—"the vision thing"

Blinder can even occur with individuals who have experienced a team graced with a SharedVision. They know the value of a vision; yet they do not pursue it, demand it, discuss it, or fight for it. They are blind to their own personal history.

## SUPPOSED SOLUTION

*Go along and get along. It's someone else's job.*

## ACTUAL SOLUTION

*Don't work on a team without SharedVision.*

Gather more information about vision experiences. Document and detail your own. Accept nothing less than a SharedVision experience, and challenge others who are willing to blithely or cynically accept less.

# ANTIPATTERN: TECHNICALITY

## PROBLEM

*People are categorized as technical or nontechnical,*
*and technical is seen as "better."*

Highly technical matters are the daily work of some part of a team. Discerning who is and who is not competent to participate in these technical discussions and decisions requires good personal judgment. An excessive emphasis on technical issues and skills, however, causes team problems to be labeled as "technical" problems, and promotes a hierarchy of values based on technical proficiency.

In a team suffering from Technicality, the following characteristics are notable:

- Interpersonal issues masquerade as technical issues.

- Team problems are seldom identified. The technical draws you away from your real work on a team.

- Sources of help for problems are neglected in the pursuit of technical solutions to nontechnical problems.

- The very concept of "technical" is hijacked in service to this ugly interpersonal discrimination system. Consequently, efficiently addressing technical issues becomes unlikely.

The penalties for enduring a life infected with Technicality include a reduced ability to get help from people who can actually help you, plus loss of team information exchange as technicals work apart from nontechnicals. Because no solutions are applied to the team's problems, these deficiencies become chronic. Genuine help—for both technical and nontechnical problems—is ignored in favor of ersatz technical solutions.

A peculiar culture emerges in the world of Technicality. People are seen as belonging to a technical or a nontechnical category. A nontechnical person does not address "technical" matters, and a technical person does not become involved in "nontechnical" issues. This separation takes the heart out of the everyday communication of useful ideas among team members and prevents the exploitation of the riches of diversity.

Technicality also undermines the value of the team's other virtues. When only one predominant value exists, a value powerful enough to separate a team that would otherwise naturally come together in unity, then everything else is necessarily valueless. In fact, many human qualities can provide more capacity to a team than technical proficiency can.[3]

Consider imagination. In creating a FarVision, it is critically important that collective imaginative powers be deployed by the team to the fullest extent possible. With FarVision, you hope to leap ahead 20 years and imagine the world in which you'll be living then. Technical stuff is not as helpful in this endeavor as is imagination.

A FarVision session should be one of the liveliest, most creative, most insightful, and most emotion-packed team meetings you ever hold. All members should be on equal footing; all have to make a huge imaginative leap. Instead of yielding creative riches, a Technicality-laden team often suffers the abandonment of imagination. Nontechnicals don't feel qualified to discuss vision of any type with the technicals, and technicals feel constrained to imagine only things in the short term and in the technical domain.

In this environment, the technical personnel are seen as the elite. The constraints imposed on them are lighter, the hours they work more flexible, their salaries larger, their futures brighter, their equipment better, their mobility greater, and their stock options more lucrative. The nontechnical personnel are second-class citizens in this world. In addition to coping with the obvious disadvantages, they are expected to act as if they don't or can't understand "technical issues," or cannot delve into the "bits and bytes." Even those who normally show the most incredible cognitive powers will suffer a momentary brain death when asked to participate in a dialogue regarding "hard-core techie" ideas. The role of the nontechnical, nonelite workers requires that they appear disabled with respect to technology. The minds, ideas, and reasoning of the technical elite are perceived to be well beyond their inadequate ken.

Technicality's penchant for corrupting an institution or team is obscured by keen protestations of equality between the technical and nontechnical disciplines. The nontechnical personnel, goes the story, are equal but different. This refrain has been heard often

*In fact, many human qualities can provide more capacity to a team than technical proficiency can.*

*Even those who normally show the most incredible cognitive powers will suffer a momentary brain death when asked to participate in a dialogue regarding "hard-core techie" ideas.*

---

3. It's likely that most resource shortages develop in teams in proportion to their practice of Technicality. Value systems that constrain abundance don't get better over time.

throughout the ages in defense of caste systems now seen as evil or, at least, suboptimal. "They make a valid contribution," say the technicals magnanimously of their lessers, "just as important as ours." The technicals' acceptance and maintenance of the unequal rewards and other prevailing conditions belie this patently weak, tired defense of an ugly status quo.

The inegalitarian nature of the techno-caste system is not maintained by brute repression, however. No obvious political or even economic terrorism keeps the system in place. Instead, it is maintained by a conspiracy of the mediocre. The erstwhile victims are willing participants, for the most part. This compliance probably arises because, by their lesser status, the nontechnical employees are able to avoid accountability for core product design, timely delivery, product quality, and virtually every other essential characteristic of success. Even so, they keep their jobs. In fact, they are often excused from understanding the product. Once an issue is deemed technical, they are no longer held accountable for it.

The technicals, for their part, acquire and hold on to the accountability for virtually all key elements, while dismissing out of hand the majority of the available minds. By taking refuge in **Technicality**, they forgo a sane practice that might otherwise ensue— namely, participation in an **EcologyofIdeas**. Instead of limiting ideas based on technical credentials, the **Technicality** team members could expansively express their ideas in a clear, articulate way and draw forth the ideas of all those around them, in a constant and rewarding quest for the very best idea, regardless of its source.

**Technicality** devolves even further. The bigotry doesn't stop at the boundaries of the techno-caste. Instead, this impulse devours its own creators by encouraging even more divisions among the team members. Most often, in each little subgroup among the technically elite, each person is considered distinctly technical. That is, each individual is deemed to be technical in a particular way or expert in a particular area, thereby erecting further boundaries to sunder the team. These ultratechnical boundaries ultimately separate every technical from every other technical. Finally, every individual is placed in his own caste.

The segregation doesn't stop there. Within each individual, technical and nontechnical alike, there are specific personal technical facets that one holds in higher esteem.

Technicality wreaks its destruction recursively. Each technical employee clings to his meager holdings, often bearing the weight of sole accountability for the related product areas. The individual is, ultimately, all alone. He has devolved into a community of one. The best case for an individual in the solitude of Technicality would be realization of his full potential as a discrete contributor. This result is highly unlikely.[4] In such an environment, each person is unnecessarily limited by his own qualities.

*Good ideas are always comprehensible to good minds when they are expressed well.* This is true without regard to technology or any other sectarian notions.

Like other bigoted human classification systems, Technicality leads to several inefficiencies and injustices:

- It effectively forbids communication of useful ideas by establishing and enforcing mostly arbitrary domains of "expertise."

- It throttles the imaginative component of SharedVision, by reducing the imagination to the technical.

Suppose Joe is assigned to integrate two programs. An engineering or technical point of view may be the best one to assess how Joe integrates his two programs. No engineering process or insight into the technical will help you understand the fact that Joe also has a personal quirk: He can get work done only between 5 P.M. and 6 A.M. When asked why, Joe mutters something about the flow of his creative "juices."

Understanding the fluid dynamics of Joe's creative "juices" is much more difficult and much less likely to be attempted than the more routine comprehension of the interfacing of programs. The

*Technicality wreaks its destruction recursively.*

---

4. The best possible outcome is especially unlikely because the uneven load of accountability leads some individuals to excessive "overwork." The realization that a person is being judged alone contributes to the overwork by creating an "A for effort" safety net.

"A FOR EFFORT"

(i.e., you failed, but
at least you wasted
a lot of effort)

FAIL CHEAP

technical work will proceed apace (constrained by Joe's oddities). The source of the systemic problem will not be addressed, however, nor will the abundant opportunities be reaped.

Now imagine that Joe also experiences "coder's block." When he isn't subject to this problem and is really cooking, considering the functionality and the quality of the code, he is by far the best programmer on the team. The number of good ideas contributed by Joe is quite high, and the number of bad ideas from others that quietly drop away after he becomes involved in a project is also high. Joe is smart and a useful team member, but his coder's block limits his programming to perhaps 20 nights per year. Even so, he will achieve the most of any team member.

The biggest gain that this team could seek would probably be to increase the number of nights per year on which Joe can "really cook." Its major problem is not technical, at least in the conventional sense. Rather than fix this problem, however, the dozens of people on the team, including Joe, blather on in technospeak, repeatedly revisiting the ostensibly technical issues. They act as if those issues are the most vital ones imaginable.

A technicality is a tiny thing, a legal detail that is so trivial that it does not hold your attention. Living within a Technicality will nevertheless cost you more than any other conceivable cultural choice, considering how many resources are wasted on elaborate and useless personal distinctions. With the pool of time and money misspent on this foolish bigotry, the team's capacity to create and sustain an aligned greatness of purpose will be insufficient.

The goal of such an enfeebled technical staff is not to "get the best ideas in the box," but rather to "get the best ideas from people who have technical bona fides in the box." The goal of the nontechnical personnel in this system is less obvious.

## SUPPOSED SOLUTION

*Control the participation of nontechnical team members.*

*The goal of such an enfeebled technical staff is not to "get the best ideas in the box," but rather to "get the best ideas from people who have technical bona fides in the box."*

*Each individual's
value is based on the
perceived degree of his
technical proficiency.*

A common mistake is to minimize the participation of nontechnical people in technical discussions and decisions. After all, the nontechnicals themselves insist on their irrelevance in technical matters. Technical people generally prefer to discuss technical matters with their technical colleagues.

This ersatz class system is no replacement for judgment or team connection. It leads to an excessive emphasis on technical issues and skills on high-tech teams. This tendency causes team problems to manifest as technical problems.[5] It also promotes a hierarchy of individual values rather than team values. Even worse, each individual's value is based on the perceived degree of his technical proficiency.

In more advanced cases of Technicality, the team members rarely reach a common understanding of how decisions will be made, how they will identify the best new ideas, or what core values the team—and, by extension, the team's product—will exhibit. In a team where Technicality reigns, a SharedVision is shared only so far. One class dominates another.

## ACTUAL SOLUTION

*Evaluate people based on results.*

Unproductive team values are forged from the same ingredients as productive team values. The way to purge a team of Technicality is to eliminate the smallish values entirely and supplant Technicality with new values. Don't evaluate people on the following criteria:

- What they know or are alleged to know

- What they did on previous projects

---

5. If the principal or only value system is technical, then strange things can happen. For example, one person might be "crazy and wreck every meeting he goes to," but all is forgiven because "He sure is good with code."

- Their political power
- What people say about them
- Your feelings about them
- Anything except their results, including their role in others' results

When deciding things for, about, or with the team, invite every team member to participate.

Each mind has infinite capacity. Careful collaboration can, therefore, bring infinitely precious rewards.

# ANTIPATTERN: RECOIL

## PROBLEM

*After achieving something of significance,*
*you experience a feeling of hopelessness, anxiety, or guilt,*
*and a sense that the achievement was without*
*meaning altogether.*

After a meaningful achievement, the individuals on a team often experience a "correction" in attitude. We call this phenomenon "Recoil," because that's what it feels like. Perhaps the empty feelings of Recoil follow the law of physics: For every action, there is an opposite and equal reaction. It seems as if some great censor in your head warns you, "Don't get used to feeling good and realizing all that potential. If you get used to feeling good all the time, just think how disappointed you'll be when everything goes to hell. Like it always does. And feeling good is not how we do things around here. Besides, this whole thing is not realistic."

The experience of Recoil shares many similarities with those of alcoholic hangover and clinical depression. Its hallmark is a "shutdown" quality. One week, a person feels as if anything is possible, and good things are probable; he feels connected and productive.

*Recoil seems to be,
partly, the psyche's
last-ditch effort at
convincing you to "go
back" to the way
things were.*

*If you expect
suboptimal behavior
to produce mediocre
results, you will
seldom be
disappointed.*

The next week, the same person feels depressed, victimized, worthless, and, most of all, hopeless. Last week's experience is viewed as, at best, an isolated special case and, at worst, a delusion. In any case, it ain't gonna happen again.

For whatever reasons, people don't change very gracefully. Psychological and behavioral change is a very messy business. Recoil seems to be, partly, the psyche's last-ditch effort at convincing you to "go back" to the way things were.

Partly, it is a way to take some time off from the effort of consolidating a new belief. When in Recoil, you may fondly look back at your earlier beliefs and behaviors, that is, those you came to see as suboptimal or not useful at all while attending a BootCamp or some other intensive learning experience. In Recoil, you might come to appreciate that at least "the quantities" of those beliefs and behaviors were known, and the outcomes of believing and applying them were somewhat predictable. Of course, if you expect suboptimal behavior to produce mediocre results, you will seldom be disappointed.

Expecting great things carries far more risk. Recoil occurs almost immediately following the SharedVision or Alignment phase of a project. It might also follow the end of a project, such as the end of a BootCamp, or any other product shipment. It could occur at numerous other points along the way, depending on the heights of joy that are reached. The more joy experienced, the greater the risk of Recoil.

## SUPPOSED SOLUTION

*Back off a bit. Be more "realistic."*
*Don't attempt to achieve at such a fast pace.*

Unfortunately, because it is not widely discussed, Recoil is seldom named and dealt with for what it really is. The world perceived while you are in Recoil is a fantasy world that is created in your head and, often, in the heads of those around you. You create this world to support your former role in the larger conspiracy of mediocrity. The idea that you must regress or inevitably "go back" to this earlier, "more realistic" world is based on fear and has little relevance to the potential of the moment.

Typically, people deal with Recoil by feeling depressed, shutting down some of their parts, and, most of all, slowing down any new, effective behavior change. Slowing down seems the worst possible— though most pervasive—surrender to Recoil. You believe the recoil-ish nonsense echoing in your mind, which insists, "That wasn't real. I can't really gain so much more. I don't even want to be so ambitious. Who do I think I am, anyway? My situation is different—I really can't do this." This tormenting line of thought typically cannot stop a true and quiescently growing commitment to yourself, and to the greater role truth will play in your life. Nevertheless, it will sap your vitality and slow your progress to a crawl.

The benefit of identifying this reaction as Recoil, and of considering its etiology and effects on your life, is that you can put the doubt to an inner vote by convening an internal Decider. That is, you can raise the issue and then decide that slowing down has no value. Or that to be most effective you must first do *X, Y,* and *Z.* Whatever. Although you probably ought not hope to escape all of the feelings of Recoil, you can choose to sidestep its most nasty effects.

## ACTUAL SOLUTION

*Get mad. Get help. Decide to recommit to greatness.*

### *Get Mad*

No one should ever talk to you in the way that you talk to yourself when in Recoil. Self-criticism of the Recoil type is profoundly unhelp-ful. Don't tell yourself, "I was wrong. I can't really be great. I am a victim. Those guys (whoever they are) were wrong, nuts, crazy, dreamers. My case is special—that is, it is especially hopeless. Others just don't understand. What was I thinking? I can't really be happy at work. Work is not fun!" These internal accusations are cruel. You would never tolerate someone speaking to one of your loved ones that way. Hurling such digs at yourself or your team does

*Why should you wait
to be happier and
have a more benign
effect on the world?*

*Anger should
accompany your
witnessing abusive
behavior, even if both
abuser and abused
are you.*

*The secret is out and
neutralized, and the
negativity is exposed
for what it really is:
useless, obviously
foolish, self-
tormenting bushwa.*

not serve much purpose. These venomous ideas can scare you into adopting the wrong change strategy, especially if it means a slower change mode. (See also the discussion of the Feedback antipattern later in this chapter.)

But who says you ought to change slowly? Why should you wait to be happier and have a more benign effect on the world? Probably, there is more than enough of everything you need right now to get going on what you want. You have every reason to be hopeful and pursue your dreams to the fullest. So get mad. Righteous anger is always an appropriate response to abuse. If you can't feel it, look deeper. If you still can't feel it, utilize the Pretend pattern.

Anger should accompany your witnessing abusive behavior, even if both abuser and abused are you. Anger will fuel your efforts to dismantle any blocking beliefs and practices. The need for self-care and courage (or most likely, any other PersonalAlignment) will demand that you handle your Recoil with angry, unyielding determination.

## Get Help

The best medicine for the Recoil bug is to connect with others. Tell someone whom you trust (and who also understands the idea) what is going on. Name it. Say, "I am in Recoil." Tell your friend what you are telling yourself in your head. These conceptually simple tactics strip the power from the punishing censor inside of you. Saying aloud the mean-spirited things you are whispering to yourself detoxifies them. The secret is out and neutralized, and the negativity is exposed for what it really is: useless, obviously foolish, self-tormenting bushwa.

Ask your friend for help in sustaining your personal drive for greatness. Your friend will also benefit from being trusted, and from being given the opportunity to review his own Recoil in the light of your experience.

## Commit to Greatness

The combination of anger and help should provide the momentum needed to break the Recoil syndrome. The triumphant power you need will be found in your intention to change and your necessary decisions to seek help and feel your anger. Will you keep your commitments to yourself and your team? Will you live all of the way, or die some of the way?

Rest assured, you will eventually grow out of—or otherwise surmount—Recoil. You will also bounce back and forth a bit from time to time. The more you practice tapping your righteous anger, AskingforHelp, and deciding in favor of your life, the shorter your encounter with Recoil. Over time, you may almost completely purge it from your existence.

## ANTIPATTERN: FEEDBACK

### PROBLEM

*There is no standardized way to gain value for your work product or personal performance from another person, or to offer your value to the work product or the personal performance of another person.*

### SUPPOSED SOLUTION

*Give or seek feedback.*

In many institutional cultures, when one person "owns" a part of a group's product, there is no standardized means for group improvement. This deficit is often ignored by "officialdom." Other informal elements (mentorship relationships, personal support networks, formal and informal design reviews, individual study, and so on) supply whatever creative and technical support a person secures while creating something.

A multitude of specified, marginally specified, and wholly unspecified communication mechanisms can be grouped under the rubric Feedback, all of which relate to the issue of aggregating critical information. The critical information flowing through an organization

*A multitude of specified, marginally specified, and wholly unspecified communication mechanisms can be grouped under the rubric Feedback.*

is extensive, diverse, and of varied utility. When we use the term "Feedback," however, we mean any process or instance wherein

*A person not accountable for a given thing or experience*
*Offers critical information regarding it*
*To the person who is accountable for its creation.*

Feedback typically requires and is usually limited to two roles: a receiver and a transmitter. Even if more than two people are involved, the additional people typically play one of those two roles. Sometimes roles may be switched in sequence, perhaps with a delay preceding the switch.

Feedback is generally launched at the initiative of one of the following:

- *The transmitter.* An individual of critical importance to another person will become a transmitter and communicate to the receiver that he has some Feedback to convey (or that person will ask the receiver if he would like some Feedback).

- *The receiver.* An individual creator will invite a person or a group for Feedback after presenting a work product.

- *The institution.* In "mandatory Feedback," the transmitter is required to transmit, the receiver is required to receive, or both are required to interact. For example, the employee review is a periodic ritual wherein the institution requires a supervisor to give Feedback to a subordinate, or vice versa. Feedback can also be mandated in any direction in a hierarchy. An institution may also solicit Feedback from one of its constituencies and require another constituency to be the receiver.

The Feedback content is ostensibly designed to provide critical support to the receivers. Possible subjects include objects created or ideas pronounced by the receiver; perceived and actual results of the receiver; matters related to the receiver's personal style; and effects thought to be caused by the receiver. The constraints on content are usually inexplicit.

In spite of the pitfalls and dependencies on the inexplicit structures on which it is based, Feedback often provides highly relevant, vitally important information to people who want it. Where the practice pays such dividends routinely, people should certainly pursue it. Although it might be possible to increase even the best results by providing greater explicitness of terms, conditions, purposes, and roles, if it works, it works.

Unfortunately, Feedback is often deficient in several important ways.

First, Feedback sessions often take place in private and typically involve only two people: the receiver and the transmitter. This privacy can create greater intimacy and safety for both individuals. It may facilitate greater depth of disclosure and increased receptivity. On the other hand, such privacy also has costs:

- The content privately exchanged in this way may be insufficiently reviewed. It is seldom produced by the collaboration of knowledgeable parties. The virtues of a more collaborative approach are not typically incorporated into the Feedback.

- The protocols and behavior patterns used in Feedback sessions are often inexplicit, which results in poor communication, miscommunication, or even manipulative communication. Although nothing can eliminate poorly intended behavior, a few basic safeguards can ensure that the quality of the transmitter's intention and the transmitter's integrity with respect to his stated intention remain consistent with the desired values.

- Supervisory Feedback is characterized by a grave power imbalance, and the common pursuit of the truth is a value that may become lost in the real-time swirl of power and authority dynamics. Without broader participation or some other design element that can smooth the bumps caused by such a polarized institutional power setup, the institution may suffer a high rate of communication breakdown.

- Two is a difficult number of people with which to create a single point of view.[6] Desired Feedback results would likely

*Feedback sessions often take place in private and typically involve only two people: the receiver and the transmitter.*

*Supervisory Feedback is characterized by a grave power imbalance.*

---

6. One person alone is a loose cannon; two people are an irresolvable fight that just hasn't happened yet; three people in agreement are a civilization.

increase should more than two people become involved in the process. Three is a more effective minimum number and, to some extent, yields results that are disproportionate to the cost of involving an additional person. Although increasing the number of roles or players will help, this strategy by itself cannot resolve all problems caused by the privacy commonly believed to be a Feedback requirement.

Second, Feedback deploys, for the most part, a one-way communication channel. Typically, the players know what kind of experience to expect. If they don't define the constraints and conditions associated with the communication pipe, and don't secure the consent of all participants beforehand, the reliability of the process is less than what it could be.

Third, what constitutes legal content for a particular Feedback session is often not negotiated or expressed a priori. Feedback content is generally limited to any one of a (usually undefined) number of aspects of the receiver's behavior or results. The criticism originates with the transmitter, or with others who use the transmitter as an agent. Typically, it is not systematically developed to any set of specifically stated and mutually accepted standards. Despite the lack of ideals or values, aspects of the receiver's life or product are judged. Presumably, these judgments are based on inexplicit assumptions of merit and demerit, which are probably unique to the transmitter. Sometimes the controlling assumptions will be the transmitter's personally distorted variants of a set of outside assumptions, which the transmitter believes to be corporately held. Occasionally, the assumptions represent superior criteria, drawn from higher-quality thinking, experience, and intuition; these assumptions are likely to be unique to the transmitter, as well.

Fourth, the only transmission control mechanism discernible in many Feedback sessions is applied when the receiver attempts to block further transmission from the transmitter or when the receiver attempts to transmit on his own initiative. The transmitter—who often enjoys a power position vis-à-vis the receiver—usually rules such attempts illegal. Thus, the receiver is shut down with the message that he is "being defensive." No other real error correction occurs in most **Feedback** events. Most notably, no standard practice tests the receiver's acceptance of the actual message intended. Because the **Feedback** content usually deals with expressed weaknesses in the receiver's behavior or products, the neurosis that originally led to the problems is often triggered in real time. The receiver therefore becomes more likely to obscure, exaggerate, or otherwise distort the transmitter's message.

Fifth, a **Feedback** transmitter typically proffers support and critical help, even though the receiver did not solicit any assistance. The transmitter will do so without fully assessing his intention. The opportunities that normally arise from the establishment of clear intention and the testing of one's benign purpose are not protected in any way, so they often become lost, to the detriment of all involved.

Sixth, the receiver has no proactive role in **Feedback**. He can ask for it and listen to it. There is no provision for investigating the content, ensuring that the receiver received the intended information, or disallowing illegal or contradictory messages.

Seventh, the transmitter or the receiver may attempt to remedy the limitations of the setup's structure with an ad hoc, ill-defined error-checking attempt. Without making a previously determined, special-purpose language available to both players, however, the probability of successful improvisation is low.

Eighth, although mandated supervisory **Feedback** often occurs predictably, more general **Feedback**—including that from supervisors—can be given at any time. A **Feedback** session can be initiated whenever the transmitter decides to do so. This approach is an enormously inefficient way to go: The act of learning proceeds with least effort when it occurs at the behest of the receiver. Conversely, personal resistance to new information increases when the receiver's feelings for timing are not considered.

Ninth, **Feedback** has evolved into an increasingly accepted practice, so that people in a community believe that they have the right to give **Feedback** to everyone else in that community. One difficulty with this emerging entitlement is that listening to someone who

*There is no provision for investigating the content, ensuring that the receiver received the intended information, or disallowing illegal or contradictory messages.*

*It seems perfectly reasonable to suspect the intention of someone who insists on "helping" you, even though you have not asked for or have declined this aid.*

*If giving Feedback is a right of the transmitter, what are the related rights of the receiver?*

wants to give Feedback to you is, therefore, becoming increasingly mandatory in contemporary work culture. In some environments, it has become politically untenable to appear disinterested when someone wants to provide Feedback.

The pressure to listen to someone who wants to give Feedback can be significant, even if you discount the interpersonal pressure coming from the person who wants to transmit and the pressure arising from your own concern about saying "no." Unfortunately, the pressure to accept Feedback is unrelated to the actual intention impelling a transmitter to deliver Feedback. It seems perfectly reasonable to suspect the intention of someone who insists on "helping" you, even though you have not asked for or have declined this aid. Still, few concessions are doled out to the individual who rejects another person's Feedback. Declining Feedback is increasingly perceived as arrogance, even in cases where it is not.

Many good reasons exist to decline a teammate's Feedback, given the poor structure and many shortcomings of the general model, as well as the unpredictability of its many variant implementations. A receiver may prefer to skip the offer because the quality of the content to be delivered is low. Perhaps the receiver merely has something else to do that would likely create greater value than the Feedback would.

People often assume that the content of Feedback is always worth hearing. This presumption of merit is derived from the fact that someone wants to deliver the message. If giving Feedback is a right of the transmitter, what are the related rights of the receiver? If you develop a reputation for being unwilling to listen to a person who wants to offer Feedback, your colleagues may ostracize you to some extent. At the least, you will be perceived to have made a tactical mistake.

Doing a poor job as a Feedback transmitter seems to entail very little risk. If someone exploits the lack of structure in Feedback to attack rather than support, what remedy does the receiver have?

Depending on the skill and wisdom of the transmitter and the capability of the receiver to accept genuinely helpful information and to discard or ignore the rest, good things can be accomplished using Feedback, even in its present form.

## ACTUAL SOLUTION

*When asked, rank the creative products of individuals and groups, detail the positive basis of your ranking, and describe any additional attributes that you believe would make the product in question perfect.*

# The Perfection Game Pattern

## PROBLEM

*Your results are not great.*

## SOLUTION

*Perfect results by thinking and telling one another what you like and what would make the results perfect.*

There are two main classes or uses of the PerfectionGame protocol: in the PerfectionGame proper and in the everyday application of the principles behind the PerfectionGame (also referred to as "perfecting" or "playing the PerfectionGame"). The former is a specific game— fun, but with serious intent. The latter will make your collecting of critical thoughts from colleagues more fun, without loss of serious intent, but with greatly increased effectiveness.

CHAPTER
FIFTEEN
THE PERFECTION
GAME
PATTERN

326

To learn this protocol and become fluent in its applications, you should first play the PerfectionGame with your team, following all rules carefully and playing it through once all the way to the end. You and your teammates will then be able to apply the protocol as desired to your everyday requirements for critical input.

Use this protocol whenever you solicit reaction or guidance—or when it is offered to you—regarding your creative product. When you are not playing the game proper, others may or may not be expected to seek the perfecting of their own created objects, as you all decide. The two cases (that is, the game and the everyday practice) differ only in terms of their setting, the time that separates iterations of the object under scrutiny, and (possibly) the taking of turns. Otherwise, the protocol is applied in exactly the same way.

Playing the PerfectionGame enables you to achieve greater expression of the entire team's values in the objects being created, and to increase the team's aesthetic alignment. Playing the Perfection Game and perfecting your products and processes provides several benefits.

## IMPROVED QUALITY

*As iterations of the object and rounds of the PerfectionGame ensue, the team will develop a shared aesthetic with respect to objects of this type.*

There will be increased aesthetic and functional value in the succeeding iterations of the object being perfected. Future versions of the object will be more reflective of the diverse sensibilities revealed by the PerfectionGame players. As iterations of the object and rounds of the PerfectionGame ensue, the team will develop a shared aesthetic with respect to objects of this type, and the perfected object will more closely reflect the team's emerging aesthetic. The aggregate aesthetic will improve upon the previously discrete aesthetics of individuals on the team. Design skills that were previously latent in the team will be revealed and made readily available. In addition, team members' anticipation of Perfection Game sessions devoted to each of the team's creative products will increase the quality in and aesthetic alignment of every creative act.

# MORE FUN

The timely exchange of critical information can be a source of joy for all concerned. Increasing your own critical awareness can feel good. Your increased understanding of your colleagues' sensibilities and critical gifts can also make for greater connection and truer collaboration with them. Likewise, your individual and the team's aggregate sense of vision for the object and its role in the team's product can be greatly enlarged. These factors will intensify the pleasurable effects of collaboration.

The pleasures of cooperative creation are more likely to happen when a team's critical exchanges are structured to minimize counterproductive elements and increase supportive ones. A team's use of the PerfectionGame will have the following effects:

*The timely exchange of critical information can be a source of joy for all concerned.*

- It will eliminate the risk of pure negation.
- It will minimize the likelihood of common interpersonal disturbances in critical discussions.
- It will emphasize the desirable "results to date" with respect to the object being perfected.
- It will require equal, specific creative contributions from all players.
- It will increase the principal creator's autonomy with respect to the next iteration of the object.
- It will require critical thinking about greatness.

# LEARNING

People who play the PerfectionGame report several changes in their outlook:

- An appreciation for the challenges implicit in the idea of "perfect"
- A richer perspective on quality associated with their work
- Reduced personal defensiveness when accepting criticism
- A more receptive attitude toward "multipersonal" creation

CHAPTER
FIFTEEN
THE PERFECTION
GAME
PATTERN

328

- An increased willingness to take creative risks

- More energy put into thinking before giving criticism

## EFFECTIVENESS

Players are more likely to give and receive helpful criticism. The idea that a human creation can be perfect is not feasible, because engaged people can always find ways to improve even the best products. Also, the aesthetics of Perfection will always change. One way to stop working as a perfectionist while still making real progress is to repeatedly play the PerfectionGame with your team on the objects you are creating.

*The idea that a human creation can be perfect is not feasible, because engaged people can always find ways to improve even the best products.*

## THE PERFECTION GAME PROTOCOL

1. Players sit in a circle.

2. Each person in the circle names a task that he believes to be simple and that he is willing to perform throughout the game—for example, "snapping my fingers," "whistling a short tune," or "acting dead."

3. The first player performs the task named in step 2. This performance has the following structure:

   – The player alerts the rest of the group to the beginning of the performance by saying, "Okay, I'm starting now." Everything the player does after this point is subject to perfecting.

   – The player performs his task.

   – The player says, "I'm done." Everything up to but not including this statement is subject to perfecting.

4. The remaining players rate the player's performance on a scale of 1 to 10, where 10 is a perfect performance of the task. The rating must be supported with critical analysis of a particular form: After saying the score (for example, "I give your performance a 7"), the scorer must state the following:

CHAPTER
FIFTEEN
THE PERFECTION
GAME
PATTERN

330

- Specifically, what about the performance was good and what earned the points in the score
- Specifically, what the performer must do in the next iteration of the performance to be awarded a perfect 10

The next player then performs his task and is rated by the rest of the group as described above.

5. Steps 1–4 are completed two more times, so that each player performs and is rated three times. Each person plays the role of critic for the rest of the team members in between each of his own performances.

### Analysis of the Perfection Game Protocol

Purely or partially negative feedback is not allowed at any point during the PerfectionGame protocol. For example, "I don't like the sound of the finger snap." The important information to transmit in this case may be something like, "The ideal sound of a finger snap for me is one that is crisp, has sufficient volume, and startles me somewhat. To get a 10, you would have to increase your crispness."

If you cannot think of a better alternative performance, you cannot withhold points. The default score is a perfect 10.

You must follow the scoring routine exactly:

- "I rate your performance $n$."
- "What I liked about it was $p, q, \ldots, z$."
- "What it would take to get a 10 from me is $a, b, \ldots, z$."

If one person breaks the protocol, the other team members must politely correct the offending person by pointing out the infraction. They must then remind the offender of the correct protocol immediately by suggesting, "I give it a . . . ," "What I liked about it was . . . ," or "What it would take to get a 10 is . . . ," as appropriate.

When playing the PerfectionGame, the team will develop a sense of the ideal performance of any given act. This aesthetic will take into account the best suggestions made, with lesser suggestions being abandoned.

Including each of the suggested improvements into the next performance rarely yields a perfect performance. The "perfecters" could be wrong about their prior feedback (not intentionally, of course), or the combination of all suggestions may have a negative effect on the performance. As the "perfectee," you must accept only the superior criticism of your performance and implicitly reject the inferior feedback.

Your ratings must not use a "dislike" to "like" scale, where 1 is "completely dislike" and 10 is "completely like." The PerfectionGame is not about whether you "like" something. The rating scale goes from 1, "The thing has no value now and I can add all value needed in my feedback," to 10, "The thing has full value, and/or I can't think of anything that would make it better." It is important to hold perfecters accountable to this type of scale and respectfully correct them if you see the dislike/like scale coming into play.[1]

In addition, the rating must be reasonable. For instance, if you rate a performance as an 8, you are saying that it is 80% perfect, and you can tell the person exactly how to gain the 20% of missing value. You must not give an 8 and then provide only 1% of the missing value.

The "what it will take to get a 10" portion of the game may not be performed in writing. It must be performed verbally with the perfectee.

If you feel an impulse to grade on the dislike/like scale; can't give a reasonable amount of value that correlates with your rating and are unwilling to raise your rating accordingly; or feel the need to write your perfecting down instead of speaking to the person, then you should pass. These impulses can contribute to a negative feedback cycle that distracts the team from achieving the desired results.

*The PerfectionGame is not about whether you "like" something.*

---

1. Perfecters can say that they like something and indicate what they like. It is only the dislike part of the dislike/like scale that distracts from the game.

# V

# Appendixes

THE CORE LEXICON,

BOOTCAMP MATERIAL,

THE CORE PROTOCOLS V. 1.0

*"I boot."*

# The Core Lexicon

One of the great simplifications available to collaborators is to establish for themselves the exact meaning of terms they deem important to their collaboration; and one of the great opportunities afforded systems developers is their unabridged right to name and define the symbols (that is, the variables and macros) that they use in the systems they write. Taking the opportunity provided by the latter in hopes of more often achieving the former, the terms important to the adoption of The Core are defined in this, "The Core Lexicon."

In cases where we felt that additional discussion of a term as defined would be useful, we added it beneath the term's definition. The use of italics separates such commentary from the definitions proper.

ABUNDANCE—A condition wherein the quantities of needed things exceed the need for them. Also, when something is in a state of true abundance, its surplus must impose no great cost on those who benefit from its availability.

*Achieving an abundant supply of the things desired by those who must do the achieving will always be an acceptable goal to them.*

ACCOUNTABLE, ACCOUNTABILITY—Acceptance of the results associated with one's behavior.

ACHIEVEMENT—The process of forming intention and the subsequent actions that lead to the establishment of the conditions intended.

ACT—To do things in a way that creates a difference; when you act, changes observable to others ensue.

AFRAID (scared)—An emotion that signals that something is unknown.

AGGREGATE—A quality collected together from all the members of a team and considered as a whole, as in *the aggregate intelligence* of the team.

ALIGN—To organize relevant elements in optimal positions in support of achieving particular goals.

ALIGNMENT—That which provides the basis for organizing elements in optimal positions relative to achieving goals.

ANTIPATTERN—A pattern that describes common solutions that yield undesirable results. A pattern that doesn't work.

AWARENESS—That which makes one present to oneself.

BELIEVE—To act as if something were true.
    *A belief is a hypothesis with legs. It can finally start planning on how to become a virtual certainty, or maybe even a known fact. It has enough value to gain a more permanent berth in your mind, and it must promise enough gain to play a more prominent role in guiding your life. To become a belief, a hypothesis must ascend over all other competing hypotheses, displace any prior related beliefs, and secure enough courage from you to let it actually govern your behavior when needed.*

*What you say you believe isn't as important as what you believe. And, obviously, you don't believe what you don't enact. Although describing, proselytizing, or otherwise articulating your beliefs in media other than your own acts can be fun, it is seldom very useful to you or anyone else. Babbling on about a value is a distraction from attaining it. Believing is not only used for framing and conducting investigation and experimentation, but for conducting actual trials. If you act as if something is true, you will shortly find out whether it is or isn't. Any reduction of effort or increase of abundance you enjoy as a consequence of your new belief is the best measure of its truth.*

*The degenerate state of believing is knowing—that is, when a hypothesis becomes "knowledge" or "certainty." Knowing is believing without regard to the truth.*

BIG IDEA—An idea regarding potential actions that solves many problems simultaneously.

BIGOTRY—Type of blindness characterized by persistent misperceptions.

BLATHER—Talk that doesn't move the team, or even the team's discourse, toward the goal. The talk may or may not be engaging.

BLOCK—In Alignment, something that obstructs the alignee from attaining a goal.

CHECKED IN—Behavior characterized by high levels of engagement, substantial presence, disclosure of self, and receptivity to others.

CHECKED OUT—Absence due to awareness of low productivity or unresolved conflicting commitments.

CHOICE—Acting in a way that selects one from among many possible actions.

COGNITION—The process of mentally structuring one's incoming stream of information.

*Cognition can be viewed as involving several steps:*

1. *The suspension of one's relevant beliefs*

2. *The analysis and integration of the information provided by one's relevant thoughts, feelings, and intuitions*

3. *The formation of hypothetical acts that might exploit the information available*

4. *The expression of the "best" acts yielded by steps 1–3*

COLLABORATE—When two or more independent agents act in concert toward achieving a stated result.

COMMITMENT—A promise of behavior or results.

CONFLICT—Unreconciled interests. Often a big idea is required to resolve conflict.

CONNECTION—A point or points of interface between people.

CONVENTION—Words or behavior conforming to socially accepted customs or style, or done by rote.

THE CORE—A collection of patterns, protocols, antipatterns, and definitions designed to increase the efficiency of teams.

COURAGE—Wise choices while feeling fear. Integrated choices.

CREATIVITY—Ideas enacted. Congealed intuition.

CULTURE—The set of traditions, laws, rules, norms, and arts characteristic of a group in a stated time period.

CYNIC—One who represses hope.

DECISION—An explicit, conscious choice. Decisions are often recorded.

DEFINITION—A statement, contained in this lexicon, of what a word or expression used in connection with The Core means.

DEPTH—A reference to the extent of levels of meaning, or degree of transcendence.

DEPTH, CHECK IN—The degree of disclosure and extent of feelings of vulnerability that result.

DISCLOSE—To reveal.

DRAMA—Neurotic behavior that is theatrical in nature and nonproductive of results.

EFFICIENCY—A value expressed mathematically as results/effort. The larger the efficiency, the greater the productivity of the effort.

*Because the practice of efficiency is a commitment to improvement in all things, a given attempt at efficiency may be more costly than earlier attempts.*

EFFICIENT—Behavior that yields the same or better results with less effort compared with prior behavior in similar circumstances.

EMOTIONS, EMOTIONAL—High-speed, personal information-processing elements consisting of one or more of four primitive feeling states: mad, sad, glad, and afraid.

*The function of emotions is to inform the person experiencing them more quickly or differently than would be done by rational thought. Emotions are slower and more vivid than intuitions, and faster and more diffuse than thoughts.*

ENGAGEMENT—Involvement with other people, work, and objects.

EVIDENCE—In Alignment, something in the behavior, affect, or results of an alignee that shows the rest of the team that he has attained, is attaining, or is working on attaining that which he wants.

FEEDBACK—Difficult to structure and often undesirable noise that usually arises in reaction to certain expressions.

FEELINGS—Emotions.

FIGHT—Use of a conflict by one or more of the interests involved to harm the other interests.

FLOW—A term given to a specific state of optimal performance, first used by Mihaly Csikszentmihalyi in his book *Flow: The Psychology of Optimal Experience* (Harper & Row, 1990).

FOLLOW—To accept benign leadership and to act as required to sustain it.

FREEDOM—The state of being wherein the pursuit of the desired is not unnecessarily hindered. Behavior that follows self-acceptance, itself often followed by the acceptance of others.

FUN/JOY/PLEASURE—Application of personal power, often associated with the exercise of connection and/or creativity.

GLAD (happy)—An emotion that signals a gain.

GOAL—That which is desired, for which one has formed intention.

GREAT, GREATNESS—That which is productive of abundant good, or goodness scaled larger. The result of sustained, passionate living.

    *Pursuit of greatness usually exhausts all accessible potential in its pursuit of the good. Greatness is generally judged by assessing the beneficence of results over the long term, and is thus the purview of history.*

HEADGAP (baseline)—The headgap baseline is the cost in time, effort, and learning for a person to apply one of his abilities to a given task when and as he desires.

HEADGAP (cost)—The increase in cost (beyond the headgap baseline) that a person would pay to apply the ability of another person.

*The cost of psychological distance (the headgap) between two people is the additional cost required for Person A to apply an ability so that it is available to Person B as if it were B's own, plus the additional cost (beyond the baseline) for Person B to gain such availability. The headgap includes any costs of the interpersonal connection between A and B, the effort A and B must make to increase their availability to each other, and the effort B must make to apply A's quality. Also the headgap incorporates the cost of erroneous transactions between A and B.*

HIGH BANDWIDTH, BANDWIDTH—The capacity of a communications channel to carry information.

HOPE—Belief in potential, usually experienced in the first stages of trust.

*Hope is really the conception of new life; it is the only antidote to cynicism.*

HYPOTHESIS—An idea about how information might be used to produce more abundance, either by reducing effort or by increasing the results of effort, or some combination of the two.

IDEA—An abstract, internal connection between things thought to be unlike, often experienced as an impulse to do, accept, or create new things or ways.

INSPIRE—To encourage more effective efforts or greater creativity. The most effective form of inspiration is behavioral; the least effective is verbal exhortation.

INTEGRITY—Transcendent congruence. Alignment of feeling, thought, word, and deed; connection with unity and without limits. The unity of thought, word, and deed.

INTELLECTUAL PROPERTY, IP—The product of imaginative effort.

*In commercial terms, IP is basically a legal fiction designed to confer the possibility of ownership over aspects of largely abstract elements. Although this type of ownership can be granted and enforced legally provided the owner adheres to certain technical procedures established by international and local law, in the context of The Core, the ownership potential of IP is neither assumed nor required.*

INTELLIGENCE—Sustained smartness. A quality that requires the consistent application of what is known to the pursuit of what is desired.

*Intelligence sometimes begins as an abstract element. Ultimately, however, all intelligence must be behavioral. That is, unapplied intelligence is stupidity.*

INTELLIGENT AGENT—A collection of dynamically available information combined with self-awareness. An intelligent agent always behaves with efficiency proportionate to the extent of intelligence in its collection.

INTENTION—Desired potential result.

INTENTIONAL—Purposeful. Behavior or expression performed with achievement of a result in mind.

INTERFACE—A point or points at which one object connects with another; the rules and protocols surrounding such engagement.

INTUITION—A precognitive awareness of emerging reality; contact with motive energy.

INVESTIGATE—Unconditional inquiry driven by real or pretended curiosity.

INVOKE—Cause to be executed.

KNOW—To know or to be certain, is to believe to a pathological degree.

*The pathology of knowing manifests itself in the "knower's" movement to expunge personal receptivity and repress the continuous experimentation and analysis that leads to learning. Learning confers vitality on the believer. Knowledge, or certainty, typically retards or even eliminates cognition in the knower. Consequently, knowing is usually an inferior interface to a world than is believing.*

LEAD—To be the first person or group to act on a belief.

LEADERSHIP—Public vulnerability. Courageous deployment of power.

MAD (angry)—An emotion that signals a problem.

MATURITY—Behavior characterized by efficiency and the absence of neurosis.

MEDIOCRITY—On average, meeting average expectations.

NEUROTIC—Behavior and/or belief that tends to defeat one's purpose.

*By this definition, it seems that all people are neurotic. The tenacious evolution of your neurotic behavior even after it has (apparently) been identified and consciously rejected (at least in the general case) is a true mystery. Still, it seems that almost all human behavior has neurotic components. Even the most successful behaviors, when deconstructed, are more like a race barely won than a purely positive succession of actions.*

PASS—To explicitly choose to forgo something.

PASSION—Compelling anger, sorrow, joy, or terror; sublime emotions. Vivid caring.

PATTERN—A pattern is a standardized way of efficiently communicating the solution to a problem in a context; it should generate something and tell you how to generate that same thing.

PERCEIVE—To acquire information via one's sensory apparatus while simultaneously maintaining awareness of the perceiving experience.

PERFECTION—That which can be improved no further.

PERSON—The smallest, discrete intelligent agent. A person is the atom of intelligence.

PLAN OF RECORD—The complete set of actions to be done. Decided by a team.

POP A LEVEL—To intentionally focus one's orientation at an imaginative level that includes but is not limited to the immediate consensual reality.

POWER—Being. New learning and new integration.

PRESENCE—A person's impact over a given time period; the experience of another's impact.

*The quality, value, and cost of your presence over time is determined primarily by (1) the differences it makes to those who interacted with you during and after the time in question, (2) the differences it made on the objects and processes involved, (3) the differences you forge in your own life by your perceptions and the interactions with others. Your degree of presence over a time and at a particular place with a particular group determines the extent of your results.*

*Presence varies: You move between having no effects whatsoever to total supremacy over the time period. Your presence is increased by self-disclosure, disclosure most effectively wrought in the medium of your behavior. If you form intentions and apply them, exercise your awareness, think and exploit whatever virtue you possess, your presence grows great. The largest increases in presence will come from timely use of your creativity. Conversely, presence is diminished by your withholding any of these things.*

PRETEND—A mental effort that superimposes newly imagined conditions in favor of actual or remembered conditions upon one's environment.

*Such pretense is almost always for the purpose of eliminating a possible personal bias or creating more productive conditions for something new by the willing suspension of disbelief. Conversely, when pretense has less intention behind it, such pretense is often meant to posit imaginary conditions that would, if accepted, establish one's lack of accountability for a result.*

PRIMITIVE—Reduced to the level of atomicity; that is, not further reducible. In a system, the primitives are the basic units of construction.

PRODUCT—Result.

PRODUCTIVE—That which generates acceptably more than it costs; could be behavior, ideas, or ingredients of any type.

PROFESSIONAL(ISM)—A style of behavior that meets expectations.

PROPOSER—A team member who has made a well-formed proposal to a team; certain rights and responsibilities accrue to a proposer for the life of his proposal.

PROTOCOL—A set of rules or standards designed to enable people or computers—singly or in groups—to connect with one another and to exchange information with as little error and using as little time as possible.

PROXIMITY—A reference to the closeness between people or objects.

RECOIL—A distressful experience following a supremely satisfying one. In Recoil, one disbelieves in the reality of the former joy and related achievements, and experiences psychological regression.

RECURSIVE, RECURSION—A property belonging to a thing that is defined in terms of itself; something that is applied to itself repeatedly.

REPRESS—To force or coerce some countervailing force to find alternative avenues of expression rather than the normal or most expedient avenues. This coercion is often done because of a real or imagined prohibition of the most direct and simplest means of expression.

RESCUE—Offering what you see as help to someone who hasn't requested this assistance.

*Rescues are words you say or actions you take that are unilateral (that is, you or you and other co-rescuers say or do something on your own initiative) and ostensibly performed on behalf of another person, even though the object of the rescue has not explicitly asked you to provide said words or actions. Most often, a rescue is a misguided attempt to change another's feeling state so as to ameliorate another's·perceived discomfort and thereby provide greater comfort for yourself.*

*Example 1: You say, "I think what Bill is trying to say is . . ."*
*Fact: Bill speaks for Bill, and you for you.*

*Example 2: Bill says, "I'm so . . . [negative self-depiction]."*
*You say, "Oh, no, Bill, you are so [positive Bill-depiction]."*
*Fact: Most likely, Bill is either (1) neurotically putting himself down, (unacceptable); (2) indirectly (which, in this case, translates to inefficiently and manipulatively) seeking your contradiction to his negative self-assessment (unacceptable); (3) accurately approaching or identifying some weakness or some darker aspect of himself (praiseworthy); or (4) simply mistaken in his self-assessment (highly unlikely), whereupon your denial would escape rescue-hood.*

*Generally, any attempt motivated by the desire to "make" someone stop feeling "negative" feelings is a rescue. All feelings are benign and transitory. Often our uneasiness with another's discomfort greatly compounds our personal discomfort.*

*Example 3: Bill says, "I need X."*
*You say, "Bill, I'll give you X."*

*Fact: You are rescuing Bill from having to show his dependency by directly asking: "Will you . . . ?" Any transaction of this type that doesn't include asking and answering has rescuing (and therefore deception) within its confines.*

*Example 4: You know Bill feels sad.*

*Spontaneously, perhaps even within a group, you start enumerating Bill's attractions. You hope it makes Bill feel better.*

*Fact: You are trying to stop Bill's sadness, if he has any, and you are telling him (and anyone else who is listening) that sadness is unwelcome to you. The basic message is "Stop the sadness!" (or whatever feeling you don't want). Although your intervention may feel courageous to you and is surely benign (you think), you are actually wasting time, injuring yourself, and prolonging or even creating Bill's angst. Such attempts at manipulative affirmation are usually transparent, and reduce the value of whatever true content they have. They injure you by tainting what you offer and diminishing the value you bring to Bill, should he ask for it. They also decrease the future value you can more purely bring to Bill or others by establishing your willingness to flatter rather than affirm. If you reward Bill's show of sadness instead of inviting his request for support, you will get more shows and fewer requests.*

**RESULT, RESULTS**—The product of intentional efforts.

**RESULTS-ORIENTED**—Behavior organized to most efficiently achieve results, that is, that which is desired.

**RICH INFORMATION, ENRICHED INFORMATION**—A set of collected facts about something of interest to a particular audience, from which local irrelevancies have been removed, and to which emphasizing and summarizing elements have been added. This information is then communicated to its audience in the most direct means possible. The person transmitting achieves special efficiencies by assuming that any prior context of trust remains stable, that earlier shared values are still shared, and that an established, common commitment to particular objectives is still active within the intended recipients of the information. These conditions allow for reduced consumption of bandwidth and time in collaborative discourse.

*High degrees of data compression can be found in a glance between two lovers. Much information is transmitted in little time with very little effort. This is due to the presumed continuity of the state of trust, shared values, and common goals of the lovers.*

SAD—An emotion that signals a loss.

SAFETY—Applied trust. Projection of the benign.

SELF—Dimensions of accountability. Empowerment.

SELF-CARE—Behavior that fulfills one's accountability for oneself.

SELF-DESTRUCTIVE—Neurotic.

*Apparently, all people carry self-destructiveness. Most instances simply result in the extra struggle and suffering you invite into your life and then oh-so-stoically endure; extreme cases have more extreme results.*

SHARED VISION—A multipersonal state of being in which the participants see and imagine the same things. Differs from a *shared vision statement*, a phrase that is used to summarize that which is seen or imagined by a team in a state of shared vision.

SKEPTIC—One who represses gullibility.

SMART—Applying what is understood to attaining what is desirable. That which is productive.

SOFTWARE—A kind of intellectual property (IP) specific to sets of organized procedures and data having the property that, when given the same parameters as input, will always produce the same results.

STUCK—Obsessing, or caught in an obsessive cycle.

*When stuck, a person will incorrectly map many evils or hindrances to the object on which he is stuck. Oversimplification of the causes of undesirable results is one symptom of being stuck. Any one or more of scapegoating, maintaining an attitude of victimhood, and the sensation of a lack of control may characterize being stuck.*

TALK—Unstructured vocalizations with widely varying signal-to-noise ratios.

*Talk is the most common way to avoid leading or following. Talking is also a strategy to prevent others from leading or following. Often, because someone wants to talk, you feel obligated to listen. This exercise represents courtesy in decay. While listening is typically a rewarding strategy, paying disproportionate attention to low-utility verbiage serves no one. Worse, seeming to pay attention positively harms all involved.*

TEAM—An intelligent agent that is super-personal. It consists of a number of persons (or teams) committed to acting in concert toward a common purpose with the highest possible efficiency.

*Team behavior always involves two activities:*

- *Pooling personal resources, especially time, information, and skills*
- *Deploying those resources in the efficient pursuit of individual and communal success and abundance*

*Also, a team is always capable of speaking with one voice.*

THINK—To intentionally monitor and guide oneself in acts of cognition.

*Often, thinking is confused with the normal process of consciousness. In the "professional" context, thinking is really a travesty of cognition. In this world, the practice of thinking seems to be characterized by detachment and based on the repression or elimination of most available information relevant to the subject of the thinking. For example, the information contained in feelings, intuitions, and other rapid-processing capabilities is taboo. This type of "professionalism" really consists of anti-thinking and emotional bigotry.*

*Rigid boundaries on thinking seem to develop when group members know—together and at the same time—that no useful information can be gleaned from their perceptions. Worse, new perceptual information may be considered dangerous to the group's well-being. As used professionally, the term "thinking" connotes antiseptic, verbal, mostly linear knowing. Typically, "thinking," as it is understood in the workplace, depends on a bias against science. This bias arises from an urge to sustain belief without ongoing experimentation. The defense of an arbitrary collection of usually second-hand knowledge against the acceptance of new, first-hand information places an enormous tax on work environments.*

THINKING—Exerting mental effort while maintaining awareness of such exertion. Thinking always includes thinking about thinking. Alternative states of consciousness do not.

TOLERANCE—Personal endorsement of something by offering no perceptible resistance to it.

TOUCHY-FEELY—Pejorative term used to demean intentional behavior that is purportedly designed to elicit or express emotions; often used prejudicially.

TRANSPARENT—That which is present but doesn't seem like it is. As opposed to virtual, that which seems present but isn't.

TRUST—Belief in connection. Accurate perception of the benign.

TRUTH—A belief that, when acted upon, is more likely to produce abundance than competing beliefs.
*Truths give way only to other truths; they do so continuously and at what seems to be an accelerating pace.*

VALUE—A positive force conducive to results.

VIRTUAL—That which seems present but isn't; as opposed to transparent, that which is present but doesn't seem like it is.

VIRTUE—A power, the application of which is particularly conducive to achieving results.

VISION—Imaginative sight. Perception in multiple dimensions.

WANTS—What is desired.
  *Goals, wants, and desires are used interchangeably in The Core.*

WASTE—Effort or expense that does not produce the desired result.

# BootCamp
# Material

I n addition to the latest version of The Core protocols, documents describing the specific rules of engagement, details on the simulation, and other miscellaneous information, BootCamp students receive the following information prior to arriving at BootCamp. BootCamp always runs for five days and nights, usually from 7 P.M. Sunday through 3 P.M. Friday afternoon. The class may include 10 to 20 students.

TO THE FIRST-TIME READER: *In January 2001, I was a student at BootCamp. At the end of the course, while giving my feedback to Michele McCarthy, I promised her I would submit a suggested attachment to the BootCamp "manual." Here it is.*

*What you are reading may well frustrate you. It did me. At first reading, the explanation of BootCamp and its assignment may seem vague. I hope you can take comfort from the fact that it is supposed to be that way. The ambiguity of the assignment, its open-endedness, and indeed the open-endedness of the entire course are what make BootCamp the success it is.*

*Your team will struggle with this assignment, just as teams in your company struggle with the complexity and ambiguity of real projects.*

*If after reading a section you find yourself saying, "Huh? I don't have a clue," I suggest you mark that section, proceed on in the book, and return to it again once you've finished reading the whole book. Or reread it after your first day of camp. Or even later in the course. Or all of the above. Many things written here become much clearer after you work on the problem for a while with your team.*

*I was skeptical about this course after my first reading of this book. Since attending BootCamp, I can assure you that this course is about tangible results in the workplace. The course, and the book, taught me more about teams and teamwork than I thought possible.*

*Bill Larson*
*February 2001*

---

## YOU AND YOUR PARTICIPATION IN BOOTCAMP

We want your BootCamp to provide a learning experience comparable to the experiences that motivated this statement from one of our students. This kind of experience will be possible if our assumptions about what you want from this course and what you're willing to do to achieve it are valid. We ask that you carefully read these assumptions and make sure that we have an accurate understanding of what we can expect from you.

1.  We assume that you *want* to participate in BootCamp.

If at any time (including now) you decide not to participate further in BootCamp, please advise a BootCamp staff member right away. We will help you arrange to leave BootCamp (or to withdraw your registration) as efficiently as possible. It is against our policy that anyone should attend BootCamp under any kind of duress. Mandatory attendance or any type of coercion also violates our written or verbal agreements with sponsoring corporate customers. This holds true whether the pressure comes from your manager, your place of employment, or any third party who applies any leverage to secure your attendance.

If you don't want to attend, it is important to everyone involved that you not attend. BootCamp has been created for your personal development. Although we are unwilling to be a party to any type of "personal development" under duress, we do believe it is wise for your managers and other leaders[1] to encourage your attendance. If you are confused about the difference between support and coercion for your participation here, we expect you to contact a BootCamp staff member immediately to help resolve this issue.

2. We assume that *you* will take care of yourself, your privacy, and your safety.

We do not insist that you participate in any activity or perform particular behaviors during BootCamp. Nor will we support any pressure or coercion from team members toward one another. If we see pressure applied within the team, and if the team does not eliminate it, we will do so, as a last resort.

As in the rest of your life, all activities here are absolutely voluntary. We will not be concerned with whether you ought to do or say something. We expect that you will act as an adult and be accountable for your own well-being. If you hear someone say, "At BootCamp they made me . . . ," you will know that this statement is untrue, by virtue of this assumption and by our consistent behavior in support of our Core protocols, which you will have opportunity to observe.

We will not "make" you do anything at any point.

3. We assume that if you choose not to participate in an activity, you will explicitly "pass" on it.

---

1. It is unwise for them to encourage anyone until they have completed a BootCamp themselves.

Passing is good, even though it may cause discomfort. A person who passes makes it acceptable for all to pass. This kind of leadership is essential to the smooth running of a team. When structured interpersonal protocols are in place, as in BootCamp, relief is always possible by exercising the right to pass.

*Note:* When a person passes, others on the team are enjoined by the protocol from questioning or harassing him in any way; nor can they mention or discuss the person who has passed, comment on the passing, or tolerate any mention of it from another. Passing is free to the passer as far as we can make it possible.

4. We assume that you want to learn about yourself and team dynamics, and that you want to understand what we understand about teams.

We have developed a thoroughly researched point of view on several issues:

- What elements are necessary for the efficient development of intellectual property by a team
- How best to transmit this point of view to a team
- How best to catalyze the required elements for team greatness in just a few days

We have helped create more than 100 high-tech teams in our quest to acquire the most advanced team knowledge available. We have developed an efficient way to transmit the knowledge to those who want it. We have rigorously studied the teams we've formed, assessed and reassessed our results, experimented with large numbers of variables in a wide variety of settings, and incorporated many generations of new learning.

In short, we've done all the things that you might do if you wholly devoted yourself to becoming a student of teams. We are absolutely committed to providing you with the most useful team knowledge and practice in the shortest possible amount of time. We will not be easily deterred from that commitment.

5. We assume you want to learn efficiently.

*We respectfully suggest that debate with the staff is not the best use of your time with us.* We encourage you to simply accept us in our teaching and consulting role.[2]

As you begin your BootCamp, you will definitely want to maximize your learning and fun and to reduce any discomfort or wasted effort. The best way to do so is simply to pretend that the teaching we provide is true. During BootCamp, you may pretend that alternative strategies that you've never imagined are the best alternatives.

If Campers suspend their natural skepticism and set aside their initial impulse to reject new ideas, they will learn more. Many people have a negative response to new information when that information requires a change in their own behavior. We recommend that you pretend that you are learning something similar when you experience this kind of response. As hundreds of our students have found, transcending the initial discomfort and acquiring the information despite one's transient feelings of resistance is a hallmark of mature, experiential learning.

It doesn't make sense to proceed unless you understand this point and have accepted the basic learning strategy described earlier. If you can escape the ruthless gravity of your own certainty long enough to experiment with the new ideas, assuming that they might actually work, before you decide whether they are useful, your learning will be the most profound, and your experience the richest. After understanding an idea, you will have plenty of time to reject it, improve upon it, or adopt it as a belief. In the experimental environment of BootCamp, acting as if new behaviors would yield new results is the optimal learning strategy.

If you cannot do that, you must not want the things we've assumed you want so far.

---

2. While efficient disputation and fruitful debate certainly have their place as learning tools, they are not appropriate here. Consider an analogy: If you wanted to learn chemistry in the shortest amount of time, you might hire a (costly) chemistry professor to teach you for, say, five days. Likely, you would not dispute his assertions about the periodic table during your five-day cram course, even if you had never heard of the periodic table and found it to be a preposterous idea.

6. We assume that you agree to adhere to The Core protocols.

7. If any of our assumptions is not true of you, then *you must* resolve that issue before proceeding.

   – You can promptly get what you need to render the assumptions true.

   – If you are at BootCamp, you can check out and immediately physically leave the BootCamp.

   – If you have not arrived at BootCamp, you can advise us of your withdrawal.

8. We assume that your attendance at the initial session at Boot-Camp constitutes your full acceptance of these assumptions and that you are psychologically and mentally capable of endorsing and fulfilling this contract.

# MISCELLANEOUS BOOTCAMP INFORMATION

BootCamp is a "simulation" environment. We simulate what goes on in the work environment. Simulations will surface issues that come up in the "real world." In the BootCamp simulation environment, you are free to try out new behaviors and beliefs when these issues arise. There is no penalty for trying something different, as this setting is purely experimental. No actual product hangs in the balance.

The more deeply immersed you become in the simulated environment, the more you will gain from BootCamp. The following activities will draw you out of the simulation if you allow them to do so:

- Leaving to go home
- Doing work from the office
- Going to work
- Carrying your cell phone/pager/e-mail device
- Getting involved in dramas at home or work while you're away
- Using alcohol or other recreational drugs

- Giving feedback about BootCamp during BootCamp
- Talking about outside work problems[3]

Although we can't prevent you from leaving to go home or to work, both of which are actions that will diminish your own Boot Camp experience (and your ultimate contribution to your team), we will insist that you not interrupt the simulation for other Boot Campers. We do not allow the use of alcohol or other drugs during BootCamp. We do not allow cell phones/pagers/e-mails/feedback or other outside disruptions to affect the class.

We support the integration of family life with work life. If you want to spend time with your family this week, we would enjoy having them visit BootCamp. This contact adds to the experience of the simulation, as opposed to your departure for home, which breaks the simulation.

## THIS WEEK'S SIMULATION

The simulation this week involves three groups:

- Your team, which consists of BootCampers and BootCamp Coaches (who have attended BootCamp at least once already)
- Consultants (played by the BootCamp staff), who are hired by your manager to help you create your product
- Managers (played by the BootCamp staff), who represent the people for whom you work and who need you to create a great product on time

After the BootCamp introduction on Sunday night, the simulation will begin. Your team will be responsible for delivering the assignment by Friday at 1 P.M. The consultants will be available by appointment if you ask for help. The managers will send faxes and/or show up periodically to track your team's progress. You may send communications to your managers by handing a fax to one of the consultants.

---

3. Unless the problem is directly related to personal work you are doing, such as your PersonalAlignment.

# HATS

We sometimes wear colored hats. You may wear an orange hat sometimes.

### *Blue Hat*

Worn by a staff member playing a character. These characters are not always explicitly supportive, but they always have some good information for you.[4]

### *Orange Hat*

Worn by a person who acts solely as an observer. Do not talk to observers or ask them to participate in any way. If you are an observer, do not participate explicitly. In particular, observers do not speak or interact physically with the team. If a staff member puts an orange hat on you, continue to observe until the staff removes the hat. Team members can put orange hats on one another.

We recommend that you give an observation report after taking an orange hat off, describing what you observed.

### *Black Hat*

Worn by a staff member playing a manager in charge of your project.

### *White Hat*

Worn by a person who has attended at least one BootCamp. White Hats might visit during your BootCamp. Their intention is to support you on your project.

---

4. A famous Blue Hat character is Rescinda, the angel of good meetings. Rescinda can control time like a VCR. Rescinda may rewind time and let you try something over, like an interaction with a Black Hat. The notable thing about the role of Rescinda is that you can always pretend you are Rescinda and rewind or pause time if needed.

*No Hat*

Worn by a staff member playing the role of a consultant, doing the utmost to help you. *A consultant will wait until you ask for help.* We will not jump in to guess what help you need. If we do jump in, we are almost certainly making a mistake. Occasionally, we may make a well-thought-out intervention. This entrance is substantially different from ad hoc engagement.

## FACILITIES LIAISON

BootCamp staff members are not responsible for facilities issues (using hotel facilities, arranging food, finding white boards, and so on). We suggest that you nominate a representative from your team to handle all facilities issues, including provision of meals. Some teams have found that picking a different person every day for facilities liaison works well. Whatever meets the needs of the team is fine with us.

Coaches-in-training on your team may not be facilities liaisons.

## ART SPACE

We recommend using the art space to help with almost any sort of problem and to achieve more connectedness with less effort. Creating individual and team art can help you achieve clarity, connect with one another, resolve conflicts, get new ideas, get bigger ideas, and so forth. Creating something is the solution to many problems. Think of art-making as a way to enlist your unconscious and as a way to provide a substitute for developing products.

When you use the art space, be sure to clean up—both the area and the tools—thoroughly each time you create anything. The goal is to respect and preserve the tools. With regard to materials, be generous with yourself. "Thorough" art seems to be the best.

When you create an art object, label it with the following information:

- A title
- Your signature
- The date
- The location

For example,

*"Chaos" by Michele McCarthy, June 1998, Seattle, WA*

The value of your artwork comes from your valuing it. By treating the things you create respectfully, you increase the probability that you will create respectable art. For many students, the most difficult part of creating art is owning that it is art and that it should be treated as such. We believe that your art has great personal and historical significance.

Many people claim that they are not artists and are not comfortable playing with art. One way to experiment with art in BootCamp is to view it as "opposite art." Whatever you think you "ought" to do, do the opposite.

"Mistakes" are impossible in art, because mistakes reflect the idea that all goals or expectations ought to come true—even if we lack the tools or the maturity to make them come true, even if we learn more another way, even if it doesn't matter, even if it would be better otherwise. The concept of mistakes is valued negatively, as if we've done something "bad." To understand this idea, think of a person close to you, who upon feeling judged by someone, states, "Sure, I've made mistakes." The voice is grudging, the tone either defensive or arrogant, the following word almost always "but," and the words hypocritical. In team art, "mistakes" are where our learning happens and where our joy arises.

One useful way to look at the act of creating something is to consider the rational, planning part of you as impeding rather than supporting great art, which flows from the unconscious. You are trying to understand and employ vast untapped parts of your being. You are looking for your potential. The unconscious is attempting to break through the block. Things that appear to be "mistakes" to your conscious self actually help your aesthetic self grab center stage and express itself.

The creative impulse escapes your rational self by producing mistakes that you may want to follow. These mistakes indicate where the action is.

- Unpainted canvas surfaces are usually ugly, including edges, unless you make them beautiful. This ugliness is recognized only when contrasted with the power and beauty of the parts you painted. One good strategy for making your art more compelling and vivid is to leave no surface untouched by you and your brush. Take this step first, and then you have the freedom to stop whenever you like. *This art hint can make a huge difference in the quality of your team art.*

- Check material labels so you know whether something is acrylic or water-soluble. (Something is water-soluble when wet; when it dries, it will stain.)

- Surfaces that are interesting are more interesting than surfaces that aren't.

- Make art as a team, if possible. Do the big work simultaneously. Align around something while you paint.

- Use your hands and other appropriate body parts to create art.

- Be careful of muddying colors, which happens when you overwork paint.

- Streaking and layering colors is very effective with acrylics. Acrylics dry within a few hours. You can paint more later.

- When doing team art, you must not "own" an area on the piece. The surest way not to own an area is to play on another area.

## STAFF

The staff members are your consultants during the BootCamp simulation.

If the consultants are not present in the room, it does not mean that we are not available. It is your responsibility to find us and get help as you need it. *The BootCamp staff will provide consulting as, and only as, you request it.* To get one-on-one assistance or any other type of consulting, ask a consultant. You will be expected to arrange a mutually agreeable time and place.

Many teams at BootCamps struggle needlessly rather than ask for help, especially at the beginning of the week. Not only is this struggle unnecessary, but it usually lasts far too long. The requests for consultants' time pile up at the end. One reason for this tendency is that you may find it highly enjoyable to be successfully creating and collaborating with your team and not want to miss any team time.[5]

As things begin to click, people connect and the juices flow, and the majority of the members of the team tend to want one-on-one experiences with BootCamp consultants. They are more willing to ask for help at this stage than at the beginning of the week. The calendar time for BootCamp is finite, and consulting schedules get crowded—like any product development endgame. Every moment seems more urgent than it is.

> *When faced with a choice between a half-hour of consulting and a half-hour of team engagement, choose the consulting. This experience will probably be more beneficial for you and your team.*

Get consulting early and often. Those who do benefit more than those who don't.

## YOUR TEAM'S ASSIGNMENT

Design, implement, and deliver a course that teaches you everything you need to know to ship great products on time, every time.

———————————————

## WHAT WE WANT YOU TO LEARN IN YOUR FIRST BOOTCAMP

———————————————

1. To successfully ask for help
2. To create high-bandwidth connection
3. To achieve shared vision

———————————————

5. Alternatively, if things aren't going well, you will find the situation so stressful and all-consuming that you won't think to connect with one-on-one consulting resources. Many of the greatest BootCamp teams have struggled until the last possible moment.

You might also learn the following:

- What is smartness, anyway?
- How to increase personal receptivity
- Levels of alignment
- Intentional greatness
- How to investigate the benign
- True results orientation
- Products: versions and visions
- Big ideas
- Functional program management
- Feeling as a source of special information
- You get what you want (no matter what you get)
- And more—BootCamp is always booting, always new

We consider three primary lessons—AskforHelp, Connection, and SharedVision—essential for your first BootCamp experience. We want you to learn these lessons well enough to make a significant difference in your life. The breadth of your learning here and the goals that you achieve with its help are completely up to you, and will reflect the choices you and your team make this week.

## ANSWER KEY

In the past, after BootCamp had concluded, graduates have said that we should have told them *x* earlier in the week, where *x* represents a certain piece of information they believed we withheld. Their feeling was that *x* would have saved them from unnecessary struggle. To ensure that we expose everything we know about how to have a great BootCamp experience, with as little discomfort and wasted effort as possible, we are providing this answer key.

If you do all of these things, BootCamp should be conceptually simple and mostly fun. It is not always easy to *change* behavior, however, even when you clearly identify the desired behavior. The difficult part about BootCamp is doing the things mentioned here, and leading others to do likewise by example and encouragement. These items are listed in rough order of their appearance during the progression of BootCamp.

1.  Yes, BootCamp is hard.

Sometimes you might feel surprised at the difficulty of the challenges of BootCamp. It may be a struggle for you to complete the week. While the ideas seem simple enough, it can prove very difficult to carry them out.

This problem arises because the BootCamp world is very different from the outside world at this point. The BootCamp world holds individuals accountable for their own destinies. At first, this idea seems far more challenging than the expectations of the outside world.

2.  Learn to recognize when you need to ask for help, and then do so, in ways that get results.

You will probably recognize this feeling as having the following qualities:

- You feel that a BootCamp consultant should be in the room at all times.

- You feel frustrated.

- You feel stalled out or that your team is stalled out.

- You feel mad, sad, or afraid.

- You feel like a victim (often of the coaches-in-training/ consultants).

- You feel like hurting someone (by yelling at someone or blaming him).

- You repeatedly think, with increasing annoyance, "Why doesn't Joe do $x$?"

- You believe, with increasing fervor, "If JoAnn would just do $x$, everything would get solved."

- You think that the consultants aren't doing enough of something.

- You think that the Black Hats aren't doing enough of something, or that they are doing too much of something.

- You ask a consultant for help, and you think that he isn't helping or you experience a feeling other than gladness at the help that is offered.

An expert at help acquisition will ask for help when things are going well. Such a person will ask so often that it may seem that he is being strange or overly dependent. Acquiring help, especially when things don't seem terrible, is really the first step to greatness. Acquiring help is not a surrender, but an advance. To practice this idea, focus on the following:

- Always maximize the help you get from someone who has more knowledge than you do about a relevant topic. For example, always maximize help from the consultants, because they have used The Core successfully many times previously, and have practiced giving help directly and efficiently.

- Always look for ways to make things more efficient. There are always methods to get more results with less effort. The key to finding these efficiencies is acquiring help.

3. Ask for help every time you need it.

You can't ask for too much help.

Sometimes when you do ask for help, you won't get the type of response you expected. Think about whether what you actually did receive was more helpful than what you expected. In other words, many times a BootCamper wants the consultants to do something, rather than doing it himself. The person therefore asks for help with the expectation that the consultants will jump in and take control. The consultants have learned that this tactic doesn't work. If you ask for help when you really want us to jump in and take over for you, we will tell you how we would do something, but we won't assume the leadership role. You must keep leading yourself and your team with our assistance; we will not lead for you.

Many times students believe that we should jump in more often and help without being asked. If you are not in alignment with the idea that it is better for us as consultants to wait to help until asked for assistance, please ask us for help in understanding this idea. We will be happy to demonstrate the efficacy of this approach in real time for you.

4.  Don't propose (with Decider) getting help. Just go get help.

Get up and leave the team if necessary. Earlier in the week, it is more likely that you will have to leave the group to ask a question or seek any help needed. The team distraction level is highest on Sunday, but decreases as the week proceeds.

5.  There is no downside to getting help. If you vote against getting help or resist help in some other way, you are working against team momentum for some reason.

6.  Ask for lessons on topics you think the team is struggling with or finds particularly interesting.

For example, you might request lessons on AskforHelp, the Decider protocol, Alignment, SharedVision, Rescuing, or the GreatnessCycle.

7.  The assignment has many levels of meaning. Thinking about it fully will make your experience more rewarding.

The assignment: Design, implement, and deliver a course that teaches you everything you need to know to ship great products on time every time. We find that the first key to understanding this assignment is to recognize that the customer is each person on your team. If each person on your team achieves what he wanted from your work on your product this week, then you will be successful. Because humans share so many similarities, if your team figures out what it needs, then it can help any other team figure out what its team members need.

This assignment is also recursive—that is, it refers to itself. The course you are creating is the course in which you are participating (BootCamp). The BootCamp protocols are designed to ensure that each person gets everything he needs to deliver great products on time, every time. In one sense, the product you deliver will be your team.

It is important, however, that your team create a product. To make money, it is important that the product at least support a business case explaining why the course should be implemented on other teams in the company, and then probably be marketed as courseware to other companies. Therefore, your final presentation should, at a minimum, state a dollars-and-cents business case. How does your team plan to make money?

In addition, we recommend creating art that illustrates the greatness of the team your course created. Use some or many forms to make great art that conveys your SharedVision and shows that your team makes great things. It would make sense that this art actively supports the course you are telling management will make them millions.

The key is to show that your course creates great teams, beginning with your team. To demonstrate greatness, your team expression must be great in every aspect.

8. Learn CheckIn, Decider, and the PerfectionGame (more deeply than you already have).

Practice these protocols with your team until you feel that you could lead a new BootCamp group in implementing them. CheckIn, Decider, and the PerfectionGame, when faithfully executed, make the Boot Camp exponentially more efficient. When complaints emerge that there isn't time for CheckIn, it means that there is only time for CheckIn.

Get help in becoming an expert on these protocols.

9. Don't work on or agree to work on a product until your Shared Vision is complete.

The Black Hats will not be happy until your team has SharedVision. That's why they hired the McCarthys to help you. Don't promise or

do anything less, even if you think it will meet the Black Hats'
needs in the short term.

In the first Black Hat meeting, the managers will ask you
whether you've been maximizing your use of the consultants, and
whether you understand and follow their advice. If you haven't,
you will feel as if you have wasted some time, because the Black
Hats will insist that you take full advantage of all your resources for
this project.

Remember:

- The Black Hats will most likely catch you when you say anything short of the truth.

- The Black Hats will be able to tell when you don't have a
  SharedVision.

- The Black Hats will always know when you didn't ask for help.

- The Black Hats will always know when you are acting as if you
  know something you don't really know.

- The Black Hats will get tougher when you get defensive, and
  they will relax when you tell the truth and are receptive.

10. Do great Black Hat work.

The Black Hats have certain requirements and behaviors for which
you can prepare yourself:

- They will insist that you maximize the help you get from the
  consultants.

- They will insist that you achieve a SharedVision.

- They will insist that you ship on time or earlier.

- They will insist that your product be "great."

- They will insist that the product succeed and that each individual learn what he needs to ship great products on time, every
  time.

- They will insist that you do what you say you will do.

- They will act like regular people. They will ultimately insist
  that you treat them like regular people. All BootCampers have

struggled with the tendency to act "weird" when the Black Hats are around.

- They will insist that you tell the truth and admit when you don't know the answer.
- They will search out inconsistencies on your team as indications of problems on the project.
- They will insist that *everything* you do be great, including meetings and communications with them.
- They will insist that you take as little of their time as possible. They have 50 other teams to manage. They are counting on you to lead yourselves.

11. Be "normal" around the Black Hats.

- When the Black Hats walk in the room, immediately welcome them and offer them a seat, coffee, and so on.
- Don't laugh at the Black Hats. They are people.
- Don't be mean, cynical, smart-assed, or otherwise unpleasant with the Black Hats. They are people.
- Don't make jokes about the Black Hats, especially in their presence.
- Don't break simulation when the Black Hats walk in by referring to "fake" or "pretend" things. Anything you do that avoids acting as if you are a real employee meeting with a real boss breaks the simulation.
- Don't expect effusive support from the Black Hats. They have provided all that you need to be a great team. Look to your existing resources, especially yourself, for support if you feel that the Black Hats aren't "supportive" enough.

12. Beware of Recoil.

Recoil occurs whenever the team or individual has achieved a success. Some equal and opposite force occurs afterward, sometimes with a delay. Recoil feels yucky—like depression, anger, misalignment, or some other form of discontent. In every BootCamp, we have seen the team experience Recoil at the following moments:

- After alignments are done and before the SharedVision is complete. This problem will take the form of an impulse not to complete the SharedVision once alignments are done.

- After the SharedVision is complete and before the team starts working on the product. This problem will show up as fighting or other ways of stalling out after the SharedVision is done.

- After BootCamp, when you see how dramatically the "false" world differs from BootCamp world. This emotion will take the form of hopelessness that you can't bring what you've learned to the "false" world, a failure to ask for help, and a belief that you can't have what you want.

The key to undoing Recoil is to name it and utilize AskforHelp. Tell a consultant, "I think I'm having Recoil. Will you help me?"

13. Create a SharedVision.

Don't do any work on the assignment until you have a SharedVision. You will need to learn CheckIn, Decider, and Alignment to get your SharedVision. Only then will your work proceed in the direction of greatness. PersonalAlignment will probably take the highest percentage of the BootCamp time. Successful completion of Personal Alignment and SharedVision will guarantee that your team is maximally productive while in the "development" phase of your project; what you used to consider the "development" phase is actually just the final stage of development.

14. Get our help with the SharedVision protocols.[6]

First, make sure that your WebofCommitment is really complete before you move on. Ask the consultants for help in determining whether the quality of the web is sufficient to move on.

Use the Passionometer protocol to help reach a state of Shared Vision and create a FarVision statement. This statement should meet the following criteria:

---

6. Get help at every point. Teams often stop asking for help once the WebofCommitment is complete, as if no more help would be beneficial.

- It should be very short and to the point (less than ten words).

- It should give the reader a picture of how the world will be different when your work is done—for example, "a computer on every desk" or "a man on the moon."

- It should be catchy and hit the reader in the gut. It should address some desire of the reader. The reader should say, "Yeah!" when he sees it and realizes the statement expresses something attractive—for example, "a wireless world."

Some fighting will likely occur during this protocol as part of the SharedVision Recoil. We recommend that a few people work on this statement while the others begin work on the product.

15. Take advantage of the benefits of your state of SharedVision.

As part of the post-SharedVision Recoil, the team will backslide into some old work habits. These habits, which were designed for coping with a world that generally lacks SharedVisions, might include the following:

- Not trusting that others' work will be acceptable if they work apart from your view; not wanting to split up into smaller groups

- Wanting to implement some particular process scheme

- Wanting to "brainstorm" instead of following the intuition of the team toward the deliverables

In the BootCamp world, once you have a SharedVision, you can drop many of the habits you've developed to control things at work. After achieving a SharedVision, we recommend doing the following:

- Just talk about good ideas as they occur. You don't have to control the discussion with a brainstorming session.

- Follow the visionaries. Some people on the team will undoubtedly have visions for product pieces; just start implementing them. There is no downside to making something while your team is in a state of SharedVision.

- Make sure that someone understands the business case for your course. How does your course translate into dollars?

- Use what you know about processes to get results on your deliverables, but don't discuss the process itself or waste the team's energy trying to gain support for a process.

- Start making things. You will find your way by creating the product. "Planning" is generally a bad idea.

- Split up into subteams. Your work will match up well because you can stay connected with one another and you share the same vision.

16. Avoid feedback.

*When you feel like you need to give feedback to the consultants or you have an idea about feedback, ask a question instead.* Most feedback we receive doesn't help improve BootCamp because it was formulated without all of the information. To help us truly improve BootCamp, make sure that you fully understand the area you are criticizing before formulating your feedback.

Also, most feedback is really about anger. We recommend getting help in solving whatever problem is causing your anger, rather than giving feedback.

17. Let yourself go.

Let yourself relax and be the greatest you can be. Let yourself reveal your full potential in these five days. BootCamp success is much more about the simple revelation of yourself and your gifts than it is about heroic effort. It is more contingent on integrity than on mastery. Find and then put the best of yourself into the product. Trust your team for this time period.

You can always change your mind about newly introduced ideas after BootCamp is over. First, however, understand these ideas and practice them until you see their advantages. If the ideas are suboptimal, you can improve them, so that they yield even greater advantages. Don't bother debating the ideas offered with the consultants or your teammates until you can execute them with fidelity to their intention. Only then will you have sufficient expertise to contribute rather than negate. Genuine contribution is always well intentioned, whereas simple negation or complex resistance is always suspect.

# BOOTCAMP IS NOT THERAPY

During past BootCamps, we have noticed that some BootCampers confuse the purpose of BootCamp with the purpose of psychotherapy. To ensure that you get the most from your BootCamp experience, it's important to underline the differences between the two. BootCamp is *not* psychotherapy. The two have different goals and different practices.

Generally speaking, therapy has the goal of optimizing your happiness. BootCamp has the goal of increasing your capacity to build products that make money.[7] Both of these goals are very important. In some cases, they may even be mutually dependent. Because of their fundamentally different aims, however, it is worth stating clearly that some practices from the psychotherapeutic world with which you may be familiar are not effective (and therefore are not tolerated) at BootCamp.[8] Therapeutic behaviors and practices are perfectly acceptable for your private edification or to do one-on-one with any individual team member or BootCamp staff member, should they want to help you in the way you desire. In BootCamp (or other team situations), however, therapy-based behaviors may often decrease your personal results in a one-on-one setting. Moreover, some are not acceptable in the group setting at BootCamp because they invariably distract the group from its fundamental purpose—getting the required work results.

---

7. Unless, of course, you work in a nonprofit capacity such as for government or charity, where the results depend on your role (but still do not align with therapeutic results). In any case, economics are involved, and surplus is better than deficit.

8. Effective therapy is a very good thing, and we recommend it for all. A thorough psychotherapeutic experience is probably more important in today's world than, for example, a college education.

# COMPARING BOOTCAMP
# WITH THERAPY PRACTICES

Therapy typically requires the constant supervision or participation of a therapist when in session. BootCamp (that is, the initial, concentrated application of The Core), on the other hand, has a tightly controlled, limited authority structure:

- BootCamp prohibits any team "supervision."
- BootCamp requires a minimal presence of the BootCamp staff.
- There are Black Hats and consultants, both roles played by BootCamp staff.
- BootCamp explicitly constrains Black Hat and consultant participation.

Things forbidden in BootCamp but allowed in many therapies include the following:

- Using a CheckIn-type element to talk about your feelings toward someone else
- "Blowing up," (that is, vivid expression of anger or rage primarily for the purpose of learning about one's own anger or rage dynamics, or to provide personal relief from same) in the group
- Blowing up at an individual in front of the group; confronting

### Black Hat Engagement Rules

- Black Hat attendance at team meetings is limited to no more than 15 minutes at a time.
- Interaction generally occurs by prearranged appointment.
- The sole Black Hat interest is the team's fulfillment of the assignment.
- Black Hats involve themselves only to the extent necessary to make assessments of the schedule, the progress against the schedule, the features of the product, and the likelihood of

team success. This includes watching for deception or delusion in the team.

## Consultant Engagement Rules

- Consultations are generally by direct request and appointment only.

- No single consultant is allowed to remain physically with the team during the majority of the time the team is in session.

- A consultant (or, more likely, a group of consultants) may occasionally intervene in a three-step process: (1) by stating that intervention is his intention; (2) by stating (or otherwise communicating) his point of view; and (3) by explicitly ending the intervention.

## Group Discussion

Analysis and discussions of "why" someone feels a particular way, especially those focused on the past or those tied up in specifics, are the bread and butter of therapy. Such discourse is all but illegal in BootCamp. BootCamp consultants may ask a person why he *does* something (whereupon the consultant should detail the inefficiencies observed). The question underlying all such questions is, "Assuming what you are doing must be done, can you do it with greater efficiency?"[9]

Therapy requires spending time discussing your own or someone else's feelings; running The Core basically prohibits this type of discussion. Emotions are revealed and named explicitly as a part of CheckIn. CheckIn is a special "time apart," and further discussion is usually unnecessary and is prohibited.

---

9. Efficiency = Benefits of Results/Costs of Effort.

## Confrontation

In some types of group therapy, confronting someone in front of the group is tolerated or encouraged. In BootCamp, it is illegal.[10] It is not acceptable in BootCamp to blow up, confront, or get "pissed off at" others in the group setting. These behaviors relate to your unresolved feelings. If you want to behave in any of these ways, you need to ask for help instead of doing so. These behaviors derail the group from getting results. Your fear and anger will spread unnecessarily, and they may create urgency sensations in others. It is important that you obtain help from outside the team so that you do not derail the group from its primary purpose of creating products.

## Presence of a Moderator

Unlike some therapy groups or settings where a psychotherapist moderates the session constantly, it is important that a BootCamp team be able to work independently, without an authority figure hovering nearby. If you feel that a consultant should be present and isn't, you need to ask for help. Find a consultant and make an appointment to talk. If the entire team wants help, find a consultant and make an appointment for that assistance. If you feel that you need a consultant, can't find one, and can't resolve your individual needs independently, check out until you either find a consultant or otherwise resolve your predicament.

This behavior is important work for you and your team. In fact, it is the primary focus of BootCamp. You must

---

10. It is nonetheless important to resolve feelings you have toward someone at BootCamp as expeditiously as possible. We find the most productive way to do so is to first get help from a staff member about your feelings. Often, the feelings you are having (which you connect with the other person) have little or nothing to do with that person per se, and you can resolve them by changing your own behavior. Therefore, you need not bother the other person (and certainly not the whole group, or members of it) to attain your desired results. Finally, although it is more rare than you might think, the occasional genuine unresolved "multipersonal" (that is, one that actually does extend beyond your individual boundaries) conflict occurs, and the consultant can help you structure the resolution of that conflict.

- Practice recognizing when you need to ask for help,

- Have the maturity to secure that help, and

- Be willing to wait if help is not immediately available.[11]

Methodical, help-seeking behavior will always get results in the world of work after BootCamp. It is important that you practice it in the BootCamp setting. You would not have the opportunity to practice this behavior if a BootCamp consultant continually "supervised" or monitored the BootCampers.

That BootCamp might produce more changes or compress normal stresses does not mean that a consultant will always attend to the team. It is important that you learn to effect major changes, live with others while experiencing major changes, and still be able to ask for help, secure that help, and exercise impulse control while doing so.

If you don't "feel safe" (typically, this means you are afraid or mad beyond your norm), it does not mean that a consultant should be around at all times. BootCamp rules and The Core provide for ample safety. Feeling "unsafe" *does* mean that you should ask for help from a consultant.

## *Check In*

Announcing your feeling state in a CheckIn provides two types of benefits: for your own interpersonal connectivity, and for the information gathering of all team members. It is a means to build presence and set connections. It is not legal to address something someone said in CheckIn or to use your CheckIns to talk about other team members. (Even if what you say seems purely positive and to

---

11. Simply accepting and feeling the urgency sensations while waiting for sought help, or even just waiting for them to pass and to be replaced by clearer thinking, are also very useful exercises. Sensations of urgency (typically, pronounced fear and anger, usually combined with enough adrenaline to create sensations of impending doom unless *something* is done), are, as a matter of course, best handled by indirect or no action (for example, by seeking help or simply thinking or meditating). Tolerance of the feelings of urgency until they subside is the best strategy. In most cases, making decisions or taking material action while feeling urgency sensations is a bad idea and yields poor results.

the point, you take a risk that is not worth the effort.) Saying your feelings helps make you present to the people in the meeting at hand and increases your own awareness, perceptivity, and receptivity. Listening to others' feelings may give you a thermometer reading of the state of your team and its members, or it may reveal other types of information, all of which can be used to increase results. Focusing on feelings after CheckIn, talking about someone's CheckIn, or talking about others in your CheckIn always distracts from results. If you need to resolve your feelings, ask for help from a consultant.

## *Alignment*

The goal of Alignment is to figure out what each person on the team wants. Alignment is not an invitation to analyze, rescue, or probe into someone's family of origin. Do not delve into what you perceive to be another's "issues" at BootCamp. This exercise distracts the team from obtaining results and is best left to an explicitly therapeutic environment. Because BootCamp is not designed to explicitly perform therapy, any inclination you have to wander into therapeutic territory with your own or someone else's alignment is always a distraction from results. When you bring your alignment to the group, your goal should be to tell the group about your thinking as efficiently and as clearly as possible—not to get support for your feelings, get ideas for your alignment, or talk about your feelings or other therapeutic issues. Those activities are AlignMe behaviors.

You perform your alignment alone, possibly using investigatory help from consultants or other team members in a one-on-one setting. The group alignment sharing time is devoted to information exchange, protocol handshakes, and clarification purposes.

Do not use an alignment to tell someone how great he is. That is a rescue.

Do not use the group's alignment time except for the purpose of maximizing results. If you feel a desire to probe into your feelings or some other alignee's feelings in front of the team, you are probably experiencing the magic of intimacy, along with the seduction of a neurotic impulse. You feel close to the person with whom you are talking or perhaps you want to be closer. Intimacy is a good thing, and it is good to want it. Nevertheless, it is neither as efficacious as achieving it privately with the same person, nor particularly results-oriented to go for it with the whole group watching. We suggest committing to getting more intimacy in your life and resisting the impulse to try to glom onto it by doing some variant behavior or playing some role in AlignMe, and thereby wasting the enormously precious group alignment time.

BootCamp is about results—products that make money. It is not *about* feelings, but *includes* feelings. Therapy, on the other hand, is often about feelings. Feelings are explicit team resources and are used at BootCamp only to the extent that they help get results.

If you are tempted to say (especially to the staff), "I've been to things like this before," we congratulate you in advance on whatever it is that you experienced. After investigating this idea many times (that is, the claimed similarity to BootCamp of other training or some organized group experiences students have experienced), we have found that the people claiming this *have* enjoyed the experience of being fully present and emotionally engaged, typically in a therapy setting, or, rarely, on a team. And this is surely good. However, we can also assure you that you have never experienced BootCamp before. BootCamp is unlike therapy or other forms of "team training." Its similarities with other "team-building" courses on the market are few in number. BootCamp is a results-oriented, team product development simulation. Even other courses called bootcamps are unlike this BootCamp. This BootCamp has never happened before. Indeed, there is nothing else "like" it—no Core protocols,[12] no product development simulation, no ground-up reinvention every time, no rejection of neurotic behavior, no building on the past and passing it on, and, most important, no you. To get the most out of your week, we recommend dropping any assumptions you may have about BootCamp or in any way generalizing from your prior experience.

---

12. Unless someone is duplicating BootCamp somewhere and we don't know about it.

# The Core Protocols V. 1.0

*TO:* Readers

*FR:* Jim and Michele McCarthy, McCarthy Technologies, Inc.

*RE:* The Core Protocols Version 1.0 Distribution

*Dear Recipient:*

*The information in this document, The Core Protocols V. 1.0, is "software for your head." Although it is a somewhat new take on how to distribute ideas, we think the medium of software, its common characteristics, and the way people view it, is the best way to disbribute any system of functional ideas and procedures. People understand that software is supposed to do something, and they also understand that successful software will likely be upgraded with better (or at least different) versions over time. You will find these things to be true of The Core protocols.*

*There are many other benefits to treating procedures as a kind of software and distributing them as software is distrubuted; but, whatever benefits there may be, they all depend on the customer receiving a perfectly faithful copy of the program to begin with. This document is your copy.*

*With computers, when you install a new program on your hard drive, you reasonably expect the files provided by the manufacturer to be a replica of the master program. Though the program may have other problems, most often the fidelity of the bits involved in your copy is not of great concern to you. With software for your head, things are a bit different. The document you are reading now is meant to support the person-to-person "copying technology" on which we depend for the promulgation of The Core protocols.*

*If someone handed you these pages prior to discussing The Core protocols with you, or e-mailed them to you, you should be aware that he or she is only behaving in accordance with his or her obligations under The Core Licensing Agreement. This License is an instance of the "GNU General*

Public License" (*www.fsf.org/copyleft/gpl.html*), and, as such, it governs the free distribution of The Core protocols, among other things.

The Core Protocols V. 1.0, distributed in its entirety within these few pages, consists of

1. This letter
2. The Core protocols
3. The Core Protocols License Agreement

These three elements constitute (wholly and inseparably) The Core Protocols V. 1.0. Later versions may well be available on our Web site (*www.mccarthy-tech.com*). The files mentioned in the License Agreement (below) consist of these three parts. All three of these parts should be included with the package you are now reading. Please note that there are many other pieces of The Core that you might find useful, especially the patterns, antipatterns, and definitions of The Core. These are published in a book[1] (wherein these words were also first published), but they are not included here, and are not governed by The Core license.

When you distrubute The Core protocols, what you distribute are the pages in this Appendix. If you decide to tell someone about The Core protocols, or to "teach" them to someone, you are, in fact, copying The Core protocols. Such verbal "copying" efforts are buggy and incomplete. They can also be very annoying, especially if the person doing the copying is evangelical. But we do think it is good to copy The Core protocols, so we've made it free of charge to do so, provided that you actually copy it: Copying The Core protocols means that you must provide all the material in this document before or at the time you attempt to impart any of the substance of The Core protocols to someone else. You must include (1) This statement from us, (2) The Core protocols, and (3) The Core Protocols License Agreement, either in writing or by e-mail (an electronic version of this document is found on our Web site at www.mccarthy-tech.com).

It's not really so many pages, and by passing them out, you won't have to explain, defend, or evangelize The Core. It's really just software. Pass it out, and people can take it from there.

---

1. *Software for Your Head: Core Protocols for Creating and Maintaining Shared Vision*, by Jim and Michele McCarthy. Boston: Addison-Wesley, 2002 (ISBN: 0-201-60456-6).

*We offer courses, BootCamps, and certification services for practition-
ers of The Core protocols, services that are detailed at www.mccarthy-
tech.com. Nothing in this distribution authorizes you to actually teach The
Core protocols, or certifies you as competent to do so. You are not authorized
to conduct a BootCamp on The Core. If you are participating in some type
of authorized course or BootCamp, your instructor will have shown you his
or her certification from McCarthy Technologies by now, which authorizes the
activity. If this hasn't happened, it is an unauthorized activity.*

*Incidentally, if you have already heard about The Core protocols from
someone who purportedly knew all about them, but you've never seen this
note, now you know something new about that person.*

*Thank you for your interest in our work.[2]*

*Jim McCarthy*
*jim@mccarthy.net*

*Michele McCarthy*
*michele@mccarthy.net*

---

2. You can find current versions of these pages plus book and video information at
www.mccarthy-tech.com.

# THE CORE PROTOCOLS

## THE CHECK IN PROTOCOL

### *The Specific "In-ness" Commitments*

When you say, "I'm in" (see "Group Check In"), you commit to the following behaviors:

- You will listen and observe fully.

- You will offer to the team and accept from the team only rational, efficient behavior.

- If the team or its members stray from the CheckIn commitments, you will mention the deviation as soon as you are aware of it and recommend alternative action. If disagreement about your perception arises, you will efficiently propose appropriate alternative action and resolve the conflict using Decider.

- You will accept explicit emotional information as valuable.

- You will be aware of your ratio of time spent effectively speaking to your time spent listening.

- You will speak only and always when you

  - Have a relevant question.

  - Require more information about the current idea. In that case, you will frame requests for information succinctly and clearly.

  - You will ask no bogus questions—that is, questions that reveal your opinions rather than investigate another's thinking. An example of a good question: "Jasper, will you say more about [whatever]?"

  - Have a relevant proposal.

  - Have an official speaking role in a Decider.

  - Have immediate, relevant value to add.

  - Are responding to a request for information.

  - Are volunteering a supportive idea to the current speaker. You will ask the speaker if he or she wants your idea before stating it. The current speaker, of course, is free to accept, investigate, or reject your offer.

- Are performing a CheckOut or a CheckIn.

- Express a better idea than the current one (idea preamble). In exchange for the opportunity to present your idea, you commit to uphold your idea until one of the following is true: (1) Your idea is shown to you to be unsuitable or inefficacious; (2) your idea is expanded in a way that includes or transcends its original value; or (3) your idea is resolved in a Decider process.

## Personal Check In

Anyone on the team can check in as, when, and if he or she desires. No permission is required to do so. In the case of a personal CheckIn, no participation beyond listening is required from other team members. When you want to check in, you say, "I'm going to check in." This activity takes precedence over any other Core activity except running a Decider session.

## Group Check In

Although the purpose of the CheckIn protocol is to facilitate the engagement of the person who checks in, it is more efficient if a general group CheckIn takes place. This situation brings the requirement that every team member will check in or pass.

Usually, a group CheckIn takes place at the beginning of a meeting or other team gathering, after a break in a long team meeting, or when the group's activities or direction is confusing or conflict-laden. Group CheckIn also occurs at the beginning of telephone meetings, in any contact between individuals, or in electronic chats. To inaugurate a group CheckIn, simply suggest, "Let's check in." You, as the invoker of a group CheckIn, must check in first.

Execution of a group CheckIn proceeds as follows:

1. Start with the invoker. Each person takes a turn when he feels it is appropriate until everyone is "in" or has "passed."

2. Each person says, "I pass," or "I feel (sad and/or mad, and/or glad, and/or afraid)." (Optionally, each person might give a brief explanation of emotional state.)

3. Say, "I'm in." This statement seals your commitment as outlined in the CheckIn commitments.

4. The group responds, "Welcome." This statement acknowledges that they heard your check-in and accept your commitment to be "in."

## *Example*

*Person Checking In:* "I feel afraid and glad and sad. I feel afraid that this new project won't be exciting or that it won't turn out well. But I feel glad that we are starting a new project. Also, I feel sad that I'm not with my family today. And I'm in."

*Group:* "Welcome."

## *Core Emotional States*

CheckIn requires that all feelings be expressed in terms of four and only four emotional states:

- Mad
- Sad
- Glad
- Afraid

Although myriad other emotions exist, all can be expressed with acceptable fidelity in terms of mad, sad, glad, and afraid.

It is not legal to check in without referencing any of the four emotional states unless you pass. Also, it is not legal to introduce emotions other than those in the four emotional states.

## *When to Use Check In*

- Check in at the beginning of any meeting. You can check in individually or call for a general CheckIn. If you call for a general CheckIn, you cannot pass and you must be the first person to check in.

- Check in when the team seems to you to be moving toward unproductive behavior.

- Check in whenever you feel the need.

### Check In Guidelines

- CheckIn creates maximal results if you express at least two feelings when checking in.

- Do not describe yourself as "a *little* mad/sad/afraid" or use other qualifiers that diminish the importance of your feelings.

- Check in as deeply as possible (where "depth" can be thought of as the "degree of disclosure and extent of feelings of vulnerability that result"); the depth of a team's CheckIn translates directly to the quality of the team's results.

### Check In Rules

CheckIn is a time apart, and is governed by these constraints:

- No discussion is allowed during CheckIn—only the welcome at the end of each CheckIn. Simply listen to each person, speak when it is your turn, and wait until everyone is done before speaking additionally. Listen and observe as deeply as possible. Gauge and note the congruency of your own emotional response to the CheckIn.

- Do not talk about your own CheckIn before or after CheckIn.

- Do not ask about, reference, or disclose another's CheckIn.

- Do not blame others for your emotions during CheckIn.

- Do not use CheckIn to talk about, yell at, get "pissed off" at, or confront another team member or anyone not present.

## THE CHECK OUT PROTOCOL

Say, "I'm checking out." Then immediately physically leave the group until you're ready to check in once again.

## Synopsis

Use your time off in a way that will allow you to return refreshed and participate fully, even though you may not feel like using your time in that way. While there is no shame in checking out, your lack of contribution should inspire concern. Give it some thought. Also, you may experience discomfort when you check out, but it will soon be lost in the greater sense of relief that you feel in living out your commitments.

Others may become alarmed by what they perceive as your abrupt disconnection, but they'll survive any momentary discomfort and even prosper in your absence. Avoid the temptation to exploit their potential for alarm by making a show of your Check Out (e.g., by dramatizing the viewpoint that *they* are driving you to check out).

## When to Use Check Out

When you need time to take care of yourself in any way (e.g., calm down, rest, or do what is necessary to return fully checked in). CheckOut gives you and your team the opportunity to be productive simultaneously when that is impossible if you remain.

CheckOut is also used when individuals need to take care of personal matters.

## Check Out Commitments

- To admit your lack of productive engagement and physically leave

- To not check out to get attention

- To return as soon as you can be productively engaged again

- To return without unduly calling attention to your return

- To be clear with the team about your checking out. (For instance, tell the entire team when you are checking out, not just one person. If you are checking out for more than an hour or so, let your teammates know when you will return.)

## *Check Out Guidelines*

CheckOut is an admission that you are unable to contribute at the present time. It is intended to help the team, not to manipulate team members. This pattern is not intended for any of the following purposes:

- To express your anger
- To cause disruption
- To draw attention
- To create drama
- To trigger others' feelings

You can tell when it's time to check out if the idea occurs to you.

## THE PASSER PROTOCOL

At an appropriate time (presumably at the beginning of some process or protocol), say, "I pass." If you know you will pass on something, you are obliged to do so as soon as you are aware of your decision. Once something is started, you can still pass.

### *Example*

A CheckIn is occurring. You don't want to check in, so at an appropriate point (earlier is better) during the process, you signal the group by saying, "I pass. I'm in."

### *Synopsis*

Passing expresses your decision not to participate in an event—that is, to opt out of a process. Passing sets a margin of safety for everyone. It takes courage.

### *Passing Guidelines*

- Passing is always permissible except during a Decider vote.
- There is no discussion about a person's passing.
- To invoke your right to pass, you must say, "I pass." Silent passing is not allowed. Silence indicates that you are awaiting your turn.

- Inevitably others will be curious. Do not explain your passing.
- You can "unpass."

## When to Use Passer

Do it when and if desired—even if you just want to see how it feels to pass.

## Passer Commitments

The following commitments are required with Passer:

- To take good care of yourself
- To not judge, shame, hassle, or interrogate anyone who passes
- To not judge, shame, hassle, or interrogate those who do not pass
- To not explain why you are passing (no matter how great the urge)

If you feel the need to "punish" the group, or you desire to use passing for some other reason than simply wanting to opt out of some activity, something more is likely afoot. You probably need to check out rather than pass. Like CheckOut, the Passer protocol should not be used for dramatic purposes. A temporary inclination to dramatics is always a good reason to check out.

# THE DECIDER PROTOCOL

1. The **proposer** says, "I propose . . .".
2. The proposer offers a concise, actionable proposal.
   - No more than one issue is resolved per proposal.
   - The behavior expected of the voters if the proposal is accepted is clearly specified.
3. The proposer says, "1-2-3."
4. All team members vote simultaneously in one of three ways:
   - "Yes" voters raise their arms or give a thumbs-up.

- "No" voters point their arms down or give a thumbs-down.
- "Support-it" voters raise their arms midway or show a hand flat.

5. Once the vote is taken, use the Decider tally procedure:

   - If the combination of "no" voters (called *outliers*) and "support-it" voters is too great (approximately 30 percent or more, as determined by the proposer), the proposer drops the proposal.

   - If any of the "no" voters states his absolute opposition to the proposal, the proposal is dead.

   - If there are just a few "no" voters, the proposer uses the Resolution protocol to resolve things with the outliers (the "no" voters).

   - Otherwise, the proposal passes.

## Guidelines

1. The proposer is responsible for tallying.

2. No one speaks during Decider except the proposer
   - When stating the proposal or
   - When using Resolution

   Or the "no" voter
   - When using Resolution or
   - When declaring his absolute "no" state.

3. "Yes" or "support-it" voters cannot speak during Resolution.

4. Voters requiring more information must vote "no" to stop the proposal before seeking information.

5. Voters do not state why they voted as they did.

6. What constitutes "too many" of a given category of votes (for example, too many "no" votes or too many "no" votes plus "support-it" votes) is determined solely by the proposer. Typically, three or four "no" votes out of ten total votes are considered "too

many" to pursue to **Resolution**. A majority of "support-it" votes suggests a very weak proposal.

7. Passing is not allowed on a **Decider** proposal. You must vote if you are present.

8. Unanimous "yes" votes or "yes" votes mixed with some "support-it" votes are the only configurations that cause a proposal to be adopted as a part of the team's **plan of record**.

9. Each team member is accountable for personally carrying out behaviors specified in a **Decider** decision, and no member has more or less accountability than any other. Each is also accountable for insisting that the behavior specified in the proposal is carried out by the other team members.

10. After a proposal passes, a team member who was not present during the vote is responsible for acquiring information about what transpired, and will also be held accountable for the decision. If the person prefers not to be accountable (that is, he would have voted "no" if present), he now must make a new proposal as soon as possible. In the meantime, the individual is bound by the decision just as if he had voted "yes."

11. When a "no" voter states that he "won't get in no matter what" (i.e., an "absolute no" vote), it means that there is no condition that the voter can imagine that would change his vote.

12. It is traditional, though not mandatory, for an "absolute no" voter to make a new proposal following the death of the proposal killed with his vote.

## *Voting*

Given a proposal, the **Decider** protocol provides three possible voting strategies:

- Yes
- No
- Support-it

"Support-it" is a "yes" vote with an attitude. It can be translated as, "I can live with this proposal. I believe that it is probably the best way for us to proceed now. I support it, even though I have some reservations. While I don't believe I can lead the implementation of this proposal, I do commit not to sabotage it."

## Decider Outcomes

Three outcomes are possible:

- *Affirmative decision.* Immediate and universal acceptance of the proposal occurs.

- *Efficient negotiation with conflicts exposed and the proposal resolved.* Finer proposals are created while the team's inclusion effort proceeds.

- *Swift elimination of unsupported ideas.* Immediate, clear, and unremorseful rejection of an idea too many people think misguided occurs.

## Decider Commitments

Decider requires the following commitments from team members:

- Actively support the decisions reached, with the behavior specified in them.

- Vote your true beliefs.

- Speak or don't speak as specified above.

- Hold others accountable for their decisions.

- Respect an "absolute no" voter. Do not pursue the voter or analyze his motives.

- Do not collect others' votes before making your own.

- Do not repeat failed proposals unless relevant circumstances have changed.

- Keep informed about Decider votes run in your absence and resolve, via Decider, your lack of support, if any, for the decisions made when you were absent.

- Reveal immediately whether you are an "absolute no" voter when you vote "no."

# THE RESOLUTION PROTOCOL

When a **Decider** vote yields a small minority of outliers, the proposer quickly leads the team, in a highly structured fashion, to deal with the outliers. The proposer's goal is straightforward and unabashedly promotes the proposal: to bring the outliers in at least cost.

1.  The proposer asks each outlier to express his requirements for joining the team in support of the proposal: "What will it take to bring you in?"

2.  The outlier has only two possible legal responses:

    – He may state, at any time after the vote, but no later than when asked the above question by the proposer, that there is "no way" he will change his vote to "yes" or "support-it." This simple declaration means that the proposal is now officially dead, and the **Decider** protocol ends.

    – The outlier may state in a single, short, declarative sentence precisely what it is he requires to be "in." In this way, he expresses a contingent commitment to see that the proposal is accepted and transformed into reality. If given what he requires, the outlier promises to drop all resistance to the proposal and to provide affirmation and support for it instead.

3.  As needed and as possible, the proposer makes an offer to the outlier. Two methods for incorporating changes into the original proposal while resolving any resulting perturbations to non-outliers' support are permitted:

    – If the adaptations to the proposal to accommodate the outlier's requirements are minor, the proposer may employ a simple, unofficial "eye-check" of the nonoutliers to see if there is general acceptance to the changed proposal. If you are opposed to this implicit new proposal, or you require a formal restatement and a new vote, you must make your requirement known during this interval.

    – If the required changes are more complex, the proposer must create and submit a new proposal that accounts for the outlier's requirements. The team reviews this proposal and conducts a new vote, and the Decider protocol begins anew.

4. "Yes" voters and "support-it" voters are not allowed to speak during Resolution.

5. If all outliers change their votes from "no" to "support-it" or "yes," then the decision to adopt the proposal is committed; it will be acted upon by the team. No further communication is required to achieve strong, unanimous consensus.

### *Resolution Commitments*

You are committed to answer the question, "What will it take to get you in?", with an actionable modification of the proposal. Explaining why you don't like the proposal, for example, is off the subject.

### *When to Use Resolution*

Use Resolution whenever a small percentage of the team votes "no" to your Decider proposal.

## THE INTENTION CHECK PROTOCOL

IntentionCheck assesses the integrity of your own (and, to a lesser extent, another's) intention. IntentionCheck evaluates conditions that tend to skew or bias your effectiveness in dealing with a given issue at the time you run the check.

1. Ask yourself, "Is my current emotional state solid, turbulent, or intense?"

2. Ask yourself, "Is my current receptivity to new information high, medium, or low?"

3. Ask yourself, "Do I understand clearly what my current purpose is?" That is, what result do I want?

4. If your emotional state is not solid, and/or your receptivity is not good, or you are not clear about your purpose, then postpone your action, or use the CheckOut protocol to get the information needed to clear up your intention before acting or speaking.

## *Synopsis*

Checking your intention prior to significant behaviors will improve the odds that your behavior will have the desired results. The most common problem in being effective is low quality of intention. By invoking an IntentionCheck on yourself or inviting investigation of your intention, you will act less with more results. This is the essence of efficiency.

## *When to Use Intention Check*

- When ambiguity or uncertainty surrounds your motive
- When your behavior seems likely to discomfort others
- When your behavior will slow others in achieving their goals
- When you are contemplating an interpersonally risky or ethically complex endeavor
- After you failed to use IntentionCheck
- When you have strong feelings about another person's behavior, are involved in it to some extent, and are about to engage with him
- When you are psychologically attached to a particular goal and believe others to be resistant to it

## THE ALIGNMENT PROTOCOL

The Alignment protocol governs behavior during alignment. It has five major steps and calls upon the PersonalAlignment, PerfectionGame, and Investigate protocols.

1. Team members begin to align themselves by applying the PersonalAlignment protocol.

All alignees start out with the same, default PersonalAlignment statement: "*I want self-awareness.*"

Spend sufficient private time in introspection and in receiving help, so you will be able to form and express your PersonalAlignment to the team.

Small groups of people can gather to listen to and investigate one another, but only after all of the individuals have spent time alone and in receiving help.

2. Team members use Investigate to help one another complete their PersonalAlignments.

Investigate is used by team members who are not currently working on their own Alignment, when they make themselves available to an alignee during the public portion of his PersonalAlignment.

3. Alignees iterate as necessary.

Your first pass at PersonalAlignment, with the support of the team in Investigate mode, will generally produce a completed PersonalAlignment, but it may yield an inconclusive result or provoke a change of heart. It may lead to a deepening of the Alignment or just confusion. It is acceptable to redo the public portion of a PersonalAlignment. Even if everything about your Alignment seemed clear, if you desire to change some or all of it, you may do so—provided that you share the changes with the team in full meeting.

4. The team improves the collected PersonalAlignment statements.

5. The team completes a WebofCommitment and integrates it into the group.

Additional factors contribute to the quality and ease of Alignment, including these physical issues.

- Alignment is best achieved in a quiet, comfortable place, away from usual workplaces and workplace stresses.

- The team will maximize its effectiveness if it performs all PersonalAlignments as a team during a single, off-site session, taking as much time as necessary (usually several days) to do the work to everyone's satisfaction.

- If one or more persons on the team can't attend the off-site meeting, the team must proceed without them.

# THE PERSONAL ALIGNMENT
# PROTOCOL

Complete the following **PersonalAlignment** exercise. You are encouraged to ask others for help early and often. Expect your helpers to use the **Investigate** pattern, and when you help others with their **PersonalAlignment**, you must use the **Investigate** pattern.

1. Ask yourself, "What do I want? What, specifically, do I, personally, want?"

2. When you think you know what you want, write it down.

3. Now ask yourself, "Why don't I have what I say I want already?" Assume that you could have had it by now. Almost always, there is some internal blocking element preventing you from getting it, or you already would have it. Write down your answer.

If your answer to the question in step 3 blames or defers accountability to uncontrollable circumstances or other people, pretend your last answer to step 3 is just a story, a myth that somehow deprives you of your full power to achieve for yourself. Before proceeding further with this protocol, you must make an imaginative leap to a more personally powerful stance. Likely, you will have to increase your self-awareness. Increase your perception and your receptivity. In any case, change *something* now about the way you have executed this protocol so far, because it hasn't worked. Then go back to step 3.

4. If your answer to the question in step 3 is more than a few words, simplify your answer, going back to step 3.

5. If your answer to step 3 doesn't refer to a personal issue:

   – Increase your commitment to yourself in this process.

   – Consider whether you are afraid and, if so, what you fear.

   – Consider whether your answer to step 3 shows integrity.

   – Change *something* now about the way you have executed this protocol so far, because it hasn't worked. Then go back to step 3.

6.  If you have gone back to step 3 several times:

    – Employ AskforHelp (again, if necessary).

    – And/or take a break and go back to step 1.

7.  If your answer to step 3 points to a problem or constraint that, if solved, would radically increase your effectiveness in life—work *and* play—you have identified a *block*.

8.  Until you are certain that what you say you want is what you really want, remain at this point. If you have remained here for a while, you are still uncertain, and your team is moving on, adopt the default alignment: that is, you want more "self-awareness" and you don't know what's blocking you. Go to step 13.

9.  If you are not certain that eliminating the block identified by your answer to step 3 will be worth a great deal of effort, go back to step 8.

10. Check out the block with people who know you and with people who know about blocks, if possible. If you are unwilling to utilize AskForHelp from your team, go back to step 8.

11. Determine what virtue would be powerful enough to shatter the block.

12. Decide whether this virtue is what you really want: the power that would yield what you *thought* you wanted (in step 1). If it is, write it down. Go to step 3.

13. Create a very concise sentence that begins with the words: "I want . . ."

14. If your sentence has unneeded words, go back to step 13.

15. This sentence is your PersonalAlignment statement. Check it out with all of your team.

16. Ask them if they can think of a shorter, more direct way to say the same thing.

17. Promise them to take specific, visible actions that will show your commitment to obtaining what you want. Tell them what they can expect to see you doing, commencing now.

18. Ask your team for help. Will they do *X*, when you signal them by doing *Y*? In your request for help, there should be specific actions you are asking them to do that will help you obtain what you want. It is very important that *you* initiate this action-reaction sequence by signaling to them that you are working on your PersonalAlignment. It is not up to your teammates to initiate status checks or police your PersonalAlignment. Ask for your teammate's help using very specific language, such as "Bill," you ask, "when I [*do something positive that demonstrates my commitment to attaining what I say I want*], will you [*show a sign of support, encouragement, and/or proffer any requested substantive help*]?"

19. Write or rewrite the following:

    – Your personal alignment statement

    – Alignment evidence

    – Support you ask for from your team

    Examples of support include the following:

    "When I say, 'This takes courage for me,' will you applaud?"

    "When I give a daily report on how I took care of myself, will you do the wave?"

    "Will you meet with me for one-half hour weekly, Bill, so I can work on this with you?"

## Personal Alignment Commitments

This protocol requires the following commitments from the alignee:

- To pass early if you are going to pass. Pass later only if you fail to pass early.

- Move to the deepest desirable point in the shortest possible time.

- Be truthful.

- Be receptive to the effective assistance of others.

- Reject assistance that impedes your progress.

- Don't just "go along," or merely humor the **Alignment** process. If you are inclined to do that, pass. This choice preserves the integrity of the experience for others.

- "Pretend" as needed. That is, try out new ideas about yourself before discarding them.

- Be accountable.

- Avoid storytelling.

- Insist that when you give your support signal, the team members follow through with their support.

## The Personal Alignment Statement

A **PersonalAlignment** statement begins with the words, "I want." The most common and successful alignment statements have the form

*"I want X", or "I want to X."*

where *X* is the virtue or power that you have decided will break through your biggest block.

## Common Alignments

The following are the most common alignments. This list is a partial list, not meant to serve as a constraint or a boundary.

*I want:*

| | |
|---|---|
| Faith | To love myself |
| Hope | To value myself |
| Passion | To feel my feelings |
| Self-awareness | To believe in myself |
| Self-care | Integrity |
| Courage | Fun |
| Wisdom | Ease |
| Peace | To accept myself |
| Maturity | To be honest with myself |
| Presence | To be patient with myself |
| Joy | |

## *Faux Alignments*

Although it is difficult to condemn a whole word or phrase to the trash heap as a faux Alignment, we have found that these "alignments" are always indicators of something amiss in the person's understanding either of PersonalAlignment or of the phrase in question.

*I want:*

| | |
|---|---|
| Confidence | To retire |
| Self-confidence | To be the best _____ |
| Self-control | To not _____ |
| Strength | Sanity |
| To solve problems | Knowledge |
| To listen | Focus |
| To be understood | Balance |
| To understand | Patience |
| Fame | Security |
| To be rich | |

## THE INVESTIGATE PROTOCOL

1. Become a detached but fascinated inquirer.

2. Ask only questions that will increase your understanding. Ask questions to acquire information. Maintain the posture of an interested person, handicapped by ignorance. (See "Intention Check" in Chapter Six.)

3. Don't ask inappropriate questions. For example, avoid the following types of inquiries:

   – Questions that attempt to lead the alignee or that reflect your agenda. This problem can arise when you have strong feelings about the subject.

   – Questions that attempt to hide an answer you believe is true.

   – Poorly thought out questions. If you are not aware of your own intention before you ask the question, don't ask it. (See the IntentionCheck protocol.)

– Questions that invite the alignee to wander off into too much analysis or irrelevant material. Questions that begin with "Why" can spur this problem.

4. Use a few formulations for your questions. Consider using the following forms:

   – "What about $X$ makes $Y$ $Z$?" For example, "What about your coding makes the experience frustrating?"

   – "How does it go when that happens?" "Will you slow down the process and describe it to me?" "Take a specific example and slow it down."

5. Ask questions only if the alignee is engaged and appears ready to learn more. If your teammate seems to be bored, stubborn, resistant, or going in circles, then stop investigating. The alignee must adhere to the commitments in personal alignment if you are to continue to any good effect. To break up this block, say, "I have a sense that I am pulling information out of you against your will. Let's take some time to think about this issue and talk about it later." You can also just be quiet.

6. Give opinions rarely and only after receiving the alignee's permission. Stick to your intention of gathering more information. If you have an interesting thought, a good idea, or theory, say, "I have an [ . . . ]. Would you like to hear it?" The alignee can then answer "yes" or "no" or state conditions under which your input would be welcome.

   If you feel that you will explode if you can't say what's on your mind, that's a good indication that you shouldn't speak.

7. Never argue during PersonalAlignment.

8. Don't talk to anyone other than the alignee.

### *When to Use Investigate*

• When an alignee asks for your help with a PersonalAlignment.

• In an Alignment situation, when an alignee has explicitly stated that Investigate questions are welcome

- In general, when you are learning about a phenomenon, with an eye toward exploiting it
- When you are working on your own PersonalAlignment.

## Investigate Commitments

- Intensify your curiosity.
- Widen your receptivity.
- Ask well-formed questions.
- Set aside your biases toward and prior experiences with the alignee. Observe the alignee with innocence and a fresh perception.
- Accept what the alignee says while perceiving more than usual.
- Do not tolerate theorizing about the alignee.
- Do not tolerate diagnosis of the alignee.
- Do not tolerate therapy during Alignment.
- Do not tolerate any distraction away from the alignee.
- Use Investigate or CheckOut.

## Examples of Investigative Questions

What is the one thing you want most from this project?

What blocks you from getting what you want?

If that block were removed, would you get what you want?

Is there some virtue that would enable you to eliminate the block?

What is the biggest problem you see?

What is the most important thing you could do right now?

If you could have anything in the world right now, what would it be?

If you could do anything in the world right now, what would it be?

How does it go when that happens?

Would you explain a specific example?

Would you slow it down into steps?

# THE WEB OF COMMITMENT PROTOCOL

The WebofCommitment protocol has four steps:

1. Each alignee should create a list that includes the following:

   - A PersonalAlignment statement

   - Positive, measurable evidence—both short-term and long-term—that will show you are getting what you want

   - Support commitments from your team in the form of (1) a specific positive signal you give to your team and (2) a specific positive show of support your teammates give to you

2. Post the list in a public place—on a bulletin board, as a poster, or in an e-mail.

3. Conduct a ceremony for the entire team to do the following:

   - Highlight each PersonalAlignment

   - Bring the PersonalAlignment process to a close (optional)

   - Celebrate the team alignment

4. Keep your commitments to one another, and track whether commitments are kept. Renew all elements as needed.

# THE ASK FOR HELP PROTOCOL

The AskforHelp protocol involves two roles: an asker and a helper.

## *Asker Role*

When you are the asker, you must inaugurate the help transaction, as follows:

1. State some form of the following question to your intended helpers: "[Name of the person you are soliciting], will you

help me [verb] [object being created, goal being reached, and so on] . . . ?"

2. If you have a specific activity or activities you desire from the helper, and especially if these are the only activities you are willing to accept, express these specifics before encouraging the would-be helper to answer your request.

3. You must always shape your help request (as in steps 1 and 2) so that you ask a question that begins "Will you . . . ?"

4. After asking for help with a Core-legal question, say nothing until your question is answered.

### *Helper Role*

When addressed directly and properly with a request for help, engage your full attention on the asker. There are only four legal responses to a valid **AskforHelp** request:

1. If you are unable to fully engage with the asker on the request for help, immediately say, "[Name of asker], I can't discuss this request right now." Then, if possible, arrange a mutually convenient time to discuss the issue.

2. If, after focusing your attention on the asker and listening to the request, you don't want to carry out (or even further discuss) the request, tell the asker, "No, I won't do that," or simply "No." Then say nothing else.

3. If you are willing to help with or willing to discuss the request, but need more information about the request, its purpose, or any specifics, ask, "Will you tell me more about the specifics of what you require?" You can then ask questions about the request to get the information you need. Once you understand the specifics, then answer "yes" or "no," which ends the protocol. Otherwise, go to step 4.

4. If you want to offer help, but believe the help requested is not what you can or should do, decline the request explicitly before

proceeding further. Answer something like "No, I won't. But I will [state the thing you think would be more helpful]. Would that be helpful to you?"

### Asker Commitments

The asker should commit to the following:

1. Have a clear intention. A person who is aware of his desire for help may often misstate this intention to secure help and somehow induce in the helper the urge to rescue the asker. (A rescue occurs when help is offered but not explicitly requested.) Examples of breaking protocol include the following:

   > "I could use a little help."
   > "I need . . ."
   > "If I had some help . . ."
   > "I want help here."
   > "Help!"

2. Be utterly clear, in your own mind and in your request, that you are the asker—the supplicant in the help transaction. This recognition is important to the helper because your asking must be freely offered, the helper must perceive that you know that he can decline the request, and the transaction must carry no penalty to the helper if he does decline.

3. State the specifics, if any, of your request.

4. Assume that the person from whom you're requesting help accepts the responsibility to say "no." That is, don't excuse your failure to ask for help by claiming responsibility for determining others' limits.

5. Don't apologize or otherwise obscure your intention.

6. Accept "no" without any additional internal or external emotional drama.

7. Accept the help offered as completely as possible. If you don't understand the value of what is offered, feel that it wouldn't be

useful, or believe yourself to have considered and rejected the idea offered previously, assume a curious stance instead of executing a knee-jerk, "But . . ." rejection.

8. Ask for something positive.

9. Accept genuine help.

### Helper Commitments

The helper should commit to the following:

1. To say "no" when you don't want to help, or even when you aren't sure you want to help

2. To say you have changed your mind and don't want to help if you begin to help and decide that you really don't want to do so

3. To fulfill completely any of your commitments to help

4. To say "no" without drama or rancor or soliciting approval from the asker

5. To offer what you believe is truly helpful if you have something that you believe would be useful to the asker, even if it is not exactly what he originally requested.

## SHARED VISION PROTOCOL

1. Envision a vision-driven life. Turn that image into a metavision (a vision of how you create and use visions) with and for your team and your institution.

2. As a team, decide what kind of world you will create. Answer two questions together: (1) How will the world be different when you finish your work? (2) What will life be like for you and your customers? From your answers create a FarVision, and write a FarVision statement.

3. Deliver one version of your product after another, and deliver each version on time. Each version must be designed to validate the single, the one and only, message you promulgate with it. The product must also palpably contribute to the increasing legitimacy of your FarVision. That is, each version must demon-

strably bring you and your customers closer to the world of your
FarVision.

## THE FAR VISION PROTOCOL

After having completed Alignment, with your team, write a statement
that best expresses for all of you what the world will look like when
your work together is done.

- *The FarVision must be imaginative.* Look as far into the future as
  possible. Twenty years is a good starting point, but the date
  chosen must be always beyond your ability to extrapolate current trends. That is, it must be the work of intention and imagination, not analysis.

- *The FarVision must be measurable.* Ideally, progress can be measured as well. The desired result may be an observable, external
  thing or event, such as "put a man on the moon." Alternatively,
  it might be softer and more difficult to measure, such as "create
  infinite, free bandwidth." Your FarVision could also be values-
  driven, which is more difficult but still possible to measure, such
  as "eliminate poverty" or "create ubiquitous radical democracy."

- *The FarVision statement should just be a few words*, ideally no more
  than ten words. If it is more than six words, ask your team to
  reevaluate it.

- *Use the PerfectionGame to perfect your FarVision.*

- *The team should unanimously support the FarVision*, using Decider.

  Examples of FarVision statements and version statements follow:

  **Put a man on the moon.**

  Version 1: Orbit the earth.

  **A computer on every desk.**

  Version 1: Software that's easy to use.

  **World peace.**

  Version 1: Peace in our country.

# THE PASSIONOMETER PROTOCOL

The Passionometer protocol provides a straightforward technique for discovering what a team cares about and how much a team cares about it. Its most common application is the creation of the team's vision statement.

1. On index cards team members write down meaningful words or phrases that they associate with the world of the team's FarVision.

2. Toss the cards onto the floor faceup. If repeats are found, throw out the extras or keep them together as a set.

3. A facilitator holds up each card (or set), and team members show their passion for the word or phrase by making noise or vivid gestures, or by another means.

4. The facilitator, with the advice and consent of the team, makes three piles of the cards based on the responses from the team as he flips through the cards one at a time:

   – Highly passionately supported

   – Somewhat passionately supported

   – No real passion

5. Repeat steps 3 and 4, using only those cards that are highly passionately supported until the cards are narrowed down to a set of five or six.

6. If the team remains stuck, repeat Passionometer on the highly passionately supported cards.

# THE PERFECTION GAME PROTOCOL

1. Players sit in a circle.

2. Each person in the circle names a task that he believes to be simple and that the individual is willing to perform throughout the game—for example, "snapping my fingers," "whistling a short tune," or "acting dead."

3. The first player performs the task named in step 2. This performance has the following structure:

   – The player alerts the rest of the group to the beginning of the performance by saying, "Okay, I'm starting now." Everything the player does after this point is subject to perfecting.

   – The player performs his task.

   – The player says, "I'm done." Everything up to but not including this statement is subject to perfecting.

4. The remaining players rate the player's performance on a scale of 1 to 10, where 10 is a perfect performance of the task. The rating must be supported with critical analysis of a particular form: After saying the score (for example, "I give your performance a 7"), the scorer must state the following:

   – Specifically, what about the performance was good and what earned the points in the score

   – Specifically, what the performer must do in the next iteration of the performance to be awarded a perfect 10

The next player then performs his task and is rated by the rest of the group as described above.

5. Steps 1–4 are completed two more times, so that each player performs and is rated three times. Each person plays the role of critic for the rest of the team members in between each of his own performances.

### Analysis of the Perfection Game Protocol

Purely or partially negative feedback is not allowed at any point during the PerfectionGame protocol. For example, "I don't like the sound of the finger snap." The important information to transmit in this case may be something like, "The ideal sound of a finger snap for me is one that is crisp, has sufficient volume, and startles me somewhat. To get a 10, you would have to increase your crispness."

If you cannot think of a better alternative performance, you cannot withhold points. The default score is a perfect 10.

You must follow the scoring routine exactly:

- "I rate your performance $n$."
- "What I liked about it was $p, q, \ldots, z$."
- "What it would take to get a 10 from me is $a, b, \ldots, z$."

If one person breaks the protocol, the other team members must politely correct the offending person by pointing out the infraction. They must then remind the offender of the correct protocol immediately by suggesting, "I give it a . . . " "What I liked about it was . . . ," or "What it would take to get a 10 is . . . ," as appropriate.

When playing the PerfectionGame, the team will develop a sense of the ideal performance of any given act. This aesthetic will take into account the best suggestions made, with lesser suggestions being abandoned.

Including each of the suggested improvements into the next performance rarely yields a perfect performance. The "perfecters" could be wrong about their prior feedback (not intentionally, of course), or the combination of all suggestions may have a negative effect on the performance. As the "perfectee," you must accept only the superior criticism of your performance and implicitly reject the inferior feedback.

Your ratings must not use a "dislike" to "like" scale, where 1 is "completely dislike" and 10 is "completely like." The perfection game is not about whether you "like" something. The rating scale goes from 1, "The thing has no value now and I can add all value needed in my feedback," to 10, "The thing has full value and/or I can't think of anything that would make it better." It is important to hold perfecters accountable to this type of scale and respectfully correct them if you see the dislike/like scale coming into play.

In addition, the rating must be reasonable. For instance, if you rate a performance as an 8, you are saying that it is 80 percent perfect and/or you can tell the person exactly how to gain the 20 percent of missing value. You must not give an 8 and then provide only 1 percent of the missing value.

The "what it will take to get a 10" portion of the game may not be performed in writing. It must be performed verbally with the perfectee.

If you feel an impulse to grade on the dislike/like scale, can't give a reasonable amount of value that correlates with your rating and are unwilling to raise your rating accordingly, or feel the need to write your perfecting down instead of speaking to the person, then you should pass. These impulses can contribute to a negative feedback cycle that distracts the team from achieving the desired results.

# LICENSE AGREEMENT

The Core Protocols V. 1.0
December 2001

Jim and Michele McCarthy, www.mccarthy-tech.com

Copyright © 2001 McCarthy Technologies, Inc.

Permission is granted to make and disbribute verbatim copies of this software provided the copyright notice and this permission notice are preserved on all copies.

Permission is granted to copy and distribute modified versions of this software under the conditions for verbatim copying, provided also that the section entitled "GNU General Public License" is included exactly as in the original, and provided that the entire resulting derived work is distributed under the terms of a permission notice identical to this one.

To protect your rights, we need to make restrictions that forbid anyone to deny you these rights or to ask you to surrender the rights. These restrictions translate to certain responsibilities for you if you distribute copies of the software, or if you modify it.

For example, if you distribute copies of such a program, whether gratis or for a fee, you must give the recipients all the rights that you have. You must make sure that they, too, receive or can get the source code. And you must show them these terms so they know their rights.

We protect your rights with two steps: (1) copyright the software, and (2) offer you this license which gives you legal permission to copy, distribute and/or modify the software.

Also, for each author's protection and ours, we want to make certain that everyone understands that there is no warranty for this free software. If the software is modified by someone else and passed on, we want its recipients to know that what they have is not the original, so that any problems introduced by others will not reflect on the original authors' reputations.

Finally, any free program is threatened constantly by software patents. We wish to avoid the danger that redistributors of a free program will individually obtain patent licenses, in effect making the program proprietary. To prevent this, we have made it clear that any patent must be licensed for everyone's free use or not licensed at all.

The precise terms and conditions for copying, distribution and modification follow.

## TERMS AND CONDITIONS FOR COPYING, DISTRIBUTION AND MODIFICATION

**0.** This License applies to any program or other work which contains a notice placed by the copyright holder saying it may be distributed under the terms of this General Public License. The "Program", below, refers to any such program or work, and a "work based on the Program" means either the Program or any derivative work under copyright law: that is to say, a work containing the Program or a portion of it, either verbatim or with modifications and/or translated into another language. (Hereinafter, translation is included without limitation in the term "modification".) Each licensee is addressed as "you".

Activities other than copying, distribution and modification are not covered by this License; they are outside its scope. The act of running the Program is not restricted, and the output from the Program is covered only if its contents constitute a work based on the Program (independent of having been made by running the Program). Whether that is true depends on what the Program does.

**1.** You may copy and distribute verbatim copies of the Program's source code as you receive it, in any medium, provided that you conspicuously and appropriately publish on each copy an appropriate copyright notice and disclaimer of warranty; keep intact all the notices that refer to this License and to the absence of any warranty; and give any other recipients of the Program a copy of this License along with the Program.

You may charge a fee for the physical act of transferring a copy, and you may at your option offer warranty protection in exchange for a fee.

**2.** You may modify your copy or copies of the Program or any portion of it, thus forming a work based on the Program, and copy and distribute such modifications or work under the terms of Section 1 above, provided that you also meet all of these conditions:

**a)** You must cause the modified files to carry prominent notices stating that you changed the files and the date of any change.

**b)** You must cause any work that you distribute or publish, that in whole or in part contains or is derived from the Program or any part thereof, to be licensed as a whole at no charge to all third parties under the terms of this License.

**c)** If the modified program normally reads commands interactively when run, you must cause it, when started running for such interactive use in the most ordinary way, to print or display an announcement including an appropriate copyright notice and a notice that there is no warranty (or else, saying that you provide a warranty) and that users may redistribute the program under these conditions, and telling the user how to view a copy of this License. (Exception: if the Program itself is interactive but does not normally print such an announcement, your work based on the Program is not required to print an announcement.)

These requirements apply to the modified work as a whole. If identifiable sections of that work are not derived from the Program, and can be reasonably considered independent and separate works in themselves, then this License, and its terms, do not apply to those sections when you distribute them as separate works. But when you distribute the same sections as part of a whole which is a work based on the Program, the distribution of the whole must be on the terms of this License, whose permissions for other licensees extend to the entire whole, and thus to each and every part regardless of who wrote it.

Thus, it is not the intent of this section to claim rights or contest your rights to work written entirely by you; rather, the intent is to exercise the right to control the distribution of derivative or collective works based on the Program.

In addition, mere aggregation of another work not based on the Program with the Program (or with a work based on the Program) on a volume of a storage or distribution medium does not bring the other work under the scope of this License.

**3.** You may copy and distribute the Program (or a work based on it, under Section 2) in object code or executable form under the terms of Sections 1 and 2 above provided that you also do one of the following:

**a)** Accompany it with the complete corresponding machine-readable source code, which must be distributed under the terms of Sections 1 and 2 above on a medium customarily used for software interchange; or,

**b)** Accompany it with a written offer, valid for at least three years, to give any third party, for a charge no more than your cost of physically performing source distribution, a complete machine-readable copy of the corresponding source code, to be distributed under the terms of Sections 1 and 2 above on a medium customarily used for software interchange; or,

**c)** Accompany it with the information you received as to the offer to distribute corresponding source code. (This alternative is allowed only for noncommercial distribution and only if you received the program in object code or executable form with such an offer, in accord with Subsection b above.)

The source code for a work means the preferred form of the work for making modifications to it. For an executable work, complete source code means all the source code for all modules it contains, plus any associated interface definition files, plus the scripts used to control compilation and installation of the executable. However, as a special exception, the source code distributed need not include anything that is normally distributed (in either source or binary form) with the major components (compiler, kernel, and so on) of the operating system on which the executable runs, unless that component itself accompanies the executable.

If distribution of executable or object code is made by offering access to copy from a designated place, then offering equivalent access to copy the source code from the same place counts as distribution of the source code, even though third parties are not compelled to copy the source along with the object code.

4. You may not copy, modify, sublicense, or distribute the Program except as expressly provided under this License. Any attempt otherwise to copy, modify, sublicense or distribute the Program is void, and will automatically terminate your rights under this License. However, parties who have received copies, or rights, from you under this License will not have their licenses terminated so long as such parties remain in full compliance.

5. You are not required to accept this License, since you have not signed it. However, nothing else grants you permission to modify or distribute the Program or its derivative works. These actions are prohibited by law if you do not accept this License. Therefore, by modifying or distributing the Program (or any work based on the Program), you indicate your acceptance of this License to do so, and all its terms and conditions for copying, distributing or modifying the Program or works based on it.

6. Each time you redistribute the Program (or any work based on the Program), the recipient automatically receives a license from the original licensor to copy, distribute or modify the Program subject to these terms and conditions. You may not impose any further restrictions on the recipients' exercise of the rights granted herein. You are not responsible for enforcing compliance by third parties to this License.

7. If, as a consequence of a court judgment or allegation of patent infringement or for any other reason (not limited to patent issues), conditions are imposed on you (whether by court order, agreement or otherwise) that contradict the conditions of this License, they do not excuse you from the conditions of this License. If you cannot distribute so as to satisfy simultaneously your obligations under this License and any other pertinent obligations, then as a consequence you may not distribute the Program at all. For example, if a patent license would not permit royalty-free redistribution of the Program by all those who receive copies directly or indirectly through you, then the only way you could satisfy both it and this License would be to refrain entirely from distribution of the Program.

If any portion of this section is held invalid or unenforceable under any particular circumstance, the balance of the section is intended to apply and the section as a whole is intended to apply in other circumstances.

It is not the purpose of this section to induce you to infringe any patents or other property right claims or to contest validity of any such claims; this section has the sole purpose of protecting the integrity of the free software distribution system, which is implemented by public license practices. Many people have made generous contributions to the wide range of software distributed through that system in reliance on consistent application of that system; it is up to the author/donor to decide if he or she is willing to distribute software through any other system and a licensee cannot impose that choice.

This section is intended to make thoroughly clear what is believed to be a consequence of the rest of this License.

**8.** If the distribution and/or use of the Program is restricted in certain countries either by patents or by copyrighted interfaces, the original copyright holder who places the Program under this License may add an explicit geographical distribution limitation excluding those countries, so that distribution is permitted only in or among countries not thus excluded. In such case, this License incorporates the limitation as if written in the body of this License.

**9.** The Free Software Foundation may publish revised and/or new versions of the General Public License from time to time. Such new versions will be similar in spirit to the present version, but may differ in detail to address new problems or concerns. Each version is given a distinguishing version number. If the Program specifies a version number of this License which applies to it and "any later version", you have the option of following the terms and conditions either of that version or of any later version published by the Free Software Foundation. If the Program does not specify a version number of this License, you may choose any version ever published by the Free Software Foundation.

**10.** If you wish to incorporate parts of the Program into other free programs whose distribution conditions are different, write to the author to ask for permission. For software which is copyrighted by the Free Software Foundation, write to the Free Software Foundation; we sometimes make exceptions for this. Our decision will be guided by the two goals of preserving the free status of all derivatives of our free software and of promoting the sharing and reuse of software generally.

**NO WARRANTY**

**11.** BECAUSE THE PROGRAM IS LICENSED FREE OF CHARGE, THERE IS NO WARRANTY FOR THE PROGRAM, TO THE EXTENT PERMITTED BY APPLICABLE LAW. EXCEPT WHEN OTHERWISE STATED IN WRITING THE COPYRIGHT HOLDERS AND/OR OTHER PARTIES PROVIDE THE PROGRAM "AS IS" WITHOUT WARRANTY OF ANY KIND, EITHER EXPRESSED OR IMPLIED, INCLUDING, BUT NOT LIMITED TO, THE IMPLIED WARRANTIES OF MERCHANTABILITY AND FITNESS FOR A PARTICULAR PURPOSE. THE ENTIRE RISK AS TO THE QUALITY AND PERFORMANCE OF THE PROGRAM IS WITH YOU. SHOULD THE PROGRAM PROVE DEFECTIVE, YOU ASSUME THE COST OF ALL NECESSARY SERVICING, REPAIR OR CORRECTION.

**12.** IN NO EVENT UNLESS REQUIRED BY APPLICABLE LAW OR AGREED TO IN WRITING WILL ANY COPYRIGHT HOLDER, OR ANY OTHER PARTY WHO MAY MODIFY AND/OR REDISTRIBUTE THE PROGRAM AS PERMITTED ABOVE, BE LIABLE TO YOU FOR DAMAGES, INCLUDING ANY GENERAL, SPECIAL, INCIDENTAL OR CONSEQUENTIAL DAMAGES ARISING OUT OF THE USE OR INABILITY TO USE THE PROGRAM (INCLUDING BUT NOT LIMITED TO LOSS OF DATA OR DATA BEING RENDERED INACCURATE OR LOSSES SUSTAINED BY YOU OR THIRD PARTIES OR A FAILURE OF THE

PROGRAM TO OPERATE WITH ANY OTHER PROGRAMS), EVEN IF SUCH HOLDER OR OTHER PARTY HAS BEEN ADVISED OF THE POSSIBILITY OF SUCH DAMAGES.

END OF TERMS AND CONDITIONS

### How to Apply These Terms to Your New Programs

If you develop a new program, and you want it to be of the greatest possible use to the public, the best way to achieve this is to make it free software which everyone can redistribute and change under these terms.

To do so, attach the following notices to the program. It is safest to attach them to the start of each source file to most effectively convey the exclusion of warranty; and each file should have at least the "copyright" line and a pointer to where the full notice is found.

One line to give the program's name and an idea of what it does

Copyright © yyyy name of author

This program is free software; you can redistribute it and/or modify it under the terms of the GNU General Public License as published by the Free Software Foundation; either version 2 of the License, or (at your option) any later version.

This program is distributed in the hope that it will be useful, but WITHOUT ANY WARRANTY; without even the implied warranty of MERCHANTABILITY or FITNESS FOR A PARTICULAR PURPOSE. See the GNU General Public License for more details.

You should have received a copy of the GNU General Public License along with this program; if not, write to the Free Software Foundation, Inc., 59 Temple Place, Suite 330, Boston, MA 02111-1307, USA.

Also add information on how to contact you by electronic and paper mail.

If the program is interactive, make it output a short notice like this when it starts in an interactive mode:

Gnomovision version 69, Copyright © year, name of author, Gnomovision comes with ABSOLUTELY NO WARRANTY; for details, type "show w". This is free software, and you are welcome to redistribute it under certain conditions; type "show c" for details.

The hypothetical commands "show w" and "show c" should show the appropriate parts of the General Public License. Of course, the commands you use may be called something other than "show w" and "show c"; they could even be mouse-clicks or menu items—whatever suits your program.

You should also get your employer (if you work as a programmer) or your school, if any, to sign a "copyright disclaimer" for the program, if necessary. Here is a sample; alter the names:

Yoyodyne, Inc., hereby disclaims all copyright interest in the program "Gnomovision" (which makes passes at compilers) written by James Hacker.

Signature of Ty Coon, 1 April 1989
Ty Coon, President of Vice

This General Public License does not permit incorporating your program into proprietary programs. If your program is a subroutine library, you may consider it more useful to permit linking proprietary applications with the library. If this is what you want to do, use the GNU Library General Public License instead of this License.

# INDEX

# ARTWORK

*Self-Portrait*
by Dan McCarthy
Seattle, WA
Spring 2001

The book's artwork, including the cover art, conceptual images, and part openers, was created by Dan McCarthy, a multimedia artist in Seattle, Washington. His work can be experienced at www.something-cool.com (e-mail: dan@something-cool.com).

Full-color originals of the artwork in this book can be seen at www.mccarthy-tech.com and are available for purchase or license as posters, paintings, or signed limited-edition prints.

*Michele McCarthy*
by Jim McCarthy
Mixed media on canvas
Woodinville, WA
Fall 2001

*Jim McCarthy*
by Michele McCarthy
Black and white photograph
Crystal Lake, WA
Fall 2000

Jim and and Michele McCarthy founded McCarthy Technologies (www.mccarthy-tech.com) in 1996 after a variety of product development, marketing, and program management positions at Microsoft. Before Microsoft, Jim worked for The Whitewater Group and Bell Laboratories, and was also a consultant. Jim is the author of *Dynamics of Software Development* (Microsoft Press, 1995). They live in Woodinville, Washington.

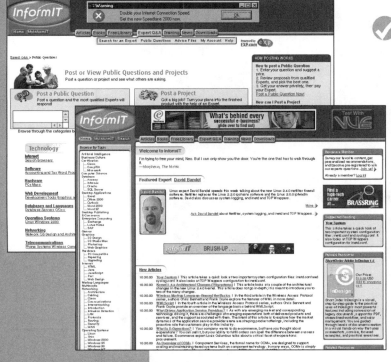

# Register

## Your Book

### at www.aw.com/cseng/register

You may be eligible to receive:

- Advance notice of forthcoming editions of the book
- Related book recommendations
- Chapter excerpts and supplements of forthcoming titles
- Information about special contests and promotions throughout the year
- Notices and reminders about author appearances, tradeshows, and online chats with special guests

## Contact us

If you are interested in writing a book or reviewing manuscripts prior to publication, please write to us at:

Editorial Department
Addison-Wesley Professional
75 Arlington Street, Suite 300
Boston, MA  02116  USA
Email: AWPro@aw.com

Addison-Wesley

Visit us on the Web: http://www.aw.com/cseng